W9-DBZ-994

The Practice of Change

Concepts and Models
for Service-Learning
in Women's Studies

Barbara J. Balliet and Kerrissa Heffernan, volume editors

Edward Zlotkowski, series editor

A PUBLICATION OF THE

AMERICAN ASSOCIATION
FOR HIGHER EDUCATION

The Practice of Change: Concepts and Models for Service-Learning in Women's Studies
(AAHE's Series on Service-Learning in the Disciplines)
Barbara Balliet and Kerrissa Heffernan, *volume editors*
Edward Zlotkowski, *series editor*

Opinions expressed in this publication are the contributors' and do not necessarily represent those of the American Association for Higher Education or its members.

ISBN 1-56377-023-7
ISBN (SET) 1-56377-005-9

Contents

About This Series

by Edward Zlotkowski

The following volume, *The Practice of Change: Concepts and Models for Service-Learning in Women's Studies,* represents the 17th in a series of monographs on service-learning and the academic disciplines. Ever since the early 1990s, educators interested in reconnecting higher education not only with neighboring communities but also with the American tradition of education for service have recognized the critical importance of winning faculty support for this work. Faculty, however, tend to define themselves and their responsibilities largely in terms of the academic disciplines/interdisciplinary areas in which they have been trained. Hence, the logic of the present series.

The idea for this series first surfaced late in 1994 at a meeting convened by Campus Compact to explore the feasibility of developing a national network of service-learning educators. At that meeting, it quickly became clear that some of those assembled saw the primary value of such a network in its ability to provide concrete resources to faculty working in or wishing to explore service-learning. Out of that meeting there developed, under the auspices of Campus Compact, a new national group of educators called the Invisible College, and it was within the Invisible College that the monograph project was first conceived. Indeed, a review of both the editors and contributors responsible for many of the volumes in this series would reveal significant representation by faculty associated with the Invisible College.

If Campus Compact helped supply the initial financial backing and impulse for the Invisible College and for this series, it was the American Association for Higher Education (AAHE) that made completion of the project feasible. Thanks to its reputation for innovative work, AAHE was not only able to obtain the funding needed to support the project up through actual publication, it was also able to assist in attracting many of the teacher-scholars who participated as writers and editors. AAHE is grateful to the Corporation for National Service–Learn and Serve America for its financial support of the series.

Three individuals in particular deserve to be singled out for their contributions. Sandra Enos, former Campus Compact project director for Integrating Service With Academic Study, was shepherd to the Invisible College project. John Wallace, professor of philosophy at the University of Minnesota, was the driving force behind the creation of the Invisible College. Without his vision and faith in the possibility of such an undertaking, assembling the human resources needed for this series would have been very difficult. Third, AAHE's endorsement — and all that followed in its wake

— was due largely to then AAHE vice president Lou Albert. Lou's enthusiasm for the monograph project and his determination to see it adequately supported have been critical to its success. It is to Sandra, John, and Lou that the monograph series as a whole must be dedicated.

Another individual to whom the series owes a special note of thanks is Teresa E. Antonucci, who, as program manager for AAHE's Service-Learning Project, has helped facilitate much of the communication that has allowed the project to move forward.

The Rationale Behind the Series

A few words should be said at this point about the makeup of both the general series and the individual volumes. Although women's studies embodies many of the same values as service-learning and thus may seem an obvious choice of academic area with which to link service-learning, "natural fit" has not, in fact, been a determinant factor in deciding which disciplines/interdisciplinary areas the series should include. Far more important have been considerations related to the overall range of disciplines represented. Since experience has shown that there is probably no disciplinary area — from architecture to zoology — where service-learning cannot be fruitfully employed to strengthen students' abilities to become active learners as well as responsible citizens, a primary goal in putting the series together has been to demonstrate this fact. Thus, some rather natural choices for inclusion — disciplines such as anthropology and geography — have been passed over in favor of other, sometimes less obvious selections, such as accounting and history. Should the present series of volumes prove useful and well received, we can then consider filling in the many gaps we have left this first time around.

If a concern for variety has helped shape the series as a whole, a concern for legitimacy has been central to the design of the individual volumes. To this end, each volume has been both written by and aimed primarily at academics working in a particular disciplinary/interdisciplinary area. Many individual volumes have, in fact, been produced with the encouragement and active support of relevant discipline-specific national associations.

Furthermore, each volume has been designed to include its own appropriate theoretical, pedagogical, and bibliographical material. Especially with regard to theoretical and bibliographical material, this design has resulted in considerable variation both in quantity and in level of discourse. Thus, for example, a volume such as Accounting contains more introductory and less bibliographical material than does Composition — simply because there is less written on and less familiarity with service-learning in accounting. However, no volume is meant to provide an extended introduction to service-learning *as a generic concept.* For material of this nature, the reader is referred to such texts as Kendall's *Combining Service and Learning: A Resource Book for Community and Public Service* (NSEE, 1990) and Jacoby's *Service-Learning in Higher Education* (Jossey-Bass, 1996).

I would like to conclude with a note of special thanks to Kerrissa Heffernan and Barbara Balliet, the coeditors of this volume. Their openness to suggestions has made working with them a very satisfying experience.

March 2000

Introduction

by Barbara J. Balliet and Kerrissa Heffernan

We open this volume with two essays that address long-standing issues in women's studies epistemology, theory, and practice. Blythe Clinchy's essay raises important questions about the virtues of two distinct educational objectives: critical thinking and connected knowing. Based on two empirical studies, the first of college women at Wellesley College and the second of the women whose stories resulted in the women's studies text *Women's Ways of Knowing*, Clinchy's essay asks us to examine whether detachment, impersonality, and argument as a mode of discourse provide a sufficient epistemological base for students, especially women students. Instead she suggests that connected knowing — presented as "imaginative attachment: trying to get behind the other person's eyes," and privileging narration rather than argument — represents an equally valuable mode of thinking and one more immediately accessible to women.

Although Clinchy's essay does not specifically address service-learning, her work holds important implications for women's studies and service-learning practitioners, as service-learning projects frequently involve students in communities in which they have no membership, no a priori legitimacy. Clinchy suggests that empathetic connection, investing in belief rather than doubt as a starting point for engaging communities and issues, holds some contradictory possibilities for students and faculty.

Within women's studies, an understanding of women in all their rich multiplicity has replaced the category of women as unitary and universal, reflective more or less exclusively of white middle-class and heterosexual women's lives. Within service-learning, collaboration has replaced the more dated vision of altruism and female selflessness. Does Clinchy's connected knowing enable students to build more effective collaborations? Certainly an awareness of the particularity of one's own knowledge and experience, firmly locating the self, could focus students on the relationship between their experiences and those that differ from theirs. Believing in the validity of different voices could enable students to listen more effectively and open them to explanations and worlds beyond themselves. But once they are open to multiple interpretations, what can they do?

We chose to juxtapose Clinchy with Bachman and Attyah to illustrate one faculty response to that question. In "Educating the Artist" Bachman and Attyah begin with the concept of voice as critical in enabling students to assert and redefine their experiences while recognizing how the world outside the classroom/studio has already shaped and constrained those experiences. Bachman and Attyah envision a seamless merger of education and practice that can contribute to provoking the political imagination, leading students to an awareness that meaning is contingent on context and interpretation. They urge their students, when making art, to employ the feminist practice of focusing on how the relationship between self and society is made, emphasizing that "because institutions and knowledge are constructed, they are capable of being changed." This entails an epistemology that begins with experience and immediately calls into question how that experience is made, directing students to challenge its construction and envision social change. In such a construct, neither experience nor its narration is sufficient. Traditional classroom notions of self-knowledge must be transcended in favor of challenging inequities and effecting change.

Bachman and Attyah's statement represents an important extension of Clinchy's work on connected knowing and offers a different way to facilitate connection. More pointedly, Bachman and Attyah offer the practice of art as another way of seeing, and envision the classroom as the place where students examine the political and transformative nature of art. They suggest that — far from being a model of singular or individual expression — art can serve a greater public good by re-envisioning power, building community, and acting as a catalyst for social change.

In Part One, "Theory and History," each essay draws on the rich history of women's activism to argue for the importance of service-learning to women's studies. Here the authors seek to present the unique locations women occupy and how those locations inform women's perspectives in service-learning. More specifically, the authors challenge the predisposition many service-learning practitioners have of identifying, defining, and presenting communities as deficient. Many of the authors in this volume challenge the destructive practice of forming relationships with "others" whom we primarily identify as "lacking" and thus funneling resources to perceived problems rather than initiating larger social and political change efforts. Women's studies offers the historical and lived perspective of turning questions of inequity into activist practice, in this way challenging the privileging of particular experiences and the authority given to those represented as privileged. In this section, the authors mount such a challenge by directing our attention to the important lessons women's history and women's studies hold for the broader service-learning community.

In her essay "A Feminist Challenge to Community Service," Tobi Walker calls for the politicization of service-learning, arguing (like Clinchy and Bachman and Attyah) that it is far easier for students to understand the immediate personal impact they can make through service than it is for them to see the value of traditional political engagement. She maintains that the gender ideology of a public/private divide, locating women firmly in the home while allocating to men the public world of politics and work, has fostered the depoliticization of service and its reduction to a private, moral, female activity. Thus, politics has historically remained distinct from service as women's community work was characterized as a form of domestic caretaking.

This historical and gendered dichotomy has had important implications for service-learning. First, the ideology of service allows us to dismiss and devalue the service work performed for pay by men and women (primarily people of color) by valorizing service as voluntary labor given freely out of an evolved moral state — a gendered imperative to care. Second, women's service and reform efforts have historically construed the communities where they took place as communities in need of help, help largely premised on middle-class norms about race, class, gender, and sexuality.

Walker points briefly to an alternative tradition represented by the black women's club movement and the Settlement House movement. Helen Damon-Moore picks up on this argument and elaborates more broadly on the historical perspective that women's history offers service-learning. Focusing on the history of mutual aid located in communities of color (including African Americans, Native Americans, and those of Chinese, Japanese, Cuban, and Mexican descent), she argues that women's studies and service-learning can create contemporary understandings and models for service that do not reflect ethnocentric and hierarchical views of the communities in which service projects are located. Both she and Walker suggest that within service-learning, gender can become a category for civic analysis as well as practice.

Like Damon-Moore, Karen Bojar identifies a trajectory arising from a particular moment in second-wave feminism as shaping many of the challenges that women's studies practitioners face. The emphasis that second-wave feminism has placed on paid work as a measure of full inclusion for women has positioned "voluntarism" and its close relative "service" as step-sisters to feminist activism. A 1973 statement by the National Organization for Women (NOW) Task Force on Volunteerism condemned service as "prevent[ing] needed social changes from occurring because with service-oriented volunteering, political energy is being used and will increasingly be used to meet society's administrative needs." Describing service as a "patchwork approach to solving massive and severe social ills," NOW signaled that the real game for women was the world of politics and paid labor, and although NOW subsequently withdrew its strictures on voluntarism, suspicions have lingered.

Bojar, writing specifically about the community college as a location for service-learning, suggests that service must be carefully attuned to the complex lives students lead and the political ground they occupy. Indeed, she suggests that for her students, commitment to community service is a lifelong project and an integral part of juggling work, family, education, and community. It is the value placed on that work that her pedagogy seeks to change. Responding to students' perceptions that putting volunteer work on a resume is "just tooting your own horn," Bojar emphasizes the social and economic power of service. For her, changing how service is perceived depends on recognizing its value, including its economic value. Drawing on the work of economist Marilyn Waring, she reports on efforts by New Zealand women activists to get tax recognition for their volunteer labor, claiming their work, time, and skills as equivalent to monies given to charity.

In Part Two, "Educating for Action," several essays argue that service-learning provides a critical opportunity for women's studies to reconnect with its activist past. Although women's studies emerged from the women's movement — part of an effort by women active in liberal, radical, and socialist circles to understand the history and experiences of women — the once purportedly seamless connections between women's studies in academia and the women's movement beyond it have become the subject of some debate. Since both the women's movement and women's studies have changed considerably over the last 30 years, their points of convergence are no longer as clearly visible or agreed on. What do scholars and theorists in women's studies have to say to women in the movement? What role should women's studies play in educating women for feminist activism?

Catherine Ludlum Foos opens this section with a compelling feminist argument that challenges even the most seasoned service-learning practitioner. Using Carol Gilligan's analysis of the moral orientations of care and justice and Morton's analysis of the service paradigms of "charity and social justice," Foos challenges the assumption held by many service practitioners that a primary goal of service is to move students along a developmental continuum from charity to social activism. In doing so she challenges the tendency in the field to judge the value of one mode of experience or interpretation as more desirable than another. Paraphrasing Gilligan, Foos argues that when practitioners present service as a continuum from a lesser point (charity) to a greater one (justice), we "silence valuable voices and impoverish our understanding." Rather, she argues, practitioners should reflect on how we have come to understand what constitutes "mature" service. She employs Gilligan's rationale for multiple meanings born of multiple perspectives and demonstrates the many ways feminist scholarship can inform service-learning.

Mary Trigg and Barbara Balliet seek to understand how reaching across boundaries of difference in communities and among disciplines distinctively shapes the nature of service-learning within women's studies. In each instance, it is the foregrounding of difference — whether in terms of gender, ethnic, national, and racial identities or as a challenge to traditional academic structures and disciplines — that creates new conditions for learning. By highlighting the incomplete institutionalization of women's studies within the academy, they also suggest that as an "outsider within," women's studies continues to struggle to delineate a space for its intellectual and activist project. As outsiders within, students entering communities and women's studies practitioners frequently find themselves the chief beneficiary of that project — even as they seek to empower others and transform knowledge.

In "Women's Studies and Community-Based Service-Learning: A Natural Affinity," Patricia Washington emphasizes the numerous natural bonds between women's studies and service-learning. As a black lesbian teaching women's studies at a predominantly white institution, Washington finds service-learning to be a valuable tool in overcoming student resistance to course objectives and materials as well as to her authority as a teacher. Washington's essay illuminates how reflecting on experience provides a basis for making change, a concept central both to women's studies and to service-learning. Considering the kinds of resistance, racism, and hostility she encountered as a new professor, Washington connects a politics of location to a pedagogy of change. Her experience becomes the basis for a critical intervention in teaching as she argues that service-learning and women's studies share a pedagogy that links lived experience with the pursuit of knowledge for the sake of promoting positive social change. Once engaged in community service, Washington's students are better able to recognize and articulate the interconnections of gender, race, sexual orientation, and class in her course Sex, Power, and Politics.

In "Educated in Agency," Melissa Gilbert uses student voices to illustrate the pedagogical journey of her students as they move from an abstract and one-dimensional view of community to a lived, deeply complex experience. Like Washington, Gilbert finds service a pedagogy that challenges student resistance and affords them an opportunity to experience "a shift in personal, collective, and activist identities." Through the intersection of women's studies and community work, Gilbert sees her students able to locate themselves as part of a larger community of women. This emerging recognition of affinity with others changes the conditions for learning and the ways students know themselves in relation to others. As a result, they form a deep commitment to the application of feminist theory in service to community.

Kimberly Farah and Kerrissa Heffernan offer another example of pedagogy in service to a community of women. Their essay describes a service-learning course in which female students confront their identities as outsiders in a specific disciplinary area. It begins with the recognition that women in the hard sciences face a struggle for access and legitimacy both in the academy and in practice. However, confronting these realities is ultimately liberating in that it allows students to acknowledge the source of their resistance to this area of study. Recognizing the historically gendered nature of knowledge in the physical sciences, the course Heffernan and Farah describe utilizes exclusively female role models (women scientists, women faculty, and women students), taking great pride in its ability to reconceptualize the learning experience and create a feminist chemistry classroom. Such a project supports Clinchy's argument that imaginative attachment is an epistemology more readily accessible to women, and it reiterates the position of Bachman and Attyah that meaning is contingent on context and interpretation.

Part Three, "Narrating the Journey," opens with Sally Zierler's remarkable autobiographical odyssey. Zierler's essay represents a well-honed tradition within women's studies — utilizing the personal to access and delineate the political. Zierler tells stories of her life as a child in segregated Baltimore, as an adolescent confronting anti-Semitism in suburbia and as a girl good at math at a time when that had to be an accident rather than a vocational direction. All these stories weave around the path of activism, a path Zierler found and followed in college and continued in her professional work in the academy. Her essay enables us to see the powerful space that women's studies and service-learning provide for students to explore identity, recognize institutional and political structures, and create solutions to social problems.

Zierler's course, The Health of Women, represents one such solution. In a professional-school setting, students are taught to evaluate the scientific research on women's health topics and then to make that information useful to a broad, diverse audience, including advocates for women's health, politicians, and women needing this information themselves. Students move from an understanding of the epidemiology of disease, diagnosis and treatment, how the experience of living with disease is gendered, to policy recommendations for both public and private use. This experience enables them to understand the institutional and political forces that shape treatment and policy as well as our very understanding of disease. Her powerful narrative reminds us how the personal informs the entire academic experience and is reflected in course objectives.

Debra Liebowitz's article highlights an international service-learning experience, a summer course that brought men and women students to Limón, Costa Rica, to teach English in a predominantly Afro-Caribbean school. She suggests the ways in which analytic tools fundamental to women's studies, particularly its analyses of identity and location, enriched their transnational service-learning experience. Students learned to use questions about the construction of identity and difference to

> interrogate the subject matter of international economic and political relations, particularly questions of globalization, neocolonialism, and foreign

policy. At the same time, attention to international political and economic dynamics helped to challenge an understanding of identity that did not include questions of nation and colonial relations.

Liebowitz's course drew in many students originally uninterested in gender or women's studies. By integrating gender analyses into an experiential and international learning program, she succeeded in meeting the challenge raised by Helen Damon-Moore of extending the reach of both service-learning and women's studies to male students. Her course also enabled students to make connections between the insights they gained about their identities and the processes of globalization that bring economic and political privilege to some nations at the expense of others.

Similarly, Eve Allegra Raimon and Jan Hitchcock utilize their experience in teaching adult learners to challenge some of the basic assumptions informing the national conversation on service-learning. Arguing that youth — especially male youth — constitute "the predominant imagined subject of current literature on service-learning," Raimon and Hitchcock reimagine the potential of service-learning in a way that places at its center their students — mostly adult women who have returned to school after having been active in their communities and after raising families. These learners, already embedded in the very communities where their service-learning projects are located, represent special service-learning resources, rather than simply service beneficiaries. Raimon and Hitchcock also found that adult women learners present special challenges to service-learning. Since, for example, they are already aware of problems in their community and are frequently experienced in efforts to solve those problems, their service-learning expectations are likely to be higher than those of other students. Raimon and Hitchcock's essay suggests how, by placing gender and age at the center of its analysis, women's studies can actually transform the national conversation about service-learning.

We conclude the volume where we started — with an essay that challenges assumptions about educational objectives and valued modes of thinking. Mary Pat Treuthart questions the long-held professional-school model of detached learning — a method in which students remain firmly outside the community and learn to "prescribe and describe." Like Zierler, Treuthart finds her "location" deeply informs her educational practice. Drawing on her experiences in advocacy and community work, she seeks to "reconnect substantive coursework [in law school] to human experience in a way meaningful for all students — and women law students in particular."

Like Heffernan and Farah, Treuthart also questions the entrenched and gendered nature of knowledge and acknowledges the power feminist studies and service-learning have to dislodge those entrenched views. In challenging the predisposition educators have of judging one mode of experience or interpretation as more desirable than another, thus diminishing the learning opportunities inherent in multiple connections, Treuthart echoes Foos. She concludes that successful service-learning faculty must "locate themselves" and provide students with an example of connecting oneself to one's work in a substantive way.

On Critical Thinking and Connected Knowing

by Blythe McVicker Clinchy

We hear a great deal about the virtues of critical thinking: how important it is to teach it, how hard it is to teach it, how we might do better at teaching it.

I believe in critical thinking, and I come from an institution that believes in it. We pride ourselves on our high standards, and we work hard to bring our students up to these standards. Often, we fail. At least I do. In the not-so-distant past, when students failed to reach these high standards, I figured it was either their fault or mine. Maybe they were lazy, preoccupied, or poorly prepared; maybe I needed to improve my teaching techniques.

But lately I have begun to think that when our students fail to meet the standards and become critical thinkers, the fault may lie not so much in them or me but in our standards. It is not that they are bad students or that I am a bad teacher, but that there is something deeply wrong about our enterprise.

There is nothing wrong with trying to teach critical thinking, but something goes wrong when we teach *only* critical thinking. Something goes wrong, at least for women students, when we subject them to an education that emphasizes critical thinking to the virtual exclusion of other modes of thought.

I have come to believe, moreover, that some of the women who succeed in such a system — who become powerful critical thinkers and, in their terms, "beat the system" by achieving summa cum laude and Phi Beta Kappa — may be as badly damaged as the ones who fail. I want to tell the stories of some of these women and I want to propose that their stories might be happier if our colleges put more emphasis on a form of critical thinking we call "connected knowing."

I draw mainly on two studies. One is a longitudinal study I did at Wellesley with my colleague Claire Zimmerman (1982, 1985a, 1985b) in which we interviewed undergraduates annually throughout their four years at the college. The other is a study I conducted with Mary Belenky, Nancy Goldberger, and Jill Tarule involving interviews with 135 women of different ages and social and ethnic backgrounds, including undergraduates and alumnae from a variety of educational institutions — which is reported in our book, *Women's Ways of Knowing* (1986). I talk most about women because that's what I know most about. When I use the word *women*, rather than *people*, I don't mean to exclude men, but in these two studies we interviewed only women.

Epistemological Positions

In *Women's Ways of Knowing* we describe five perspectives on knowledge that women seem to hold. Like William Perry (1970), we call these perspectives "positions." Our positions owe much to his and are built on his, but they do differ. Our definitions of the epistemological positions emphasize the source, rather than the nature, of knowledge and truth. Reading an interview we asked ourselves such questions as:

- How does the woman conceive of herself as a knower?
- Is knowledge seen as originating outside or inside the self?"
- Can it be passed down intact from one person to another, or does it well up from within?
- Does knowledge appear effortlessly in the form of intuition or revelation, or is it attained only through an arduous procedure of construction?

I need to describe two of these positions to set the stage for talking about critical thinking and connected knowing. They are familiar to all who teach.

Received Knowledge. Some of the women we interviewed take a position we call *received knowledge*. Like Perry's "dualists," they rely on authorities to supply them with the right answers. Truth, for them, is external. They can ingest it but not evaluate it or create it for themselves. Received knowers are the students who sit there, pencils poised, ready to write down every word the teacher says.

Subjectivism. A second mode of knowing we call *subjectivism*. Subjectivists have much in common with Perry's "multiplists." Their conception of knowledge is, in a way, the opposite of the received knowers': Subjective knowers look inside themselves for knowledge. They are their own authorities. For them, truth is internal, in the heart or in the gut. As with Perry's multiplists, truth is personal: You have your truths, and I have mine. The subjectivist relies on the knowledge she has gleaned from personal experience. She carries the residue of that experience in her gut in the form of intuition and trusts her intuitions. She does not trust what she calls the "so-called authorities" who pretend to "know it all" and try to "inflict their ideas" on her.

The subjectivist makes judgments in terms of feelings: An idea is right if it feels right. In the Wellesley study, we asked students how they would choose which was right when competing interpretations of a poem were being discussed. One said, "I usually find that when ideas are being tossed around I'm more akin to one than another. I don't know — my opinions are just sort of there. . . . With me, it's more a matter of liking one more than another. I mean, I happen to agree with one or identify with it more."

Many of our students, specially in the first year, operate from both positions, functioning as received knowers in their academic lives and as subjectivists in what they refer to as their "real" or "personal" lives. Some students make finer discriminations than this and operate differently in different parts of the curriculum: They may adopt a posture of received knowledge as they approach the sciences and move into subjectivism as they approach the gray areas of humanities.

As a developmental psychologist, I have learned to respect received knowledge and subjectivism. Some of the received knowers described a time in their lives when they were incapable of learning from others, when they could not make sense of words spoken to them. They are thrilled, now, at their capacity to hear these words and store them. And subjectivists spoke movingly of having freed themselves from helpless dependence on oppressive authorities who used words as weapons, forcing them to accept as truths principles that bore no relation to their own experiences; for these women, it is a genuine achievement to define their own truths based on their own experiences.

But clearly, both positions have limitations. When such women are my students rather than my research informants, the limitations of the positions seem to loom larger than the virtues. When I am teaching Child Development, for example, I do not want students to swallow unthinkingly Piaget's interpretations of his observations, but I do want them to pay close attention to what he has to say. I do not want them simply to spout off their own interpretations and ignore the data. Students who rely exclusively on received or subjective knowledge are in some sense not really thinking. The received knower's ideas come from the authority; the subjectivist's opinions are "just there." Neither has any procedure for developing new ideas or testing their validity. As a teacher, I want to help these students develop systematic, deliberate procedures for understanding and evaluating ideas.

Separate Knowing

We have identified two broad types of procedures for such understanding. *Separate knowing* we could just as easily call "critical thinking." Some just call it "thinking." We used to, too, but now we claim it is only one kind of thinking.

The heart of separate knowing is detachment. The separate knower holds herself aloof from the object she is trying to analyze. She takes an impersonal stance. She follows certain rules or procedures to ensure that her judgments are unbiased. All disciplines and vocations have these impersonal procedures for analyzing things. All fields have impersonal standards for evaluating, criteria that allow one to decide whether a novel is well constructed or an experiment has been properly conducted or a person should be diagnosed as schizophrenic.

We academicians tend to place a high value on impersonality. Some of us, for example, pride ourselves on blind grading: We read and grade a paper without knowing who wrote it, to ensure that our feelings about a person do not affect our evaluation of the product. In separate knowing, you separate the knower from the known. The less you know about the author, the better you can evaluate the work.

When a group of us were planning a series of lectures in a team-taught freshman interdisciplinary course, some of us tried to entice the man who was lecturing on Marxism to tell the students about Marx as a person. The lecturer argued that Marx's biography was irrelevant to his theory and only would lead students astray. He finally, grudgingly, agreed to, as he put it, "locate Marx" within an intellectual tradition; that was as personal as he was willing to get.

Separate knowing often takes the form of an adversarial proceeding. The separate knower's primary mode of discourse is the argument. One woman we interviewed said, "As soon as someone tells me his point of view, I immediately start arguing in my head the opposite point of view. When someone is saying something, I can't help turning it upside down." Another said, "I never take anything someone says for granted. I just tend to see the contrary. I like playing devil's advocate, arguing the opposite of what somebody's saying, thinking of exceptions to what the person has said or thinking of a different train of logic."

These young women play what Peter Elbow (1973) calls "the doubting game." They look for what is wrong with whatever it is they are examining — a text, a painting, a person, anything. They think up opposing positions. The doubting game is very popular in the groves of academe.

Teachers report, however, that they often have trouble getting their women students to play the doubting game. Michael Gorra, who teaches at Smith College, published a piece in the *New York Times* (1988) entitled "Learning to Hear the Small, Soft Voices." Gorra complained that he has trouble getting a class discussion off the ground because the students refuse to argue either with him — when he tries to lure them by taking a devil's advocate position — or with each other. He tells about an incident in which two students, one speaking right after the other, offered diametrically opposed readings of an Auden poem. "The second student," Gorra writes, "didn't define her interpretation against her predecessor's, as I think a man would have. She didn't begin by saying, 'I don't agree with that.' She betrayed no awareness that she had disagreed with her classmate, and seemed surprised when I pointed it out."

Gorra has found the feminist poet Adrienne Rich helpful in trying to understand this phenomenon. In her essay "Taking Women Students Seriously" (1979), Rich says that women have been taught since early childhood to speak in "small, soft voices." Gorra confirms:

Our students still suffer, even at a women's college, from the lessons Rich says women are taught about the unfeminity of assertiveness. They are uneasy with the prospect of having to defend their opinions, not only against my own devil's advocacy, but against each other. They would rather not speak if speaking means breaking with their classmates' consensus. Yet that consensus is usually more emotion, a matter of tone, than it is intellectual.

I have had similar experiences, and a few years ago I might have described and analyzed them in much the same way; but our research helps me see them somewhat differently. It is not that I do not sympathize with Gorra; I do, and I value what he is trying to teach. Separate knowing is of great importance. It allows you to criticize your own and other people's thinking. Without it, you couldn't write a second draft of a paper; without it, you are unable to marshal a convincing argument or detect a specious one. Separate knowing is a powerful way of knowing.

Argument, furthermore, is a powerful mode of discourse. We all need to know how to use it. Our interviews confirm Gorra's sense that many young women are reluctant to engage in argument; and I agree, and so would many of the women, that this is a limitation. But argument is not the only form of dialogue, and if women are asked to engage in other types of conversation — to speak in a different voice, to borrow Carol Gilligan's (1982) phrase — they can speak with eloquence and strength.

Gorra may not know about this different voice, as I did not, because, like most of us professors, he does not invite it to speak in his classroom. In his classroom, as in most classrooms run by teachers who pride themselves on encouraging discussion, discussion means disagreement, and the student has two choices: to disagree or remain silent. To get a somewhat different slant, Gorra might want to dip into another of Adrienne Rich's essays, "Toward a Woman-Centered University" (1979), in which she says that our educational practice is founded on a "masculine, adversarial form of discourse," and she defines the problem of silence not as a deficiency in women but as a limitation in our educational institutions.

I agree: Argument is the only style of discourse that has found much favor in the groves of academe. But there is a different voice.

Connected Knowing

In our research, we asked undergraduate women to respond to comments made by other undergraduates. We asked them to read the following quotation — "As soon as someone tells me his point of view, I immediately start arguing in my head the opposite point of view" — and tell us what they thought about it. Most said they did not like it much, and they did not do it much.

These women could recognize disagreement, but they did not deal with disagreement by arguing. One said that when she disagreed with someone, she did not start arguing in her head but instead started trying to imagine herself into the person's situation: "I sort of fit myself into it in my mind and then I say, 'I see what you mean.' There's this initial point where I kind of go into the story and become like Alice falling down the hole."

It took us a long time to hear what this woman was saying. We thought at the time that she was just revealing her inability to engage in critical thinking. To us, her comment indicated not the presence of a different way of thinking but the absence of any kind of thinking — not a difference but a deficiency. Now we see it as an instance of what we call *connected knowing*, and we see it everywhere. It is clear to us that many women have a proclivity toward connected knowing.

Contrast the comment illustrating connected knowing with the one illustrating separate knowing. When you play devil's advocate, you take a position contrary to the other person's, even when you agree with it, even when it seems intuitively right. The women we interviewed ally themselves with the other person's position even when they disagree with it. Another student illustrates the same point. She said she rarely plays devil's advocate: "I'm usually a bit of a chameleon. I really try to look for pieces of truth in what the person says instead of going contrary to them. Sort of collaborate with them." These women are playing what Elbow (1973) calls the believing game: Instead of looking for what's wrong with the other person's idea, they look for why it makes sense, how it might be right.

Connected knowers are not dispassionate, unbiased observers. They deliberately bias themselves in favor of what they are examining. They try to get inside it and form an intimate attachment to it. The heart of connected knowing is imaginative attachment: trying to get behind the other person's eyes and "look at it from that person's point of view." This is what Elbow means by "believe." You must suspend your belief, put your own views aside, try to see the logic in the idea. You need not ultimately agree with it. But while you are entertaining it you must, as Elbow says, "say yes to it." You must empathize with it, feel with and think with the person who created it. Emotion is not outlawed, as in separate knowing, but reason is also present.

The connected knower believes that in order to understand what a person is saying, one must adopt the person's own terms and refrains from judgment. In this sense, connected knowing is uncritical. But it is not unthinking. It is a personal way of thinking that involves feeling. The connected knower takes a personal approach even to an impersonal thing such as a philosophical treatise. She treats the text, as one Wellesley student put it, "as if it were a friend." In Martin Buber's (1970) terms, the text is a "thou" — a subject, rather than an "it," an object of analysis.

The separate knower takes nothing at face value, whereas the connected knower, in a sense, takes everything at face value. Rather than trying to evaluate the perspective she is examining, she tries to understand it. Rather than asking, "Is it right?" she asks, "What does it mean?" When she says, "Why do you think that?" she means, "What in your experience led you to that position?" and not "What evidence do you have to back that up?" She is looking for the story behind the idea. The voice of separate knowing is argument; the voice of connected knowing is narration.

Women spend a lot of time sharing stories of their experience, and it sometimes seems that first-year college students spend most of their time this way. This may help account for the fact that most studies of intellectual development among college students show that the major growth occurs during the first year.

Thinking With Someone

When I say that women have a proclivity toward connected knowing, I am not saying that women will not or cannot think. I am saying that many women would rather think with someone than against someone. I am arguing against an unnecessarily constricted view of thinking as analytic, detached, and divorced from feeling.

Similarly, I am not saying that connected knowing is better than separate knowing. I want my students to become proficient in both modes. I want to help them develop a flexible way of knowing that is both connected and separate. Bertrand Russell — no slouch at critical thinking — shares this view. In his *History of Western Philosophy* (1961), he says, "In studying a philosopher, the right attitude is neither reverence nor contempt." Also, "you should start reading with a kind of 'sympathy,'" he says, "until it is possible to know what it feels like to believe in his theories." Only when you have achieved this, according to Russell, should you take up a "critical" attitude. Russell continues: "Two things are to be remembered: that a man whose opinions are worth studying may be presumed to have had some intelligence, but that no man is likely to have arrived at complete and final truth on any subject whatever. When an intelligent man expresses a view that seems to us obviously absurd, we should not attempt to prove that it is somehow true, but we should try to understand how it ever came to seem true" (39).

This integrated approach — neither reverent nor contemptuous, both attached and detached, appreciative and critical — is the ideal. Judging from our interviews, the student is helped to achieve this integrative approach when the teacher uses an integrated approach, when the teacher treats the student in the way Bertrand Russell suggests the reader should treat the philosophic.

First believe, then doubt. When we asked students to tell us about teachers who had helped them grow, they told stories of teachers who had "believed" them, seen something "right" in their essays, tried to discern the embryonic thought beneath the tangled prose or the beautiful sculpture within the contorted lump of clay. These teachers made connections between their own experiences — often, their own failures — and the students' efforts. Once this had occurred, once the teachers had established a context of connection, the students could tolerate — even almost welcome — the teachers' criticism. Criticism, in this context, becomes collaborative rather than condescending.

I am trying to learn to be this kind of teacher; I have not found it easy. It is easier for me to tell a student what is wrong with her paper than what is right. I can write good specific criticism in the margins; my praise tends to be global and bland: "Good point." Connected teaching means working hard to discern precisely what is "good" — what my colleague Mary Belenky calls the "growing edge" — in a student's thinking. Connected teaching is pointing that out to the student and considering what might make a small "next step" for her to take from there. This kind of teaching is anything but blind; it does not separate the knower from the known. The point is not to judge the product — the paper — but to use the paper to help you understand the knower: where she is and what she needs.

When we asked women to describe classes that had helped them grow, they described classes that took the form not of debates but of what we called "connected conversations" and the women called "real talk." In these classes, each person serves as midwife to each other's thoughts, drawing out others' ideas, entering into them, elaborating on them, even arguing passionately, and building together a truth none could have constructed alone.

Current research involving interviews with men may show that learning is different for many of them. We are interviewing men and women about their attitudes toward separate and connected knowing. Although we have only begun to analyze the data, it looks as if men, on the whole, are more comfortable than women are with the adversarial style. Some men's responses to our questions about connected knowing reflect an ambivalence similar to the women's attitudes toward argument. These men say they know they ought to try harder to enter the other person's perspective, but it is difficult and it makes them uncomfortable, so they do not do it much.

It is possible that men like this might feel as constricted in the kind of connected class discussion I envisage as the women seem to feel in the classroom at Smith. In a connected class, these men might grow silent, and the teacher might worry about what in their upbringing had inhibited their intellectual development.

But not all the men would be silent. Although our research suggests that the two modes may be gender-related, with more men than women showing a propensity for separate knowing and more women than men showing a propensity for connected knowing, it is clear that these modes are not gender-exclusive.

When I first started speaking after the publication of our book, I had a fantasy that a nine-foot male would rise at the end of my talk and launch a devastating attack on our ideas. This has not happened. What has happened is that a normal-sized man rises and says, "Why do you call it 'women's' ways of knowing? I'm a connected knower, too. Why won't you include me?"

A college should be a place where, to paraphrase Sara Ruddick (1984), people are encouraged to think about the things they care about and to care about the things they think about. A college that values connected knowing as well as critical thinking is more likely, I believe, to be such a place.

Note

This essay appeared previously in a 1989 issue of *Liberal Education* (vol. 75, pp. 14-19).

References

Belenky, Mary F., Blythe McVicker Clinchy, Nancy R. Goldberger, and Jill M. Tarule. (1986). *Women's Ways of Knowing.* New York, NY: Basic Books.

Buber, Martin. (1970). *I and Thou.* New York, NY: Charles Scribner's Sons.

Clinchy, Blythe, and Claire Zimmerman. (1982). "Epistemology and Agency in the Development of Undergraduate Women." In *The Undergraduate Woman: Issues in Educational Equity,* edited by P. Perun, pp. 161-181. Lexington, MA: Lexington Books.

———. (1985a). "Connected and Separate Knowing." Paper presented at the Eighth Biennial Meeting of the International Society for the Study of Behavioral Development, Tours, France.

———. (1985b). "Growing Up Intellectually: Issues for College Women." *Work in Progress, No. 19.* Wellesley, MA: Stone Center Working Papers Series.

Elbow, Peter. (1973). *Writing Without Teachers.* London: Oxford University Press.

Gilligan, Carol. (1982). *In a Different Voice: Psychological Theory and Women's Development.* Cambridge, MA: Harvard University Press.

Gorra, Michael. (May 1, 1988). "Learning to Hear the Small, Soft Voices." *The New York Times Sunday Magazine,* pp. 32, 34.

Perry, William G. (1970). *Forms of Intellectual and Ethical Development in the College Years.* New York, NY: Holt, Rinehart and Winston.

Rich, Adrienne. (1979). *On Lies, Secrets, and Silence: Selected Prose, 1966-1978.* New York, NY: W.W. Norton.

Ruddick, Sara. (1984). "New Combinations: Learning From Virginia Woolf." In *Between Women,* edited by C. Asher, L. DeSalvo, and Sara Ruddick, pp. 137-159. Boston, MA: Beacon Press.

Russell, Bertrand. (1961). *History of Western Philosophy.* London: George Allen and Unwin.

Educating the Artist: A Political Statement

by S. A. Bachman, with D. Attyah

Whether I am teaching high school, college, or graduate school, my pedagogy rests on my respect for students' voices, experiences, and cultures, coupled with an awareness that schools do not exist outside of societal conventions, but rather inherit them. Because I understand the limitations of the classroom, I value what is possible within it. My goal is to use the studio-class as an interdisciplinary site where the capacity for personal expression, critical thinking, and self-critique is expanded in the process of artmaking. Students are encouraged to take creative risks, interrogate received texts, question the status quo, and challenge the voice of the teacher. Sometimes this creates tension or conflict, but I accept this as inherent in the process of students and teachers renegotiating knowledge and traditional roles.

My teaching also reflects my feminism in style as well as substance. Nancy Schniedewind (1983) once wrote, "Feminism is taught through process as well as formal content." As a feminist teacher, I implicate myself by sharing my influences, values, and experiences, and I have a commitment to fostering meaningful relationships with and among students that continue beyond the specific course. Because I value the ongoing dialogue and interaction that teaching provides, I resist the temptation to impose my viewpoint. Instead, I respond to each student (or class) on his or her own terms, while acknowledging my perspective and allowing it to inform the discourse.

The relationship between my teaching and my art is one I am continually trying to understand. In both situations I am trying to understand the forces that affect and constitute my daily life. In my studio practice I am involved in an internal dialogue. When working collaboratively, I dialogue with other cultural workers, and in the classroom, with students or coparticipants. All of these interactions reflect a desire to engage in the process of self-inquiry and critical thinking, and all are involved with the production and exchange of experience and meaning. Furthermore, as an artist and teacher, I utilize the concept of voice to assist in the defining, redefining, and asserting of experience while examining how women and men are constrained by patriarchy.

I view both teaching and artmaking as transformative cultural work and believe both interactions should lead to questions rather than silence.

THINK AGAIN Statement

S.A. Bachman and D. Attyah

The official story is that THINK AGAIN are artists who strike back at mainstream ideas that perpetuate injustice.

The unofficial story is that THINK AGAIN are angry artist. We've lived through ACT UP, WHAM, and WAC. We still wear too much black. We have the Guerrilla Girls hanging up all over our homes. We're still angry that conservative backlash, corporate culture, and public complacency have conspired to create a culture of political apathy. And we believe that queer liberation demands creating alliances between ethnic, racial, sexual, and economic communities.

As artists and educators our concerns have always focused on:

- How culture is created.
- Where the so-called mainstream is and what kind of power it has.
- Where the political debate needs to be centered.
- And how the right so effectively obscures ideological and economic injustice.

We still live in an age where the central means of communication are owned by the elite and where people are

While traditional art education and art practice have fostered individual expression, commodification, and solitude, I believe both activities can contribute to reenvisioning society and building community, and can serve as catalysts for social change. I agree with Henry Giroux (1992), who wrote that "critical pedagogy needs to regain a sense of alternatives by combining a language of critique and a language of possibility." In my teaching as well as my art, I share a commitment to combining those languages.

This is not to suggest that my teaching is not influenced by theory. I have been influenced by critical education theory and feminist theory as well as by what is generally referred to as postmodern theory. These theories share assaulted by the media – at home via television, at work via the web, at school via reading programs sponsored by Joe Camel and Disney. Our culture makers, Calvin Klein, Pat Robertson, Steven Spielberg, and Jeff Koons, can all pay top dollar for a platform. And let's face it, whatever visual space hasn't been bought, the state owns.

In the early 90s we both made changes in our artwork. We *"extended the document,"* made *"interactive installations,"* and taught courses with words like *"dialogue"* and *"discourse."* Now, at the millennium we return to strategies we used in the 80s. We realize the place for us again now is in the street. We believe that printed matter and wheat-paste can still incite people to THINK AGAIN. We think that low tech still works and we're committed to giving out our work for free.

Unlike some public artists, who work for extended periods in one community, THINK AGAIN has chosen to deal in the sound bite. When we're in the street, most of our encounters are for 35 seconds, and our longest conversations are about 15 minutes. We explain what we know about the "welfare witch-hunt" and we wonder if we're going to get screamed at for handing out offensive postcards. The images that we think are shocking, people say, "this is great." The ones we think are funny enrage. The sticker we think is brilliant, most people don't get.

With every new project we rethink our strategies from the ground up. We're skeptical that billboards can change

a concern for the relationship between the subject and society and emphasize that because institutions and knowledge are constructed, they are capable of being changed.

My pedagogy reflects my belief that social change is possible and education is at the core of that transformation. Unlike traditional education theory, critical or radical education theory refuses to accept prevailing power relationships and embodies a critical and transformative view of social structures. I use feminist theory in the classroom as a context in which the ongoing debates surrounding postmodernism can be considered. Correspondingly, I utilize deconstructive theory because it has demonstrated that meaning is minds or that postcards prompt political action. We routinely complain that 30,000 postcards can't possibly have an impact, especially when The GAP has plastered every inch of public space with their ads. And we wonder about all this as the Christian Coalition pays $74,000 per anti-queer page in *USA Today*.

We continually ask ourselves how much can anyone expect of a work of "political art"? Our conviction is that art can serve to provoke the political imagination.

And, just when we feel we've had an impact, Disney airs a program about how Cinderella has been misunderstood by feminists.

In the end, we've been surprised at what can get said in 35 seconds and we're finding that our connections to individuals, communities and organizations are building with rapid speed. Beyond the sound bite on the street, our postcards strive to be something between the one-liner and the editorial. Ultimately, the most coveted place for our artwork is not at MOMA, but on the refrigerator – which is where we hope our stuff ends up after going through the mail.

The good news is that in the contest of cultural meaning we're a small interventionist blip on the screen. The bad news is that WAL-MART, The GAP, and the Christian Coalition aren't backing down. But neither is THINK AGAIN.

always constructed, received, and delivered. Deconstruction theory assists in the creation of a dialogue where accepted meanings are reexamined, modified, and possibly abandoned. The awareness that meaning is contingent on context and interpretation — a notion that resonates in service-learning — can have a profound impact on the art student.

Theory also contributes to building a common language so that together as students, teachers, artists, and citizens we can question the social relations and conditions of which we are a part. Theory can facilitate an educational process that values critical thinking, identities, and the intellectual dimensions of art practice. I have a deep commitment to integrating theory within

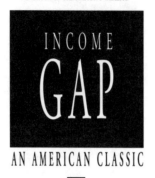

IN 1998, THE U.S. REVOKED THE RIGHTS OF IMMIGRANTS, REVOKED WELFARE, AND KICKED ONE MILLION CHILDREN INTO POVERTY. IN THE SAME YEAR, THE WEALTHIEST 10% OF AMERICANS OWNED OVER 70% OF THE NATION'S WEALTH.

INCOME GAP

AN AMERICAN CLASSIC

THINK AGAIN

"I'm sick of minorities getting all the breaks."

"If I were black, I'd have gotten the job."

WHITE MEN CAN'T COUNT

95% of senior management jobs are still held by white men.

The average white person's net worth is ten times that of black's.

For every $1 earned by white men, black men earn 74¢, black women 64¢.

67% of black families don't make the country's average income.

Which one of these people is abusing welfare?

THE RACIST MYTH: lazy, black, oversexed, single mother, with 4 kids, looking for a hand-out.

ADJUST YOUR STEREOTYPES:
- only 38% of AFDC recipients are black
- less than 1.2% are teenagers under 18
- the average recipient has only 2 children
- most stay on welfare an average of 2 yrs
- welfare constitutes 1% of federal budget

THE CORPORATE MYTH: it's a free market and corporations don't receive tax dollars.

REALITY CHECK:
- Exxon claimed $3 million in tax deductions on the Valdez oil spill
- Lockheed received $1 billion to cover plant shutdowns and relocations
- in total, profit-making corporations grab $170 billion per year in federal funds.

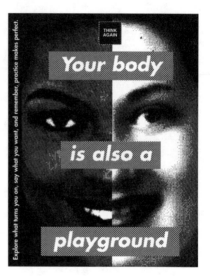

THINK AGAIN

Your body

is also a

playground

Explore what turns you on, say what you want, and remember, practice makes perfect.

studio courses and believe this strategy can contribute to a climate where the "aesthetics of theory" and the "theory of aesthetics" are valued equally.

Paulo Freire (1970) has said that critical teaching in dominant institutions means that teachers are always living a contradiction. This is also true for artists of conscience exhibiting within dominant institutions. Despite the recognition that museums, galleries, and public space represent a confluence of bureaucratic, personal, and social forces, these need not be viewed as exclusively oppressive. I believe these institutions also present an opportunity for critical work, and artists need to weigh continually contradictions, limitations, and compromises against the potential for meaningful exchange.

Note

This paper was first given in 1994 as part of a panel at Tufts University entitled "Educating the Artist." The ideas in this talk were inspired by the writings of Richard Bolton, Suzi Gablik, Henry Giroux, David Trend, and Kathleen Weiler.

References

Freire, Paulo. (1970). *Pedagogy of the Oppressed.* New York, NY: Continuum.

Giroux, Henry. (1992). *Border Crossings: Cultural Workers and the Politics of Education.* New York, NY: Routledge.

Schniedewind, Nancy. (1983). "Feminist Values." In *Learning Our Way: Essays in Feminist Education,* edited by Charlotte Bunch and Sandra Pollack. Trumansburg, NY: Crossing Press.

A Feminist Challenge to Community Service:
A Call to Politicize Service-Learning

by Tobi Walker

For several years, I split my life between graduate school and feminist activism.[1] I was enrolled in the women and politics Ph.D. program at Rutgers University, a curriculum deeply influenced by current feminist theory. The other half of my time I spent at the Center for the American Woman and Politics (CAWP), a think tank that studies and advocates for women's participation in political institutions. Although both parts of my life focused on women and politics, they occupied completely different worlds; I could spend the morning reading Judith Butler and the evening talking to the Women's Political Caucus or the Federation of Republican Women. I often felt as if I personally embodied the theory-practice divide.

However, these two worlds came together for me in considering community service as a tool of citizenship education. Here, feminist critiques of citizenship theory, analyses of the public-private split, and the study of women's history could find real-life resonance in my professional work and teaching. I could see why, and how, theory mattered and could use these insights to envision better practice. In this paper, I will explore the ways in which feminist theory caused me, first, to look critically at community service and then to formulate a service-learning pedagogy that is avowedly political.

My interest in service-learning comes from my work at CAWP, developing and administering programs that encourage young women to get involved in politics and policy making.[2] Informing my work at CAWP is the belief that citizenship involves participating in politics — whether as a grass-roots activist, a government employee, or an elected or appointed official. Many students I have worked with are themselves disconnected from politics but actively involved in service. These students easily understood the difference they could make helping at a soup kitchen. Less clear was the connection between the issues they cared about and the world of politics and policy making. Subscribing to the general public disillusionment with politics, many of these young women believed that getting involved in service was both easier and safer. Service activities were more manageable than the compromise and conflict of politics. Through service, students saw the immediate impact of their work and came away gratified.

Such young women reflect the current national interest in service. Long gone are the images of Peace Corps hippies slogging through the mud. National organizations with sophisticated visual images, websites, and advertising dollars market "idealism through service" to the so-called "slacker" generation. Corporations proclaim their commitment to voluntarism in advertising and annual reports. From the daily calisthenics of the City Year program to the high gloss of *Melrose Place* star Andrew Shue's "Do Something," service is hip. Even MTV has jumped on the bandwagon, filming a *Real World* series around glamorous young people performing service activities in Boston.

The academy has also embraced service, proclaiming it the pedagogy of citizenship. Decrying young people as "excessively inward-looking and insulated from adult responsibilities" (Moskos 1988: 110), scholars and politicians have called for new ways for young people to fulfill their civic responsibility. Civic education through service has brought together political scientists and theorists, scholars in education, college and school administrators, federal and state policymakers, and nonprofits. Influenced by these academic debates, the Clinton administration created a national service program called AmeriCorps. There has been a huge explosion of service-learning at colleges and universities across the country, while more high schools now require community service for graduation. Service, combined with classroom learning, has become the supposed solution to making education more meaningful, reminding young people of their obligations as citizens, making students "more human," teaching the skills necessary to live in a democratic society, rebuilding an ideal of national cohesion, and saving communities in need.[3]

The image of thousands of young people marching into the nation's troubled communities to "do good" inspires a great deal of positive feeling, flattering media attention, and grandiose rhetoric. Helping battered women to find shelter, feeding the homeless, maintaining national park trails, and all the other work community service participants do is important and necessary. The focus on citizenship, emphasizing rights and obligations, reminds us of the best of the idea of community: our connection to each other, our mutuality, our shared responsibility for creating a better society. These ideas are of central concern to feminists, whose theories and critiques of "autonomous man" emphasize our interconnection and whose commitment to social justice informs much of their scholarly and activist work.

This being the case, challenging the idea that educators should use service to foster citizenship seems downright curmudgeonly. However, it is my contention that educators, and feminists in particular, must cast a critical eye on service as a pedagogy of citizenship. Given the many feminist critiques of citizenship theory, it is crucial that feminist educators carefully consider those pedagogies that claim to educate and shape citizens. An exploration of the historical and theoretical roots of community service theory reveals an intellectual tradition that is heavily masculinized and fails to consider the historical relationship between women, service, and politics.

Yet it is this relationship that offers the best lessons for connecting service to social change.

Citizenship, Community, and Service

What does it mean to be a citizen? What do citizens do? What are the values embodied in citizenship? What activities mark one as a citizen? What are a citizen's rights? What are a citizen's obligations? In American political culture and thought, the definition of a citizen — these behaviors, values, and actions — has included some members of the polity and excluded others. From 18th-century arrangements that only white, property-owning males could vote, to the exclusion of blacks from many aspects of politics, economics, and society, to modern debates about the role of women in the national military, questions about what some individuals and groups can and cannot do because of their identity have shaped our national debate about citizenship.

Feminist scholars have long been concerned that the ways that citizenship has been defined and practiced have excluded women. As Jones writes:

> . . . the characteristics, qualities, attributes, behavior, and identity of those who are regarded as full members of the political community — are derived from a set of values, experiences, modes of discourse, rituals and practices that both explicitly and implicitly privilege men and the "masculine" and exclude women and the "female." (1990: 781)

My own first question, then, when confronting community service theory, was whether Jones's analysis rang true. Where were women and women's experiences in the discourse? Readings on women and politics painted a rich picture of women's historical and contemporary involvement in service, but that involvement was startlingly absent from the contemporary discussion of community service. A review of more than 120 books and articles on community service theory and practice found only a handful of writers who mentioned women, most simply asking the question "Why are more female students than male students involved in service activities?"[4] Gender as a category of analysis was absent.

If, then, community service as practiced by women has not been the text on which contemporary community service is based, what is? Its roots are in one of the most gendered of citizenship acts — the military. Community service theorists trace the idea of service as a way to educate citizens to William James's essay "The Moral Equivalent of War." In the essay, James argued that war and military service have inculcated the central values of citizenship: "Martial virtues must be the enduring cement; intrepidity, contempt of softness, surrender of private interest, obedience to command, must still remain the rock upon which states are built" (1967: 668).

A pacifist, James needed to devise another means to teach those same citizenship values. He advocated mandatory service work: "an army enlisted against Nature . . . our gilded youths would be drafted off, according to their choice, to get the childishness knocked out of them, and to come back into society with healthier sympathies and soberer ideas" (1967: 669). Contemporary community service theorists have built on this idea of military service as the model for citizenship education.

For Moskos, described as the "leading proponent of the idea of citizenship through national service" (Gorham 1992: 8), military service teaches citizens about obligations to the nation-state and about loyalty to the social whole. By focusing on citizen obligations, Moskos reflects the concern of many democratic theorists who argue that citizenship has been defined only by rights. These theorists want to replace liberalism's rugged individual, who is concerned only with pursuing his or her self-interest, with a philosophy that emphasizes shared values and the obligations and duties of the individual to the whole. Moskos develops a line of thought "in which private interests are subordinated to the public good and in which community life takes precedence over individual pursuits" (Gorham 1992: 8).

Although this approach may appeal to many feminists who have also challenged liberalism's rational individualism, Young's (1986) work reminds us that community can be a problematic concept. The quest for community necessarily excludes, defining some individuals as "inside" and some as "outside." Striving for community can also reduce subjects to what is common among them, denying differences. Young writes:

> In the U.S. today, identification as a member of such a community also often occurs as an oppositional differentiation from other groups, who are feared, or at best devalued. . . . Racism, ethnic chauvinism, and class devaluation, I suggest, grow partly from a desire for community; that is, from the desire to understand others as they understand themselves and from the desire to be understood as I understand myself. (1986: 12-13)

Young is careful to point out that the idea of community is not inherently racist. Rather, within a racist and masculinist society, the definition of the other is made on racial and gendered lines.

Moskos also highlights the ways that military service creates citizen loyalty to the social whole and the nation-state, reflecting another theme in community service theory. A deep worry about the legitimacy of U.S. political culture, where relatively few people vote, many people evade taxes, and economic self-interest is paramount, pervades community service theory.[5] At the center of this worry is "concern with the unraveling of America's social consensus in which the pursuit of politics is based upon class, race, gender, or sexual preference, a veritable 'democratic overload'" (Moskos 1988: 8). Particularized identities — race, class, gender, often called "special interests" — are a threat to democratic institutions. It is up to governmental and educational systems to create new forms of civic education that move citizens past their group identities and, instead, foster loyalty to a civic ideal.

Janowitz (1983), another key community service theorist, argues that civic education fails when it does not overcome the effects of ethnic and racial "communalism," his term for black, Hispanic, and Native American nationalism or separatism. He argues that even though communalism has contributed to increased political participation, it has also "presented [the] specter of a series of cleavages that would weaken national citizenship and democratic political institutions" (107). Community service theory posits what Jones has identified as a central feminist concern with citizenship theory, a call to "subordinate the specific bonds of gender, race, and class — indeed, all particularized identities — in favor, most often, of a national identity and loyalty to the state" (Jones 1990: 781).

Yet we know from the practice of community service that people live, work, and practice politics in communities that are often defined by identity. Sites where people come together to participate in society — churches, temples, and mosques; ethnic social groups; gay and lesbian community centers — are all places where people unite because of some shared part of their identity. Rather than erase those differences in pursuit of an overarching commitment to the nation-state, community service theorists might look to those places as sites to engage citizens in politics and create coalitions that can bridge differences for the sake of commonly desired social change.

My readings in community service theory left me deeply unsatisfied. I am not interested, either pedagogically or politically, in erasing students' identities in pursuit of some myth of citizenship. For me, it is particularly important that those who have been disenfranchised because of their identities claim political participation as a central act of citizenship. And though I am an advocate for participation in political institutions, my goal is not the inculcation of loyalty to those institutions. Rather, I am interested in academic and experiential techniques that both challenge and prepare students to use those institutions to foster social change.

Women's history offers a different model for service as citizenship education. Looking to women's history demonstrates two important lessons to anyone interested in service-learning. First, women's history of activism points to the ways in which service becomes "depoliticized" as a private activity that is both purer and more moral. When women's activity is reduced to private, it is not a challenge to the traditionally male world of politics. Feminist revaluations of women's work as public work can give us a model for service that is highly political. Exploring the history of women's activism also challenges us to think about the ways that service constructs the "served" as needy and enforces certain norms of behavior that are gendered, raced, and classed.

Learning From Women's History

I am always struck by the student who works faithfully every week at the local shelter, but refuses to call or write her member of Congress during votes on welfare reform because "it just won't matter." She expresses tremendous disgust and disillusionment, complaining that politics is dirty, corrupt, conflictual, and too filled with compromise. Her decision not to engage in politics speaks volumes, pointing to the ways in which public decision making has become distanced from citizens. Nevertheless, it also speaks to the power of the ideology of service. The solution to the social problems of hunger and homelessness is individualized as simply the volunteer efforts of individuals. The focus tends to be on how this one student can make a difference without necessarily understanding or addressing larger social conditions. This move away from politics toward service has long struck me as a reversal of generations of women's activism, where service galvanized women's involvement in politics and advocacy.

Community service has historically been a key way for women — largely excluded by custom and socialization from public decision making — to make a difference in their communities. From the black women's club movement to the founding of settlement houses in urban areas to the campaigns to control alcohol, women have a rich and varied history of involvement in public life through service.

Historically, these service activities have been wrapped in a perception of women's moral authority. Women drew on domestic virtue, religious piety, and the ideology of motherhood as justification for their involvement in public questions. Their activity in the community was defined as virtuous service; men's activity was the messy, contested work of politics and public life. However, the equation of women's public work with morality has had long-term consequences for women's power and equality. When women's work is "moral" or "care-taking," it is too often pushed aside as social housekeeping and is less of a challenge to male political power. Such definitions divide service and politics, creating a dichotomy concretized in a gendered split. This dichotomy fosters the notion that service is nonpolitical, virtuous, and nonconflictual.

When service is conceptualized as safer and purer than politics, it categorizes service and politics as two distinct activities. This distinction exists in today's service movement; Julia Scatliff, former executive director of a network of university service programs, told Loeb, a chronicler of the 20-something generation, that

> the service movement's task was "to help the person lying bleeding in the street, to put our hands over the aorta and stop the flow." COOL would leave the larger issues, she said, up to America's national leaders, who would respond when they heard sufficiently powerful testaments of need. (Loeb 1994: 236)

Such a dichotomization has caused many community service educators to avoid politics, undermining the possibility of recognizing service as politics or of educating students for social change. For example, Terry Russell, the general counsel at the Corporation for National Service (CNS), in describing why CNS prohibited AmeriCorps participants from attending as AmeriCorps participants a "Stand for Children" rally in Washington, D.C., wrote:

> National service has to be nonpartisan. What's more, it should be about bringing communities together by getting things done. Strikes, demonstrations and political activities can have the opposite effect. They polarize and divide.[8]

This statement reflects a troubling tendency within the community service movement to conclude that politics is evil. Such a belief allows — no, *requires* — students to abdicate their responsibility to confront larger social problems. It perpetuates the myth that service itself is not a political activity. Yet we need only consider that the service activities the CNS prioritizes — education, crime prevention, health, housing, the environment — are some of the most important and contested political issues in our communities. As feminists, we should worry when these issues, long sites of activism, are privatized as areas of pure service and that our students are being discouraged from acting politically in ways that might obviate the need for their service.

Privatization and glorification of service also create the misperception that service always has a beneficial impact. Lessons from women's history remind us about the potentially negative consequences of service. Scholars have explored the ways in which women's service and reform work construed communities as lacking and therefore in need of service. Often, the service enforced norms of middle-class "Americanness" loaded with set ideas about gender, race, and class. Whether the focus was religious instruction (Scott 1990), controlling sexual behavior (Ryan 1979), instruction into the ways of American life (Karl 1983), or controlling male vice by controlling alcohol (Blocker 1985; Dannenbaum 1984), service and reform were as much about regulating behavior as they were about ameliorating material conditions (Mink 1990).

Finally, one could argue that the current celebration of the service experience can be seen by feminists as an advantageous situation, a valuation of the caring work that women have historically performed. Yet, why is service only celebrated when performed without compensation? Service jobs in the economy, held primarily by women and men of color, are overlooked and undervalued. The same is true with service to the family, again primarily women's work. We do not reward service in any market or policy arena, and yet, in community service rhetoric, citizenship itself depends on it.

From Service to Politics

There are alternative ways of looking at service, ways that consider how it can engage people in politics. Historically, service evolved into political activity for some women as they grew disillusioned with social reform efforts to change behavior and attitudes through individual action. Reformers turned to legislative and policy change to address their concerns. This shift in focus contributed to a growing movement of women demanding access to formal political rights and culminated in the suffrage campaign. Particularly in the Progressive Era, women pursued public policy strategies; national federations of black and white women's clubs began developing policy agendas on issues such as conservation, food safety, factory inspection, child labor, and the minimum wage (Scott 1990). In addition to helping set a legislative agenda, some women active in service and reform moved into formal positions of authority. The Illinois Women's Alliance, organized by a women's union, forced the Chicago City Council to appoint five women as inspectors to ensure that city health codes were met (Sklar 1990). Hull House activist Florence Kelley helped forge a cross-class alliance that led the charge for anti-sweatshop legislation, and then spent four years as chief factory inspector for the State of Illinois (Sklar 1990). Many contemporary women leaders also cite their volunteer community experience as a key motivator for their involvement in the political process.[9]

Bringing Service and Politics Together: A Classroom Model

Authors such as John McKnight (1989) and Ivan Illich (1990) have challenged the contemporary community service movement, arguing that the provision of service does little to empower communities to make change. However worthy, serving food in a soup kitchen is often simply a band-aid that does little to confront the social, economic, or political systems that create and sustain hunger. What would service look like if we threw away the bumper sticker "Practice Random Acts of Kindness" and replaced it with "Practice Calculated Acts of Social Justice"?

Community service has a more radical potential if seen as a prepolitical step, demanding that individuals confront both the causes and results of social issues. Young people working with communities see economic injustice, racism, sexism, violence, poverty — and hope, justice, equality, and activism. By working with other community members, they can confront and break stereotypes. Community service can awaken in all participants a sense of social justice and social concern. By using service-learning techniques that challenge societal institutions and teach advocacy skills, young people can channel their concerns into larger social efforts, using policy and activism to address the root causes of many social needs.

What might such practice look like in a classroom? A few years ago, I developed a service-learning course called Becoming a Public Citizen. The course was designed to explore the connections between service and policy making.[10] In addition to a standard three-credit course, students participated in a four-hour-a-week service placement at the community agency of their choice, for which they earned one credit.[11] In the classroom, they studied participatory democracy, asking such questions as: What does it mean to be a citizen in the American polity? What are the expectations of democracy?[12] How have disenfranchised groups challenged these expectations?[13] We then looked at service-learning as a technique for educating young people for citizenship, asking what advocates expected students to gain from their service experiences and also reading authors who challenged the idea of service.[14]

During each class, we discussed the students' placements. We talked about their agencies' clienteles, governance structures, and fundraising strategies. Students explored the ways in which these agencies were embedded in a complex layer of government, foundation, and corporate policies and regulations that affected their approaches to social problems and the service they could provide. Students came to see how the provision of service was itself political. These discussions also provided an opportunity for students to raise questions about their roles in service. Some students discussed what it meant to be a middle-class, white student working with inner-city, Spanish-speaking children, or what happened when they left their placements at the end of the semester, a particular concern for students working with children. We talked about the limits of their work, and the difference they could make.

The class also read and discussed service in women's history. Students read accounts of women's service and activism and explored how women, when denied formal access to the public sphere, exercised authority and power. They also explored the ways in which service work prompted women to move into public life, and discussed some contemporary women leaders who became involved in politics through their service activities.

Students were required to select a public policy question of concern to them that was also related to their community service placement, to fulfill the requirements of a research project. A student teaching computer skills to Girl Scouts did her research on federal efforts to build "women in science and math" curriculums. Another student working at a women's health clinic conducted research on federal health care reform. Students were required to describe their policy questions and identify key advocacy organizations, elected officials, bureaucracies, and boards or commissions that addressed these questions, as well as actually present different approaches to addressing the questions. To round out their research, each student identified and interviewed at least two leaders — one who held a formal leadership position and one who was a community advocate. The research gave students a sense of the complicated policy structures that define issues and offer solutions.

However, theoretical and historical exploration and research were only part of the class goals. The class was also designed to encourage students to act. From my NEW Leadership (National Education for Women's Leadership) experience, I knew many students did not understand how citizens engage in the political process, nor did they have advocacy skills to draw on. Through case studies, we explored the skills necessary for political participation at the grass-roots level. Students then read skills-development articles on organizing and advocacy skills, and participated in an issue-based campaign workshop.

To link their service, academic study and research, and political practice, students developed action plans for public advocacy or public education campaigns around their research. I described this project to the students as follows:

> For example, if you have been working at a soup kitchen, and have done your research on state initiatives to alter food stamp regulations, your advocacy campaign should focus on those issues. Remember: Your audience is not the clients of a social service agency; this is not a service plan. In other words, do not develop a plan that trains volunteers to assist clients in filling out food stamp applications. Rather, your advocacy campaign might focus on policy change, on reaching the leaders in government: helping to create or support a piece of legislation, or getting food kitchen clients onto a community board, or organizing a petition to encourage the city's development commission to improve grocery store access.

Some students did little more than start a letter-writing campaign, whereas others developed wonderfully creative advocacy strategies. One student filmed public service announcements highlighting the importance of women's education. Another student used carpet remnants, with the tag line "Don't sweep adult education under the rug," as the centerpiece of a lobbying campaign. In her course evaluation, one student observed that her project "taught [her] to think creatively, to think about how to get people's attention and present a valid argument."

The service experience was an invaluable lesson for these students, despite its limited duration (40 hours over the semester). Through direct experience, research on regulations and legislation came to life. The theoretical and historical readings provided a basis for understanding the relationship between service and citizenship as politics. However, service linked to classroom reading and research was still not enough. Though the students would have stopped there, they also needed assignments that took them the next step — thinking about larger issues and building the skills and knowledge needed to craft solutions. We should not be using service simply to educate students to address social problems, we should be teaching students to solve those problems through politics.

Notes

1. My thanks to Kathleen Casey, Kathy Kleeman, and Ruth B. Mandel for their comments on this article. Additional thanks to Susan J. Carroll for her comments on an earlier version of these ideas.

2. CAWP's core program in this area, NEW Leadership (National Education for Women's Leadership), was developed in 1991 and has involved more than 300 students from across the country. The program's curriculum includes learning about women's historical and contemporary participation in politics and policy making; exploring leadership in a diverse society; connecting with women leaders making a difference in the public sphere; building leadership skills; and practicing leadership through an experiential project. More information on the program can be found at <http://www.rci.rutgers.edu/~cawp/newl/ywlihome.htm>.

3. Service-learning in higher education takes many forms. I want to differentiate between those educators who use experiential learning to provide practical experience in a field (for example, pre-med students who work in a hospital) and those who claim service-learning as a way to inculcate citizenship values. It is the latter school of thought that has the richest theoretical tradition, steeped in political philosophy, and the most influence on national policy debates in the field of community service. Central texts include *Strong Democracy* by Benjamin R. Barber (University of California Press, 1984); *Gratitude* by William F. Buckley, Jr. (Random House, 1990); *National Service: What Would It Mean?* by Richard Danzig and Peter Szanton (Lexington Books, 1986); *National Service Pro & Con* by Williamson Evers (Hoover Institution Press, 1990); *The Reconstruction of Patriotism* by Morris Janowitz (University of Chicago Press, 1983); *A Call to Civic Service* by Charles Moskos (Free Press, 1988); and *The Civic Imperative* by Richard Pratte (Teacher's College Press, 1988).

4. The one notable exception is Gorham (1992), who draws on feminist democratic theory but not women's history.

5. See, for example, Carnegie Task Force 1989; Coleman 1974; Harrison 1987; and Silberman 1990.

6. For a discussion of this point, see Baker 1984; McCarthy 1990; Scott 1990; and Welter 1966.

7. On this point, also see Pascoe 1990; Ryan 1979; and Scott 1990.

8. I also find it ironic that at this historic moment, when women and men of color are beginning to make inroads into formal decision-making positions, power as expressed by political activism is "out" but service is "in."

9. See, for example, Kunin 1994.

10. The course was co-taught with Dr. Ruth B. Mandel, director, Eagleton Institute of Politics, and Board of Governors Professor of Politics, Rutgers University. The course was funded through a two-year grant from the Rutgers Office of the Vice President for Undergraduate Education.

11. These placements were organized by Rutgers's Citizenship and Service Education (CASE) program, the university-wide service-learning program.

12. Readings included John Dewey's "Search for the Great Community" and Thomas Jefferson's "Letter to Samuel Kercheval," both in *Education for Democracy,* Benjamin R. Barber and Richard M. Battistoni, eds. (Kendall/Hunt, 1993); and Alexis de Tocqueville's "That the Americans Combat the Effects of Individualism by Free Institutions" and "Of the Use Which the Americans Make of Public Associations in Civil Life," in *Democracy in America,* Richard D. Heffner, ed. (Penguin, 1956).

13. Readings included Martin Luther King, Jr.'s "Give Us the Ballot — We Will Transform the South," in *A Testament of Hope,* James M. Washington, ed. (Harper, 1986); Carole Pateman's "Feminism and Democracy," in *Education for Democracy,* Benjamin R. Barber and Richard M. Battistoni, eds. (Kendall/Hunt, 1993); Richard Reeves's "Canandaigua," in *American Journey* (Simon and Schuster, 1982); and Cornel West's "Introduction," in *Race Matters* (Vintage, 1994).

14. Readings included Theresa Funiciello's "Filling the Gap: A Charitable Deduction" and "City Silos and the Pop-Tart Connection," in *Tyranny of Kindness* (The Atlantic Monthly Press, 1993); Paul Rogat Loeb's *Generation at the Crossroads* (Rutgers University Press, 1994); and Carrie Spector's "Empty the Shelters: Anatomy of a Struggle," in *Who Cares?* (Winter 1995, pp. 40-43).

References

Baker, Paula. (1984). "The Domestication of Politics: Women and American Political Society, 1780-1920." *American Historical Review* 89: 620-647.

Blocker, Jr., Jack S. (1985). "Separate Paths: Suffragists and the Women's Temperance Crusade." *Signs* 10(2): 460-476.

Carnegie Task Force on Education of Young Adolescents. (1989). *Turning Points: Preparing American Youth for the 21st Century.* New York, NY: Carnegie Council on Adolescent Development, The Carnegie Corporation.

Coleman, J. (1974). *Youth: Transition to Adulthood.* Chicago, IL: University of Chicago Press.

Corporation for National Service. (June 17, 1996). *National Service News*, p. 4. Available at <http://www.cns.gov>.

Dannenbaum, Jed. (1984). *Drink and Disorder.* Urbana, IL: University of Illinois Press.

Gorham, Eric B. (1992). *National Service, Citizenship, and Political Education.* Albany, NY: State University of New York Press.

Harrison, Charles. (1987). *Student Service: The New Carnegie Unit.* Princeton, NJ: The Carnegie Foundation for the Advancement of Teaching.

Illich, Ivan. (1990). "To Hell With Good Intentions." In *Combining Service and Learning*, edited by Jane Kendall and Associates, pp. 314-320. Raleigh, NC: National Society for Internships and Experiential Education.

James, William. (1967). "The Moral Equivalent of War." In *The Writings of William James*, edited by John J. McDermott, pp. 660-670. New York, NY: Random House.

Janowitz, Morris. (1983). *The Reconstruction of Patriotism.* Chicago, IL: University of Chicago Press.

Jones, Kathleen. (1990). "Citizenship in a Woman-Friendly Polity." *Signs* 15(4): 781-812.

Karl, Barry D. (1983). *The Uneasy State.* Chicago, IL: University of Chicago Press.

Kunin, Madeleine. (1994). *Living a Political Life.* New York, NY: Knopf.

Loeb, Paul Rogat. (1994). *Generation at the Crossroads.* New Brunswick, NJ: Rutgers University Press.

McCarthy, Kathleen D. (1990). "Parallel Power Structures: Women and the Voluntary Sphere." In *Lady Bountiful Revisited: Women, Philanthropy, and Power*, edited by Kathleen D. McCarthy, pp. 1-34. New Brunswick, NJ: Rutgers University Press.

McKnight, John. (January/February 1989). "Why 'Servanthood' Is Bad." *The Other Side*, pp. 38-40.

Mink, Gwendolyn. (1990). "The Lady and the Tramp: Gender, Race, and the Origins of the American Welfare State." In *Women, the State, and Welfare*, edited by Linda Gordon, pp. 92-122. Madison, WI: University of Wisconsin Press.

Moskos, Charles. (1988). *A Call to Civic Service.* New York, NY: Free Press.

Pascoe, Peggy. (1990). *Relations of Rescue.* Oxford: Oxford University Press.

Ryan, Mary P. (Spring 1979). "The Power of Women's Networks: A Case Study of Female Moral Reform in Antebellum America." *Feminist Studies* 5: 66-85.

Scott, Anne Firor. (1990). "Women's Voluntary Associations: From Charity to Reform." In *Lady Bountiful Revisited: Women, Philanthropy, and Power*, edited by Kathleen D. McCarthy, pp. 35-54. New Brunswick, NJ: Rutgers University Press.

Silberman, C. (1990). *Crisis in the Classroom.* New York, NY: Random House.

Sklar, Kathryn Kish. (1990). "Hull House in the 1890s: A Community of Women Reformers." In *Unequal Sisters,* edited by Ellen Carol DuBois and Vicki C. Ruiz, pp. 109-122. New York, NY: Routledge.

Welter, Barbara. (1966). "The Cult of True Womanhood, 1820-1860." *American Quarterly* 18: 151-174.

Young, Iris Marion. (Spring 1986). "The Ideal of Community and the Politics of Difference." *Social Theory and Practice* 12: 1-26.

———— . (January 1989). "Polity and Group Difference: A Critique of the Ideal of Universal Citizenship." *Ethics* 99: 250-274.

———— . (1990). *Justice and the Politics of Difference.* Princeton, NJ: Princeton University Press.

Political Science 440
Rutgers University
Fall, 1996

BECOMING A PUBLIC CITIZEN
CONNECTING COMMUNITY SERVICE AND PUBLIC LEADERSHIP

Instructors:	Ruth Mandel and Tobi Walker
Office:	Eagleton Institute of Politics, Douglass Campus
Office Hours:	Ruth Mandel: by appointment
	Tobi Walker: Mondays, noon to 2:00 or by appointment
Office Phone:	828-2210, exts. 228 and 230 respectively

Course Description

In this seminar, we will explore the links between community service and public leadership, which we define as making a difference in one's community, state, and nation through government and public policymaking. Historically, community service has been the means by which women left the private realm and entered the public world. We will ask whether that connection still exists and how it can be strengthened. Students will participate in a service experience in the community and explore public policymaking and women's leadership in the classroom. Through a research paper and the development of a public advocacy campaign, students will apply academic skills and community experience to the world of public policymaking.

We will begin the course by looking at notions of participatory democracy. What does it mean to be a citizen in the American polity? What are the expectations of democracy? How have these concepts been challenged by marginalized populations? We will then look at service as a technique for educating young people for citizenship. What are the pedagogical expectations of service? What are the challenges to the concept of service?

Our focus will then shift to the role that service and voluntarism has played in women's history. Denied formal access to the public sphere, how did women exercise authority and power? How did women's service work prompt women's access to public life and how does that reflect in contemporary politics?

We will then turn to ways that students can use their service experience to engage in mainstream political activity by examining the skills necessary for political participation. Finally, we will consider political interest and motivation among the "twenty-something" generation. Studies show that young people have less interest in politics then ever before. Why? How can young people be motivated and galvanized to make a difference?

This course has five objectives:
1) to make a connection between academic and extra-curricular interests and the public arena;
2) to understand the theoretical expectations of democratic citizenship and challenges to those concepts;

3) to carefully consider the dynamics of service learning and its consequences;
4) to discover the ways that service has moved women into the public arena;
5) to explore the various roles one can play in the political process and to expand opportunities for connecting to that process.

Course Requirements

This will be an intense and highly participatory class that will require everyone's involvement. Students will be expected to read each week's selections completely and critically and to be active participants in class discussions.

Community Service

This course has a community service requirement. You will volunteer 4 hours per week for 10 weeks in a community service placement in an issue area of interest to you. The placements will be organized by the CASE program. You will receive one additional credit, but you must register for both this class (790:440:03) and for the community service placement (790:400) and attend all scheduled trainings conducted by the CASE program.

Community service credit will be graded separately from classroom activities. You will be expected to keep a simple log of your activities during your volunteer hours and submit the log to the instructors on December 2nd. Community service hours must be completed by November 25.

Paper

One major paper is required for this class. Students will select a public policy question of concern to them and related to their community service placement. Each student will identify and interview at least two leaders who share an interest in the policy question. One of the leaders must hold a formal leadership position and one must be a community advocate.

The paper should describe the policy question and identify the key advocacy organizations, elected officials, bureaucracies, and boards or commissions which address the issue. The paper should present the varying approaches to addressing the issue. However, in the end the author should take a stand on the issue and advocate for a preferred approach to solving the problem, whether that be through improved implementation of current policies, support for proposed legislation, or a different policy approach. The author's proposed solution will then be the basis of her/his action plan.

To facilitate the writing and research process, the papers will be graded in a "rolling fashion," with bibliographies, interview questions, and a rough draft due during the semester. By October 7th, students will submit in writing their paper topics and arrange a meeting with Ms. Walker to discuss the topic and their preliminary ideas. No later than October 21st, students will submit a bibliography. No later than October 28th, students will submit the names of the two people they wish to interview and a list of interview questions; these *must be approved* before interviewing can proceed. A rough draft of the paper is due November 18th.

To provide students with more feedback on their papers, as well as provide experience in constructive feedback, students will participate in a group review process. Students will be assigned to groups of three and rough drafts will be exchanged among group members. Reviewers have one week to read the paper and make comments. Reviewers will be provided with a series of questions which will guide their feedback. One copy of the review will be given to the paper writer and a copy should be submitted to the instructors.

All component parts must be submitted on time; lateness will affect the grade. The papers are due December 9th. *There are no exceptions to this deadline; for every day the paper is late, the grade will be reduced by one letter.*

Action Plan

In order to explore how to relate academic study and research with political practice, students will also develop an action plan for an advocacy campaign around the issue each has researched. Each student will present her/his action plan in class during the last two weeks of class. We will discuss these action plans in more detail later in the semester.

Readings

Readings are available for purchase from Joanne on the second floor of the Eagleton Institute of Politics.

Instructors' Expectations

1. Utilize the assigned readings, lectures, and discussions for the research papers, action plans, and community service experiences.
2. Bring the community service experiences into the classroom as a basis for questions and discussion.
3. Submit all written assignments on time, typed, and proofread. The instructors will expect students' writing to conform to the rules of grammar, punctuation, and spelling of standard written English.

Breakdown of Seminar Grade

15% Attendance and Participation
15% Bibliography, Interview Questions, & Rough Draft
 5% Reviews
40% Paper
25% Action Plan

Dates to Remember

September 14	CASE Orientation (mandatory)
October 7	Paper Topic Due
October 21	Bibliography Due
October 28	Interview Names and Questions Due
November 18	Rough Draft Due (3 copies)
November 25	Reviews Due
November 25	Community Service Hours Completed
December 2	Placement Logs Due
December 9	Paper Due/Action Plan Presentations
December 18	Action Plan Presentations

Class Schedule

September 9: **Course overview, discussion of community service placements, and introduction of basic concepts**

September 16: **A Basis for Discussion**

Harry C. Boyte and Kathryn Stoff Hogg, *Doing Politics: An Owner's Manual for Public Life*, Minnesota: Hubert H. Humphrey Institute of Public Affairs, 1992.

Sara M. Evans, "Women's History and Political Theory: Toward a Feminist Approach to Public Life," in Nancy A. Hewitt and Suzanne Lebsock (eds.), *Visible Women*, Urbana: University of Illinois Press, 1993, pp. 119-140.

Oliver Sacks, "The Revolution of the Deaf," in Benjamin R. Barber and Richard M. Battistoni (eds.), *Education for Democracy*, Iowa: Kendall/Hunt Publishing Company, 1993.

September 23: **Citizens, Community, Democracy**

John Dewey, "Search for the Great Community," excerpted in Benjamin R. Barber and Richard M. Battistoni (eds.), *Education for Democracy*, Iowa: Kendall/Hunt Publishing Company, 1993.

Thomas Jefferson, "Letter to Samuel Kercheval," in Benjamin R. Barber and Richard M. Battistoni (eds.), *Education for Democracy*, Iowa: Kendall/Hunt Publishing Company, 1993.

Alexis de Tocqueville,"That the Americans Combat the Effects of Individualism by Free Institutions," and "Of the Use which the Americans Make of Public Associations in Civil Life," in Richard D. Heffner (ed.) *Democracy in America*, New York: Penguin Group, 1956.

September 30: **Citizens, Community, Democracy**

Martin Luther King, Jr., "Give Us the Ballot -- We Will Transform the South," in James M. Washington (ed.) *A Testament of Hope*, San Francisco: Harper, 1986.

Carole Pateman, "Feminism and Democracy," in Benjamin R. Barber and Richard M. Battistoni (eds.), *Education for Democracy*, Iowa: Kendall/Hunt Publishing Company, 1993.

Richard Reeves, "Canandaigua," *American Journey*, New York: Simon and Schuster, 1982.

Roger M. Smith, "Beyond Tocqueville, Myrdal, and Hartz: The Multiple Traditions in America," in *American Political Science Review*, vol. 87, no. 3, September 1993, pp. 549-566.

Cornel West, "Introduction," *Race Matters*, New York: Vintage Books, 1994, pp. 3-13.

October 7:   **Community Service: Educating Future Citizens**   *Paper Topics Due*

Bryan Barnett and Grace Losso, "For Self and Others: Some Reflections on the Value of Community Service," *Getting the Most from Community Service*, New Jersey: The Civic Education and Community Service Program, 1991, pp. 19-24.

Brad Belbas, Kathi Gorak, and Rob Shumer, "Commonly Used Definitions of Service Learning: A Discussion Piece," October, 1993.

William James, "The Moral Equivalent of War," in John J. McDermott (ed.), *The Writings of William James*. New York: Random House, 1967, 660-671.

Matthew Moseley, "The Youth Service Movement: America's Trump Card in Revitalizing Democracy," *National Civic Review*, Summer/Fall, 1995.

October 14:   **Library Session**   *Meet in Douglass Library*

October 21:   **Critiques of Service and "Charity"**   *Bibliography Due*

Theresa Funiciello, "Filling the Gap: A Charitable Deduction," and "City Silos and the Pop-Tart Connection,"*Tyranny of Kindness*, New York: The Atlantic Monthly Press, 1993.

Eric B. Gorham, "National Service, Political Socialization, and Citizenship," *National Service, Citizenship, and Political Education*. Albany: State University of New York Press, 1992, pp. 5-30.

Paul Rogat Loeb, "Tangible Fruits: The Community Service Movement," in *Generation at the Crossroads: Apathy and Action on the American Campus*, New Brunswick: Rutgers University Press, 1994, pp. 231-247.

Carrie Spector, "Empty the Shelters: Anatomy of a Struggle," *WhoCares*, Winter, 1995, pp. 40-43.

October 28:   **Women's Voluntarism and Moral Authority**   *Interview Names and*
                                                                              Questions Due

Catharine Beecher, "The Peculiar Responsibilities of American Women," in Nancy F. Cott (ed.) *Roots of Bitterness*, New York: E.P. Dutton & Co., 1972.

Karen J. Blair, "Sorois and the New England Women's Club," *The Clubwoman as Feminist*, New York: Holms & Meier Publishers, Inc., 1980.

Paula Giddings, "To Be a Woman, Sublime": The Ideas of the National Black Women's Club Movement (to 1917)," *When and Where I Enter: The Impact of Black Women on Race and Sex in America*, New York: William Morrow and Company, 1984, pp. 95-118.

Barbara Welter, "The Cult of True Womanhood, 1820-1860," *American Quarterly* 18:151-74.

November 4: **From Service to Reform: Women Entering the Public Sphere**

Paula Baker, "The Domestication of Politics: Women and American Political Society, 1780-1920," *American Historical Review* 89 (1984) p. 620-647.

Mary Pardo, "Mexican American Women Grassroots Community Activists: 'Mothers of East Los Angeles,'" *Frontiers*, vol. Xi, no. 1, 1990, pp. 1-7.

Ann Firor Scott, "Women's Voluntary Associations: From Charity to Reform," in Kathleen D. McCarthy (ed.) *Lady Bountiful Revisited*, New Brunswick: Rutgers University Press, 1990.

November 11: **Women in Contemporary Politics**

Susan J. Carroll, "The Politics of Difference: Women Public Officials as Agents of Change," *Stanford Law & Policy Review*, 5 (Spring, 1994), pp. 11-20.

Tamara Jones, "A Candidate's Uneasy Station in Life," *The Washington Post*.

Celinda C. Lake and Vincent J. Breglio, "Different Voices, Different Views: The Politics of Gender," *The American Woman 1992-1993*, New York: W.W. Norton, 1992, pp. 178-201.

Joseph P. Shapiro, "The Mothers of Invention," *U.S. News*, January 10, 1994.

November 18: **Political Advocacy** *Rough Drafts Due*

Guest Speaker: Christy Davis, state director, U.S. Senator Frank Lautenberg

Nancy Amidei, *So You Want to Make a Difference: Advocacy is the Key*, Washington DC: OMB Watch, no date.

Kim Bobo, Jackie Kendall, Steve Max, "Direct Action Organizing," in *Organizing for Social Change*, Washington: Seven Locks Press, 1991, pp. 2-48.

November 25: **A Life in Politics** *Reviews Due*
Community Service Hours Completed

Madeleine Kunin, *Living a Political Life*, New York: Alfred A. Knopf, 1994, Chapters 2, 3, 4, 7, and 11.

December 2: **Apathy and Activism in the 20-Something Generation** *Placement Logs Due*

Susan B. Glasser, "Do 20somethings Hate Politics?" *WhoCares*, Fall, 1994, pp. 20-28.

Harwood Group, *College Students Talk Politics*, Ohio: Kettering Foundation, pp. 1-30.

Paul Rogat Loeb, "The World of Activists: Communities of Concern," in *Generation at the Crossroads: Apathy and Action on the American Campus*, New Brunswick: Rutgers University Press, 1994, pp. 207-230.

December 9:   **Oral Presentation of Action Plans**   ***Papers Due***

December 18:   **Final Exam Period/Oral Presentation of Action Plans**

Class meets 8:00 am to 11:00 am.

The History of Women and Service in the United States: A Rich and Complex Heritage

by Helen Damon-Moore

Service-learning courses have proliferated in the field of women's studies and appropriately so; at its best, service-learning fosters political awareness and activism in ways that can profitably reinforce and extend the women's studies curriculum. Community service and service-learning offer our students not only the opportunity to express care while learning experientially but also the opportunity to take risks and to explore their identity while working with, rather than for, others. Relatedly, women's studies courses are rooted in a long heritage of voluntarism and service in the United States, as are courses in other disciplines. But that heritage is more complicated in women's studies because (1) the discipline is grounded in the second-wave feminist movement that began in the 1960s; (2) second-wave feminism featured a negative stance on women volunteering; (3) throughout history women's experiences in service have varied by age, race, and class; and (4) service has been defined differently at different points in time even within cultural groups. Exploring these complicating factors is critical to understanding the history of women's service in our country, which in turn serves as a necessary backdrop to understanding best practices in women's studies service-learning courses today.

This article will demonstrate the need to define service and voluntarism in ways that give credence to and analyze the experience of women of all cultural and class backgrounds in the United States. For the purposes of the discussion at hand, to volunteer is to "choose to act in recognition of a need, with an attitude of social responsibility and without concern for monetary profit, going beyond one's basic obligations"(Ellis and Noyes 1990: 4). Different types of voluntarism have traditionally been characterized in patriarchal U.S. culture in a hierarchical fashion, starting at the bottom with direct service and progressing to policy making, fundraising, administrative volunteer work, and advocacy; hence trustees have traditionally enjoyed a higher status than have simple "volunteers."

Women have suffered from this ranking in two ways. First, such a hierarchy devalues women's direct service work, and second, it does not include mutual aid, which is the most common form of service for many racial and class groups in the United States. Women are central to the history of service, but their experiences are not monolithic; this article will demonstrate that privileged women have tended to judge and sometimes intrude on the lives of those they have sought to help, whereas volunteers of lesser means have tended to provide mutual aid to their peers and to reach out to men as well as to women. Knowing the specifics of women's gendered history of service can help practitioners of service-learning to avoid the elitist mistakes that some female volunteers and some feminists have made in the past.

History of Service

Historical studies of service generally commence with the organized acts of charity European men and women began to perform in the late 1700s and early 1800s (McCarthy 1990; Scott 1991; Shaw 1991). Predating this type of service by many years, however, was the mutual aid model dominant among many Native American tribes as far back as we know. Such tribes operated as large extended families that stressed cooperation over competition (Rauner 1991-92). Mutual aid went beyond one's immediate family to encompass the larger organized group. Colonization of Native American land by Europeans made mutual aid even more necessary. A similar pattern of mutual aid characterized the response of Africans imported as slaves beginning in the late 17th century. Thus situated, black women and men operated as "communities within communities" in which an extended pattern of mutual aid helped to "ameliorate the harsh conditions of their enforced bondage" (Albrecht and Brewer 1990: 8; Shaw 1991: 11).

The colonial period in general was distinguished by a relative lack of organized charity. European women's charity work grew out of church and friendship groups and was a result of women's desire, first, to help others like themselves in reduced circumstances — generally widows and orphans — and second, to fill a gap in the social structure resulting from a lack of governmental assistance (Crooks 1981). In organized groups, women created community institutions such as orphanages, homes for widows, schools, and poorhouses. Though well-intentioned, these women often made gratuitous distinctions between the worthy and the unworthy poor. Those whom they considered worthy included the working poor and others who had become the victims of unfortunate circumstances beyond their control, such as illness or unemployment. Those whom the women considered unworthy included people who appeared unembarrassed by their poverty, took advantage of charity, made themselves obvious by panhandling or overindulging in drink, or who simply appeared to be suspicious foreigners (Scott 1991).

In spite of such distinctions, women of privilege were filling critical gaps in the social structure, and they were participating in the public world of the emerging nation in one of the few ways available to them. Meanwhile, men of privilege, who had more outlets for public activity, were less likely to give time than money to others and were more likely to come together for ritualistic rather than service reasons.

This gendered pattern of uneven participation in the world of service and mutual aid extended to the African-American community, where women were more likely than men to participate in direct service activities. Although men of privilege volunteered less than women because of other opportunities for public and civic life, black men may have participated less for the opposite reason; namely, because they were devalued by and excluded from activity in society at large. Nineteenth-century free urban blacks, predominantly women, created antislavery groups, libraries, and literary societies for self-improvement. They also created groups to help the poor and the sick, and to bury the dead. These included the Benevolent Daughters, the Daughters of Africa, and the American Female Bond Benevolent Society of Bethel. Exclusion from the larger society spurred black women to take a broader view of needs within their own cultural group (Rauner 1991-92; Scott 1991). Indeed, this pattern appears repeatedly in U.S. history for those of Chinese, Japanese, Cuban, and Mexican extraction as well.

Around the turn of the century, W.E.B. DuBois conducted the first research on the nature of black voluntarism. He found that churches and clubs were the main venues for mutual aid and charitable work of all kinds (Rauner 1991-92). He also found heavy participation in service among African Americans at all socioeconomic levels, a trend confirmed by recent research demonstrating that black service organizations tend to be more heterogeneous than are parallel organizations of European-American women (Hine 1990; Scott 1991). Respectful partnerships with such heterogeneous organizations or groupings can provide modern-day opportunities for achieving feminist goals.

Top-down kinds of service and self-improvement efforts characterized European-American women's activity in the late 19th century. Women founded literary societies and clubs — such as the New England Women's Club and Sorosis — which in turn helped to create libraries, hospitals, placement bureaus, kindergartens, and youth programs. In addition, European-American women followed African-American women in creating antislavery societies, and moral aid and reform continued to flourish, especially through the Great Awakening and other forms of religious revivalism. Women continued in the years 1860 to 1900 to be viewed as the keepers of civic virtue in the country. Such a view in turn helped to reinforce the notion that men were not, an attitude echoed today in the much higher rates of service participation among college women than men (both through cocurricular service programs and in service-learning courses).

Women in the latter half of the 19th century were consciously using volunteer and activist work to expand their base of power — a process that culminated in the turn-of-the-century founding of the General Federation of

Women's Clubs and the beginnings of the settlement movement. Composed at first largely of white women of privilege, the settlement movement was distinguished from earlier assistance efforts by an attitude of "serving with" rather than simply "helping." Settlement workers such as Jane Addams and Florence Kelley lived in the neighborhoods they sought to assist, and they learned to listen to and plan with their neighbors rather than for them (Sklar 1995). This model is more pertinent than ever 100 years later, when students, faculty, and staff are working in neighborhoods, not as residents, but as researchers, tutors, providers of child care, etc. Emulating the holistic approach of the settlement movement could strengthen current community projects by encouraging a varied approach that would encompass service-learning courses, community service projects, and community action research.

Complicating the settlement scene at the turn of that century was that some women were paid for their work in settlement houses, laying a foundation for the development of the social work profession that would expand so rapidly in the 20th century (Fitzpatrick 1990). This expansion, in turn, laid the foundation for what would later become a divisive distinction between paid and unpaid service work in the United States.

The turn of the century saw the continued establishment by both women and men of parallel service organizations, especially by Japanese Americans, who created the Japanese-American Citizen's League to help immigrants cope with discrimination, and Mexican Americans, who through the Alianza Hispano-Americana volunteered to help one another learn English, find jobs, and preserve their Mexican cultural ties (Rauner 1991-92). Cuban-American charity groups in Florida evinced class divisions, with more prosperous women reaching out to those below them in ways that paralleled the Anglo community, whereas women from lower socioeconomic backgrounds tended to offer mutual aid to their peers as well as assistance to those back in their homeland (Hewitt 1990a). It behooves women's studies faculty to seek out and support groups like these that might be open to partnerships; they are not always visible nor are their leaders. Belenky, Bond, and Weinstock (1997) suggest the existence of "a tradition that has no name," a type of invisible leadership among women "who devote themselves to drawing out the voices of the silenced and making communities more nurturing places to live" (3), and they recommend working as often as possible with such powerful women.

For a long time, service to others continued to be confined generally to one's own cultural group. A disastrous experiment in cross-cultural "help" suggests the problems that could arise when crossing such cultural and gendered boundaries. In the 1880s Richard Henry Pratt launched a well-intentioned but misguided attempt to "serve" American Indians by creating boarding schools to re-educate them. This effort to give the "blanket Indians" the language, appearance, religion, and manner necessary to succeed in white culture grew into a veritable movement that stretched over decades. Built on the ethnocentric, racist assumption that Anglo culture was superior in every way, it was also sexist in its assumption that the way to save young male Native Americans from themselves and their culture was to save the girls first, who might then in turn save the boys and men. Practitioners of service-learning in women's studies must be vigilant in their efforts to consult and plan projects with community members and not for them, to monitor the projects, and to help students reflect regularly, thus making sure that ethnocentric views of the Other are not distorting their work.

Efforts to socialize young people of European descent were less radical, but they became pervasive in the United States with the rapid spread of Boy and Girl Scouting. Boy Scouting originated in England in 1908 as a way to promote both an efficient citizenry and imperial privilege (Rosenthal 1986). Boy Scouts was promoted by men in this country who were nervous about boys and men becoming "soft," whereas a main focus of Girl Scouts was giving girls an alternative to being "overdriven in the schools" (Low 1919: 6). The main goal for both groups seems to have been to reproduce a middle-class combination of initiative and obedience, but Scouting did nonetheless engage both men and women in service to children and young people (MacLeod 1983).

Service efforts in the early decades of the 20th century revolved around the wars, Depression relief, and New Deal efforts under the careful eye of Eleanor Roosevelt on behalf of Franklin Delano Roosevelt. During World War II, women served overseas in various military groups such as the WACS and the WAVES, and with the USO. Many more women served back home, either as volunteers keeping service networks afloat or for pay in war work. When the war ended, many African-American and Anglo women wished to continue working. Rebuffed by the government and patriarchal popular culture, many of these women channeled their energies into service roles instead. Longstanding organizations such as the NAACP and the League of Women Voters benefited from this infusion of displaced energy. African-American women continued to work for the rights and needs of women, men, and children, whereas Anglo women volunteered increasingly in ways that paralleled their family's development, i.e., in schools, churches, and youth organizations.

The post-war United States saw the growth of national service programs such as the Peace Corps, VISTA, and the Retired Senior Volunteer Program. Activism was the watchword for many groups in the 1960s and 1970s as women and men collaborated to fight for African-American, Hispanic-

American, Native-American, and Asian-American rights. At least some young women were galvanized by their heightened awareness of issues and their experiences of sexism in these activist groups and spun off to create their own women's groups (Evans 1989).

But the fight for women's rights also engaged older women, a number of whom joined forces to found the National Organization for Women (NOW) in 1966. NOW's focus on economic equality led the group in 1973 to urge women not to provide free services in the form of volunteering (Kaminer 1984). Thus volunteer activity for women of privilege — work that had signaled a larger arena of influence at the turn of the previous century — was seen by women of privilege 70 years later as a means of exploiting women who, NOW believed, deserved to be paid for their work. (Volunteer activism on behalf of women's issues was acceptable.) Even though NOW purported to speak for all women, advocating paid work and discouraging volunteer work did not speak to American women from a range of cultural backgrounds who already had to work for pay and who had less time for mutual aid activities than they would have liked.

Implications

The academic discipline of women's studies grew out of the movement that produced NOW and other more liberal and radical groups that critiqued U.S. culture and advocated change. Today, scholars such as bell hooks criticize women's studies for becoming more and more removed from its activist origins and entrenched in academic and theoretical constructs. Service-learning provides an ideal channel for connecting women's studies to the community, but we must proceed cautiously as we implement this form of experiential education. Key questions harkening back to NOW's objection to voluntarism include the appropriate relationship between paid and unpaid labor and the fact that women continue to volunteer in our society more frequently than men. Women's studies practitioners are obligated to consider the role of voluntarism and service-learning in our capitalistic, patriarchal culture and to encourage our students to do the same. Why have we needed voluntarism throughout U.S. history, and why today? Does our service work support structural change or are we simply helping to maintain the status quo? What is the proper relationship between paid and unpaid labor? The answers to these questions will vary, but asking them is critical to thoughtful and productive service-learning.

In addition, we need to work with our faculty colleagues and community service directors to engage men as well as women in service. Service-learning and community service projects are ideal venues for learning about gender, and we must move beyond teaching mainly women about gender issues to engage men in similar considerations. Mentoring programs informed with both academic and experiential, gendered perspectives are ideal for this purpose. For example, two years ago students at Cornell College worked with sixth- and seventh-grade girls to found the GIRLSS (Great Intelligent Real Ladies Showing Support) discussion, activity, and service group. The group grew out of research and discussion in several women's studies and education classes, and is firmly grounded in both feminist and educational theory. But the group was cofounded with the middle school counselor and the middle school girls themselves, who helped to create the group's mission statement and name. Some current GIRLSS group mentors are education and women's studies majors, but mentors are also drawn from the college's larger pool of community service volunteers. The GIRLSS group has provided the mentors as well as the girls many opportunities for learning about gender — a fact recognized by young men attempting to create a parallel group for boys. Unfortunately, the same curricular base for a boys' group is not readily available, and male mentors are finding it difficult to articulate the group's identity.

They are, however, working to do so, and men at Cornell College are also responding to the call to serve as Lunch Buddies, a program that pairs college students with local elementary students to eat lunch and play at recess once a week. Out of 115 college students who serve as buddies, 47 are men, a number suggesting that men will answer the call of service if asked in effective ways. And it is productive on both sides: One college buddy testified recently that "the more we mentor children, the more we need to know about ourselves"; meanwhile, in a scenario repeated in several classes, a first-grade buddy has stopped beating up other children in his class because he doesn't want to disappoint his college friend. Thus the mentoring program, which engages males and females, is helping put pressure on the college to provide a broader curriculum to explore men's as well as women's identities as gendered people.

Conclusion

To avoid the elitist voluntarism that has arisen at times in the past, we need to privilege the knowledge that grows out of experience and mutual aid, such as that demonstrated by the Daughters of Africa in the 19th century, and we need to look for ways to serve with, rather than simply helping, others, as did Jane Addams and the settlement workers. Otherwise, we run the risk of exploiting the communities we seek to assist and to learn from, and of perpetuating injustice rather than fighting it. Service-learning at its best can and should be a route to connecting the academic understandings gained through women's studies with the needs and the strengths of the communities of which we are a part. As Neururer and Rhoads write, "Community service [and service-learning] can be an act of caring that attempts to bridge the gap between the self and the other, between individualism and community, between notions of an ethic of care and an ethic of justice" (1998). Our students in women's studies stand poised, ready to bridge these gaps.

References

Albrecht, L., and R.M. Brewer. (1990). *Bridges of Power: Women's Multicultural Alliances.* Philadelphia, PA: New Society Publishers.

Belenky, M.F., L.A. Bond, and J.S. Weinstock. (1997). *A Tradition That Has No Name: Nurturing the Development of People, Families, and Communities.* New York, NY: Basic Books.

Crooks, J.B. (Spring 1981). "The Role of Women in Volunteerism: A Short History." *Voluntary Action Leadership,* pp. 22-28.

Ellis, S.J., and K.H. Noyes. (1990). *By the People: A History of Americans as Volunteers.* San Francisco, CA: Jossey-Bass.

Evans, S. (1989). *Born for Liberty: A History of Women in America.* New York, NY: Free Press.

Fitzpatrick, Ellen F. (1990). *Endless Crusade: Women Social Scientists and Progressive Reform.* New York, NY: Oxford University Press.

Hewitt, N.A. (1990a). "Charity or Mutual Aid?: Two Perspectives on Latin Women's Philanthropy in Tampa, Florida." In *Lady Bountiful Revisited: Women, Philanthropy, and Power,* edited by K. McCarthy, pp. 55-69. New Brunswick, NJ: Rutgers University Press.

————. (1990b). *Women's Activism and Social Change: Rochester, NY, 1822-1872.* Ithaca, NY: Cornell University Press.

Hine, D.C. (1990). "We Specialize in the Wholly Impossible: The Philanthropic Work of Black Women." In *Lady Bountiful Revisited: Women, Philanthropy, and Power,* edited by K. McCarthy, pp. 70-93. New Brunswick, NJ: Rutgers University Press.

Kaminer, Wendy. (1984). *Women Volunteering: The Pleasure, Pain and Politics of Unpaid Work From 1830 to the Present.* Garden City, NY: Anchor Press.

Low, Juliette. (1919). *Girl Scouts as an Educational Force.* Washington, DC: Government Printing Office.

MacLeod, David I. (1983). *Building Character in the American Boy: The Boy Scouts, the YMCA and Their Forerunners 1870-1920.* Madison, WI: University of Wisconsin Press.

McCarthy, K., ed. (1990). *Lady Bountiful Revisited: Women, Philanthropy, and Power.* New Brunswick, NJ: Rutgers University Press.

Rauner, J. (1991-92). "Multicultural Perspectives in the History of American Volunteerism." *The Journal of Volunteer Administration* 1: 1-8.

Rhoads, Robert, and Julie Neururer. (1998). "Alternative Spring Break: Learning Through Community Service." *NASPA Journal* 35(2): 100-118.

Rosenthal, Michael. (1986). *The Character Factory: Baden-Powell and the Origins of the Boy Scout Movement.* New York, NY: Pantheon.

Scott, A.F. (1990). "Most Invisible of All: Black Women's Voluntary Associations." *The Journal of Southern History* 56(1): 3-22.

————. (1991). *Natural Allies: Women's Associations in American History.* Urbana, IL: University of Illinois Press.

Shaw, S. (1991). "Black Club Women and the Creation of the National Association of Colored Women." *Journal of Women's History* 3(1): 10-25.

Sklar, Kathryn Kish. (1995). *Florence Kelley and the Nation's Work.* New Haven, CT: Yale University Press.

Service-Learning and Women's Studies:
A Community College Perspective

by Karen Bojar

Women's studies is ideally suited for service-learning. The discipline in its early stages was intertwined with an activist commitment to better women's lives. A wide range of services for women — shelters for battered women, rape crisis centers, and legal assistance for women experiencing job discrimination and sexual harassment — all grew in tandem with women's studies as an academic discipline. Some women's studies programs have retreated from this earlier connection to activism to focus instead on theoretical issues, but in most programs the commitment continues.

As a teacher at an urban community college for the past 23 years, I can personally attest to the particular relevance of service-learning to the field of women's studies. Both areas are vitally important to me in my professional life, and I have channeled most of my energy in their direction. In 1988 I developed — and since then have taught — Community Involvement: Theory and Practice, a course that provides students with the opportunity to earn academic credit through service work linked to reading, writing, and reflecting on the social meaning and value of their experiences. In this course, my students have been overwhelmingly female, and they frequently report that their commitment to community service has been a lifelong pursuit, in many cases growing out of deeply rooted family traditions.

I also codeveloped and have taught an introduction to women's studies, incorporating into it an optional service-learning module. Some of my students have taken both courses concurrently and have attested to the ways in which the service-learning course complements the women's studies course. In the following pages, I would like to argue, first, that service-learning is particularly relevant to community college students despite some particularly acute difficulties they must deal with; second, that service-learning is of particular value for women students; third, that the content of women's studies courses is closely linked to the issues frequently at the core of the reflective component in service-learning.

Service-Learning and Community College Students

Most community college students have deep roots in their local communities and are not likely to leave after completing their education. They frequently approach service work not out of a sense of noblesse oblige, but rather to help and, in some cases, to transform their own communities. The service ethic runs deep in many working-class and minority communities. Thus, service-learning programs in community colleges serving large numbers of working-class and low-income students can draw on these rich traditions to the benefit of both the surrounding community and the students themselves.

However, there are also special constraints. Many students are under great pressure to juggle work, family, and school. Even with the carrot of academic credit, many students simply cannot find the hours in the week to do service work. As one student told me, "I would love to take your Community Involvement course, but I can't deal with one more thing to arrange, one more thing to keep track of." Even with various supports, the difficulties loom large for many of our students.

Also, faculty have heavy teaching loads and few of the perks that accompany academic life in four-year settings. Under these circumstances it is not so easy to integrate a service-learning component into one's courses. I was able to do so because of a wide range of contacts I developed over the years in my second life as a community activist, but not every faculty member with an interest in exploring service-learning has these personal networks.

In order to assist faculty and students in developing service-learning options, community colleges must have a service-learning resource center. A small office with even a part-time staff person can provide the information and support necessary. Fortunately, with the help of a grant from Pennsylvania Campus Compact, we were able to develop this support at the Community College of Philadelphia. With an administration strongly supportive of service-learning, the college assumed responsibility for the center after the grant ended. But even with this support, heavy teaching responsibilities often lead to a situation in which my colleagues, like my students, say, "I can't deal with one more thing. I can't deal with incorporating one more thing into my teaching life, I'm on overload as it is."

Service-Learning and Women Community College Students

Although such service programs are of potential value for *all* students, my experience attests to their special value for women students. In my Community Involvement course, my students have been, over the years, overwhelmingly female, and they frequently report that their commitment to community service goes back a long way. The opportunity to receive academic credit for service validates this commitment, while the integration of community service into the curriculum gives the students an opportunity to reflect on what has been an especially meaningful part of their lives. My students have welcomed the chance to place their own service experiences in a broad historical/cultural context through exploring the rich literature on service organizations in American society.

I have been struck both by the importance of community service in women's lives and by the tendency to undervalue that experience. Failure to recognize the value of women's service work is often shared by women themselves. Many of my female students have a long history of informal service — what they call "just helping out in the neighborhood." Frequently, toward the beginning of my class many students will say they've never done any community service, because they don't think of their work as "service." But it soon comes out that they have a long history of "just helping out" — bringing meals to infirm, elderly people; taking care of neighborhood children; acting as a general resource for people in need in their communities.

Affluent upper-middle-class women are much more likely to participate in organized community service — and to get the recognition that comes with it. This is the kind of activity that can be put on a resume and used to advantage in a variety of ways. So many of my students (many of whom are from low-income families) have said that it never occurred to them to put community service activities on their resume. As one woman said, "Isn't that just tooting your own horn?" This self-effacing note that has informed many women's characterizations of their service work has no doubt contributed to some feminist unease with community service.

Yet, as mentioned above, some women have performed service work seeking just such an opportunity to "toot their own horns" and have quite openly sought recognition for their efforts. Service has obviously had a range of meanings and fulfilled a wide variety of functions for women. I suspect it will become increasingly important as our population ages and we have growing numbers of healthy, retired women.

As Betty Friedan (1993) has noted in her book *The Fountain of Age*: "The most important predictors of vital age are satisfying work and complexity of purpose" (222). Friedan tells us that such work need not be paid employment; rather, what is needed is "a project that structures one's day and keeps alive all those important human ties and sense of personhood" (222). Women who have spent years working as volunteers in a variety of service organizations are especially well-equipped to get through their later years and to enjoy the freedom to pursue developed personal interests — a freedom most of us do not have in paid employment.

Indeed, many women in the labor market have used service work as a means of compensating for what is lacking on the job and thus as an outlet for underutilized talents. In service activities, individuals have a measure of choice and control not available to many in their jobs. For some women, confined to a pink-collar ghetto and denied options for meaningful work in the paid labor force, community service has been a salvation, functioning as what Sara Evans and Harry Boyte (1986) have called "a free space" — an environment in which they can "learn a new self-respect, a deeper and more assertive group identity, public skills and values of cooperation and civic virtue" (180).

The Content of Women's Studies Courses as Itself a Focus of Reflection

The Importance of Volunteer Work in United States Women's History

Women's studies courses lend themselves particularly well to service-learning. It is impossible to teach United States Women's History without paying considerable attention to the history of women as volunteers and the close connection between participation in service and the advancement of women. Certainly, the history of service-oriented voluntarism has been largely a history of women's efforts. Susan Ellis (1990), in her comprehensive history of voluntarism, *By the People: A History of Americans as Volunteers*, notes that:

> Any historical look at volunteering must pay attention to the issue of women as volunteers. Until the twentieth century women had very limited opportunity for impact except through volunteering. What becomes increasingly apparent through a closer look at the history of volunteering in the United States is that women have made vital contributions to every aspect of the country's growth, contributions that deserve permanent recognition. (10)

This impressive record has become a source of controversy among many contemporary feminists because of the highly gendered nature of traditional volunteer work. The lines of demarcation, of course, are not clear-cut, and many volunteers did not conform to traditional gender roles. However, historically, most women have gravitated toward the less prestigious forms of volunteer work such as social service or charitable work, whereas men have been drawn to more prestigious, potentially career-advancing service such as political activism or service on boards of directors.

However, the major difference may not be so much the type of volunteer work as the relative importance of such work for men and for women. For men, most service organizations have been a small part of their lives; for women, such organizations have been an alternative ladder of advancement. Before the mid 20th century, volunteer work, for many well-educated women, was the only possible entry into public life. One consequence, as Anne Firor Scott (1991) has pointed out, is that the women who devoted their lives to a "career" of service were often especially talented individuals:

> As long as women had virtually no access to the professions or business, the leadership of voluntary associations was of an extremely high caliber. All the ability that in the male half of the population was scattered in dozens of directions was . . . in the female half, concentrated in religious and secular, voluntary associations. (180)

Another important feminist text that explores the crucial role of service work in the history of American women is Nancy Cott's *The Bonds of Womanhood: Women's Sphere in New England* (1977) — an exploration of the role of the church in the development of civic skills for 19th-century women. Historically, charitable work sponsored by religious organizations has been the major focus of American women's service efforts; indeed, in the early days of the republic, the only focus. Such charitable work reinforced traditional gender roles, yet religious-based charitable work also served as a vehicle for mounting a challenge to traditional roles.

While women in such organizations certainly did perform the kinds of service traditionally thought to be women's province, nevertheless, as Nancy Cott has noted in her exploration of the role of the church in the development of 19th-century women's civic skills, service-oriented activities in religious-based organizations helped women to enter the public sphere. Their activities enabled them to acquire some of the public citizenship skills thought to be the sole province of men. Cott has argued that work in "benevolent" societies led to the development of what many years later would be labeled a feminist consciousness:

> Women . . . examined as fully as men the American penchant for voluntary organizations noted by de Tocqueville in the 1830s. But women's associations before 1835 were all allied with the church, whereas men's also expressed a variety of secular and civic, political and vocational concerns. (133)

Cott quotes Harriet Martineau, an astute British observer, who speculated that American women "pursued religion as an occupation" (138) because they lacked other outlets for exercising their intellectual and social skills. Cott tells us that in their religious service associations

> women wrote and debated and amended constitutions, elected officers, raised and allotted funds, voted on issues, solicited and organized new members; in other words, they familiarized themselves with the processes of representative government in an all-female environment, while they were prevented from doing it in the male political system. (155)

Thus, according to Cott, religious activities can be seen as a means used by New England women to define themselves and their place in the community, in contrast to men, whose sense of self and social role were more likely to be defined by worldly occupations. Finally, it is important to note that many of the skills developed and much of the energy generated by women's participation in religious organizations were channeled into the 19th-century suffragist movement, which culminated in the 19th Amendment to the Constitution, granting women the right to vote. Although 19th-century religious-based service organizations themselves never questioned traditional gender roles, they enabled individual women to develop the skills needed to contest such roles. For 19th-century white women, the church was a school for citizenship in the same way that the church functioned for African-American men and women.

Possible Assignment: Students can be encouraged to explore the extent to which participation in civic life has enhanced their own job skills and career options. They can also interview women they have met through their service work and question them about the relationship between their service work and their personal and professional growth.

Many of my students involved in church-related service activities have found it particularly rewarding to trace connections between their experiences and the historical patterns traced by Cott. Students can be asked to explore the extent to which religious organizations still function as schools for citizenship, as vehicles for developing leadership skills, now that women have a range of opportunities in secular organizations and are no longer dependent on religious organizations as a means of developing their skills.

Connections Between Service Activities and a Feminist Approach to Economics

The energy and talent that women have poured into service have seldom received adequate recognition — neither recognition for the individuals involved nor recognition for the social and economic value of the work itself. Most of my students have never thought about the economic value of their service work. Marilyn Waring, a New Zealand economist, has written a brilliant and eminently readable analysis of global economics in which she argues for the inclusion of women's unpaid labor — including those countless hours of community service — in computing gross national product. According to Waring, "in the United States in 1980, 52.7 million women participated in voluntary work that was valued at $18 billion. It was not calculated in the nation's accounts" (1988: 69).

Waring also reports that women in New Zealand have mobilized around the issue of recognition for service work, including tax recognition: "These women have argued that while the overwhelmingly male donations to charity are claimed as tax deductions, the overwhelmingly female capital donations of time, skills, and labor are not tax-deductible" (139). Although we are not likely to see our own tax system accommodate such considerations, there has been increasing recognition on the part of employers of the value of service experiences. According to Waring:

> *Eleven of the top 17 employers in the greater area recognized volunteer experience in hiring . . . the California Department of Fair Employment and Housing, for example, carries the following as a regulation on prior work experience: "if an employer or other covered entity considers prior work experience in the selection or assignment of an employee, the employer or other covered entity shall also consider prior unpaid volunteer work experience." (1988: 323)*

As I have already noted, many of my students have never considered the social and economic importance of their contributions and in many cases have not thought about marketing their service experience. They are gratified to see that what had been unacknowledged is now being recognized — in large part due to the efforts of the women's movement.

Possible Assignments: Students are asked to evaluate the feasibility of Waring's policy recommendation that tax deductions be offered for the value of service contributions and discuss other ways in which women's service efforts could be rewarded.

Service and Women's Lives: A Lens for Exploring Conflicts in Contemporary Feminist Thought

I have become convinced that the ambivalent responses of feminists to community service is an extremely useful lens for exploring conflicts in contemporary feminist thought. The debate about service work is intimately bound up with the difference/sameness debate running through feminist thought of the past 150 years or so. Traditional community service is more likely to be valued by "cultural feminists" or "difference feminists," who value women's different voices and concerns and tend to emphasize women's special attributes. Service work is most likely to be viewed with suspicion by that strand of feminist thought that focuses on the struggle for equality based on the premise that men and women are fundamentally the same and should be treated the same in the public sphere. Such "equal rights feminists" usually adhere to individualist values; cultural feminists, to communitarian values.

A helpful way to characterize the difference/sameness split is to conceive of the divide in terms of "minimizers" versus "maximizers." As Ann Snitow (1990) has put it:

> *A common divide keeps forming in both feminist thought and action between the need to build and identify "woman" and give it solid political meaning [the maximizers] and the need to tear down the very category "woman" and dismantle its all too solid history [minimizers]. (9)*

Minimizers have tended to be suspicious of service-oriented voluntarism; maximizers have tended to celebrate women's "ethic of care."

A traditional service-oriented attitude — informed by just such an ethic of care — was once a unifying value among women, shared by women of all social classes. Many women continue to value this ethic of care, and in some cases see it as an explicitly feminist project. Most of my own students are more likely to be drawn to this position, to find themselves more attracted to cultural feminism than to equal rights feminism and, at least on a theoretical level, to find communitarian values more appealing than individualist ones. The NOW critique of community service is, for many, at variance with their own experience of volunteer work and at odds with some of their basic assumptions. However, with the opening of what were once exclusively male professions to middle-class women, increasing numbers of women have joined men in pursuit of individual fulfillment and success. As a result, the once universal ethic of care is now far less a unifying concept among women — indeed, perhaps to some extent, it has served to open a class, as well as a theoretical, fault line.

A commonplace of contemporary social thought is that the middle class (or perhaps more accurately the upper-middle class) values competitive individual achievement, whereas the working class values an ethic of solidarity (see Sennett and Cobb 1972). Such oversimplifications can be dangerous, but my research and experience tend to confirm the existence of some such overall pattern. As I indicated above, my working-class and low-income students are much less likely to be suspicious of the ethic of care than are my middle-class colleagues. In a recent *Sojourner* article on the not-so-hidden injuries of class, Mary Frances Platt (1994) expressed a sentiment I think I have heard in the voices of some of my students:

> Unlike our [working-class] feminists, middle-class feminism does not participate in the "give all that you can and we will give that back to you" circle. Godlike importance is placed on individual needs getting met, as we have been brainwashed into believing the class-privileged concept that care-giving is a women's disease and not an ethic to be honored. (27)

Most of my students have not had Platt's extensive experience in feminist organizations and do not share her sense of betrayal, but most would similarly object to viewing "care-giving [as] a women's disease." Many of my students want it both ways — wanting the respect and compensation men have enjoyed for their work, yet wanting to honor and to continue the uncompensated voluntary service tradition. Their ambivalence (which I share) reflects the profound ambivalence of many feminists about the equality/difference debate underlying the controversy regarding women's service work.

The opposition position was formally presented in the much-quoted 1973 statement from the National Organization for Women's (NOW) Task Force on Volunteerism:

> Essentially NOW believes that service-oriented [voluntarism] is providing a hit-or-miss, Band-Aid, and a patchwork approach to solving massive and severe social ills which are a reflection of an economic system in need of an overhaul. More than this, such volunteering actually prevents needed social changes from occurring because with service-oriented volunteering, political energy is being used and will increasingly be used to meet society's administrative needs. (NOW Task Force on Volunteerism 1973: 2)

Yet, such service-oriented voluntarism continues despite expanded options for women and rejection of the service ethic by some segments of the organized women's movement. Even in the early 1970s, some middle-class feminists recognized the personal rewards of service, such as opportunities for career exploration and development of job skills. Doris Gold (1971), for example, wrote that

> feminist women can use the volunteer structure for their own ends, experimenting with its training and mind-expanding opportunities to nourish a more conscious identity. Voluntarism in new dress . . . must be judiciously altered to fit [a] woman's growing need for real work in a real life. (398)

The subtext here appears to be that such work is okay if your purpose is to further your own personal or career goals, but not if your motive is to help others. Such an emphasis on the potential career benefits for the individual rather than on the benefits for the community being served suggests a fundamental mistrust of service-oriented activities.

NOW has since changed its bylaws to remove its prohibition against such activities. Indeed, from a current vantage point, the 1973 NOW statement may seem somewhat extreme, but it does raise some important questions and reflects a legitimate (and prescient) concern that a parsimonious government will abdicate its responsibilities to its citizens and try to substitute "hit-or-miss" volunteer efforts for much-needed social programs. Although my students acknowledge the seriousness of the issues raised by the NOW statement, most think it misses something extremely important — the mutually reinforcing relationship between direct service and advocacy for social change. The political energy that NOW wants to encourage is often developed as a consequence of the experience of direct service. Determination to attack a social problem at its roots can be an outgrowth of the experience of such service, and the experience of service itself a way of informing and shaping advocacy.

Ironically, while NOW was focusing on the negative aspects of traditional volunteer work, a new, insidious form of volunteer work was emerging — volunteering on the job. The self-sacrificial "Mother Teresa syndrome" criticized by equal rights feminists now crops up in paid employment. This syndrome is mainly confined to professional women — very few of my students report experiencing it — and appears to be most prevalent in the less prestigious professions such as teaching and social work.

What this syndrome involves for many women in such professions is that their jobs have become in many ways like volunteer work, as they put in far more time than can and should be expected. A professor at a *community college*, exhausted by round-the-clock student advising and unable to ease students out of her office after their allotted 15-minute appointments, has to all but abandon her own research projects. Even those women professors who spend less time with students and thus manage to make time for their research nonetheless fall victim to this syndrome. One young faculty member who cut back on her commitment to her students felt extremely guilty about her decision: "Some of my best friends spend an incredible amount of time with students, and I know they think I am hopelessly insensitive and careerist. So maybe I do have more time for my work, but a lot of my energy is sapped by guilt."

"Volunteer time" on the job can become really insidious when a woman's job is also her cause; some of the most compulsive people in this category are directors of women's studies programs and directors and staff of women's advocacy groups. I think I first realized the pervasiveness of such behavior during a board meeting of a small nonprofit reproductive rights group of which I am a member. A student who had been hired on a part-time basis to write a grant submitted a request to be paid for overtime. Initially, we were nonplussed. Overtime? Who asks for overtime when working for a worthy cause? One board member noted that she had just spent 80 hours the previous week working on a grant for her agency, and she had never thought of asking for overtime. But upon reflection, we soon agreed it was a very reasonable request — especially from a part-time employee — although as one board member said, "Getting paid for overtime is not part of the culture of the organization."

Possible Assignments: Students should consider whether the 1973 NOW statement reflects a legitimate concern that the government will abdicate its responsibilities to its citizens and try to substitute volunteer efforts for much-needed social programs. Or whether such a statement fails to recognize a mutually reinforcing relationship between direct service and advocacy for social change? Can the political energy NOW wants to encourage develop as a consequence of the experience of direct service? In what ways does the experience of service itself inform and shape the advocacy role? To what extent should social services be provided by voluntary organizations?

Students should also consider whether, as Mary Frances Platt has charged, denigrating "care-giving [as] a women's disease and not an ethic to be honored" does not itself represent a "class-privileged" attack (1994: 27). Is valuing "caring and connection" a trap — a "compassion trip" as Margaret Adams (1971) has called it? Or is the ethic of "competitive individual achievement" an even greater trap? Is the woman who organizes much of her life around service work and puts community involvement before career goals buying into stereotypical notions of "true womanhood"? Should her choice be valued less than that of the feminist corporate lawyer who works an 80-hour week and is poised to break through the glass ceiling?

Finally, students should examine the extent to which they and other women of their acquaintance have "volunteered" on the job. They should consider the issue of when service to others becomes self-exploitation and how one can best balance personal needs with a desire to give to others.

References

Adams, Margaret. (1971). "The Compassion Trap." In *Woman in Sexist Society*, edited by Vivian Gornick and Barbara K. Moran, pp. 401-416. New York, NY: Basic Books.

Cott, Nancy. (1977). *The Bonds of Womanhood: Women's Sphere in New England*. New Haven, CT: Yale University Press.

———. (1988). *The Grounding of Modern Feminism*. New Haven, CT: Yale University Press.

Ellis, Susan. (1990). *By the People: A History of Americans as Volunteers*. San Francisco, CA: Jossey-Bass.

Evans, Sara, and Harry Boyte. (1986). *Free Space*. New York, NY: Harper and Row.

Friedan, Betty. (1993). *The Fountain of Age*. New York, NY: Simon and Schuster.

Gold, Doris. (1971). "Women and Voluntarism." In *Woman in Sexist Society*, edited by Vivian Gornick and Barbara K. Moran, pp. 384-400. New York, NY: Basic Books.

Platt, Mary Frances. (August 1994). "Class Truths." *Sojourner Women's Forum*, p. 27.

Scott, Anne Firor. (1991). *Natural Allies: Women's Associations in American History*. Urbana, IL: University of Illinois Press.

Sennett, Richard, and Jonathan Cobb. (1972). *The Hidden Injuries of Class*. New York, NY: Vintage.

Snitow, Ann. (1990). "A Gender Diary." In *Conflicts in Feminism*, edited by Marianne Hirsch and Evelyn Fax Keller. New York, NY: Routledge.

Waring, Marilyn. (1988). *If Women Counted: A New Feminist Economics*. San Francisco, CA: Harper and Row.

The "Different Voice" of Service

by Catherine Ludlum Foos[1]

A controversial question within the field of service-learning is whether service-learning experiences should focus primarily on promoting social change toward a more just society. One author gives an implied answer when she identifies as one of the defining features of service-learning "a social justice rather than a charitable framework" (Varlotta 1996: 26). Even though defining charity right out of the picture might be an extreme view, a more moderate view is that charity and social activism exist on a developmental continuum, with charity at the "beginning" end — the place where students can get their feet wet and develop a desire to do service — and social activism at the developmentally "mature" end of the spectrum. This view implies that the goal of a service-learning program should be to encourage students to move away from charity and toward social activism.

The notion that there is a developmental continuum running from charity to justice, however, has been challenged (Morton 1995). Morton interviewed students, faculty, administrators, and community partners regarding their understanding of their community service and what motivates them to do service. In doing so he found that "the ideas of a continuum and progress from charity to advocacy do not square with how people do service or why they do it" (21). Instead, Morton describes charity and social justice as distinct paradigms of service, each with its own internal coherence and integrity.[2] "Each paradigm has 'thin' versions that are disempowering and hollow, and 'thick' versions that are sustaining and potentially revolutionary" (24). One reason this question is significant is that the view we take regarding the nature and telos of service will influence the way we structure service-learning placements and programs. There is a presumption, at least for many, that an integral part of service-learning is educating for moral and civic development. If we are to have much hope of being successful (except accidentally), we need a clear idea of the nature of the moral and civic development we are seeking.

This debate regarding charity and social justice is strikingly similar to the discussion that has been going on for more than a decade regarding the roles of justice and care in an understanding of moral development and moral reasoning. In 1982, Carol Gilligan published *In a Different Voice*. In this book she revealed a blind spot in the dominant way of describing moral development. For many years, discussions of moral development had concluded that females do not develop to the same level as males. For instance, in the theory of Lawrence Kohlberg (1981), moral development is a three-stage process (with substages) beginning with egoism, progressing through a view of morality as social conformity, culminating in an understanding of morality as the consistent application of universal principles of justice. In Kohlberg's scheme, females seldom reach the level of moral maturity; they tend to remain in the middle stage of social conformity, basing their moral reasoning on particulars of the social context rather than on abstract universal principles. Gilligan claims her research shows that women are not necessarily reasoning deficiently, but rather differently. She describes women's moral reasoning as a distinct paradigm within which to interpret moral questions rather than as a deficient mode of (men's) moral reasoning. Within that paradigm, she identifies stages that parallel the three-stage developmental process outlined by Kohlberg: an egoistic stage *(Orientation to Individual Survival)*, a conventional stage *(Goodness as Self-Sacrifice),* and a postconventional, principled stage *(The Morality of Nonviolence)* (Gilligan 1977: 489-509; see also Gilligan 1982: 64-105). She dubs the approach to moral reasoning based on abstract principles the *justice orientation* to morality, and the contextual, interpersonal approach the *care orientation.*

The history of the debate regarding charity and social activism as orientations to service and service-learning contains interesting parallels to the debate regarding moral development. In each case, two approaches were identified, with one being labeled inferior, the other representing a more "mature" approach. With each, a researcher "listened to the voices" of those who engage in the supposedly inferior paradigm and found that many of the voices spoke in a very "mature" manner. This person then redescribed the two approaches, presenting them not as stages on a continuum but as distinct paradigms. With so many parallels, it seems reasonable to explore the scholarly discussions that have arisen from Gilligan's work to illuminate our understanding of the relation between charity and social activism and the notion of *mature* service.

Care and Justice

Gilligan's work is set within the context of a tradition that has systematically devalued women in many ways, including their moral capacities. The dominant tradition in morality, referred to by Gilligan as the justice tradition, defines morality in terms of a commitment to general principles that govern all morally relevant interactions. This tradition is characterized by several key features. One is its abstractness. Morality, according to this view, is tainted by the contingent details of a particular situation. Morality is defined in terms of *universalizability.* "The . . . two features of moral judgments . . . [are] prescriptivity and universalizability" (Hare 1978: 340). Another key feature is its understanding of the moral agent as essentially autonomous, and the primary moral value for the justice perspective is *equality* among autonomous agents.

What Gilligan found by listening to the "different voice" of women, however, was not that women are incapable of reasoning about moral issues in the manner depicted above, but that they have a distinctly different way of conceptualizing moral problems.[3] The reasoning can be every bit as complex and sophisticated, but the notion of what is to be considered is different. A key feature of the care perspective is that it is contextual; care-based reasoning is based not on applying abstract principles to generalized situations but on dealing with each situation in its concreteness and uniqueness. Another distinction is that, from the perspective of care, the moral agent is seen as being concerned with relationships. Importantly, these relationships are fundamentally defined not as freely chosen relationships of equals but as, in many cases, unchosen relationships of unequals. Thus the chief value for the care perspective is not equality but attachment.

> From a justice perspective, the self as moral agent stands as the figure against a ground of social relationships, judging the conflicting claims of self and others against a standard of equality or equal respect. . . . From a care perspective, the relationship becomes the figure, defining self and others. Within the context of relationship, the self as moral agent perceives and responds to the perception of need. The shift in moral perspective is manifest by a change in the moral question from "What is just?" to "How to respond?" (Gilligan 1987: 23)

Once Gilligan articulated the notion of care as a distinct paradigm from the traditional view of morality as grounded in general principles, a debate arose regarding how these two paradigms might be related. Is care superior to justice, or vice versa? Is care a special case of justice, or vice versa? Are care and justice in conflict? On this question I am substantially in agreement with Marilyn Friedman (1993). Friedman argues that justice and care, while indeed pointing to distinct *orientations* to moral reasoning, ought not to be conceptualized as indicating two separate spheres of morality itself, because justice and care are mutually implicatory. "It seems wise both to reconsider the seeming dichotomy of care and justice, and to question the moral adequacy of either orientation dissociated from the other. Our aim would be to advance 'beyond caring,' that is, beyond *mere* caring dissociated from a concern for justice" (Friedman 1993: 267).

The theory of John Rawls (1971) shows how justice and care entail each other. Rawls describes his theory as one in which "the guiding idea is that the principles of justice for the basic structure of society . . . are the principles that free and rational persons concerned to further their own interests would accept in an initial position of equality as defining the fundamental terms of their association" (11).

The "initial position of equality" referred to above comes about by means of a heuristic device Rawls dubs the "veil of ignorance" (1971: 12). Rawls asks us to envision ourselves in the original position referred to in social contract theory; the pregovernmental state of affairs in which every person has complete liberty and is a law unto her or himself, a position we voluntarily give up in order to come together and live in a well-regulated society. To the original position of classical contract theory Rawls adds the notion of a veil of ignorance: Parties to an original agreement to establish a society and laws to govern it are completely ignorant of the position they will occupy in that forthcoming society. The purpose of this is to ensure that any decisions made behind the veil of ignorance are not motivated by a desire to tailor society to benefit one's own specific circumstances. While this may look unrealistic at first glance, it has tremendous theoretical power. Rawls is in no way making any empirical claims about how we *do* arrive at our principles; rather, he is presenting a means by which we *could* develop principles of justice that, he claims, would reflect our intuitive sense of justice as nearly as is humanly possible. In a limited sense, this is what we already do; this is really just a sophisticated version of putting oneself in the other person's shoes. A key difference is that behind the veil of ignorance one has to put oneself in *every* other person's shoes. A just society is one in which one would be content to live, and whose laws and institutions one would be willing to embrace, no matter what segment of society one occupied or what disadvantages one suffered.

Although the description of the original position and the veil of ignorance is not intended as a description of a historical event by which principles of justice were established, it is intended as a device that could be employed to establish principles of justice. If this is indeed a workable theoretical framework, however, it is necessary to articulate the empirical conditions required to make it feasible. Rawls addresses this need to a certain extent in part three of *A Theory of Justice*. "Conceptions of justice must be justified by the conditions of our life as we know it or not at all. . . . However attractive a conception of justice might be on other grounds, it is seriously defective if the principles of moral psychology are such that it fails to engender in human beings the requisite desire to act upon it" (1971: 454-455). Thus part three includes a discussion of moral psychology and development. It is at this point that the notion of *care* enters in.

According to Rawls, a commitment to a sense of justice arises out of an attachment to, and a desire to please, individual persons who desire that one act in certain ways. He describes a child whose parents clearly communicate their love for her. This, in turn, leads the child to love and trust the parents. As a result, the child desires both to please the parents and to emulate them.

Similarly, if these parents teach and, importantly, model principles of justice, the child will grow to adopt those principles as her or his own. Conversely, a child who grows up in a loveless home will not develop an attachment to principles of justice (462-467). To use Gilligan's terminology, Rawls presents an ethic of care as being the condition of the possibility of a society governed by principles of justice.

At this point it is tempting to draw the oft-drawn conclusion, that justice is the moral orientation of public life, and care the moral orientation of private life. Indeed, this certainly seems to be Rawls's conclusion.

> The conception of acting justly, and of advancing just institutions, comes to have for him [that is, the child-become-adult] an attraction analogous to that possessed before by subordinate ideals [namely, ideals of personal attachment]. . . . But even though moral sentiments are in this sense independent from contingencies, our natural attachments to particular persons and groups still have an appropriate place [namely, the private sphere]. (1971: 473, 475)

It is misleading, however, to think that an ethic of care can thus be restricted to the sphere of private morality. Not only is care a necessary component for producing just people, it is also necessary for generating just institutions. The original position as described by Rawls seems unlikely to yield truly just institutions if care is not given a place behind the veil of ignorance.

This strategy for establishing laws that provide equal liberty and adequate sustenance for all helps to counterbalance the human tendency to restrict rights and privileges to those groups approved by the group in power. However, if we assume, as Rawls intends, that real human beings are applying this heuristic, we must recognize that they will only include in their list of positions they "might" occupy in society those positions they can relate to sufficiently to see as possibilities for themselves. Just as Rawls does not expect people behind the veil of ignorance to ask "What if I were a farm animal?" so, too, people who believe that those of a certain category (black, gay, etc.) are on a *completely different level* from themselves will not even ask "What if I were X?" The evolution of our sense of justice, from applying to white men, then all men, then men and women, has been not an evolution of our sense of what justice *requires* but an evolution of our sense of the *scope* of justice. Each group has gained acceptance into the ranks of full rights bearers because members of the group in power have come to experience a sense of relatedness to those in the other group, an ability to see that "that could be me." In other words, for justice to realize its full range, an element of care is required.

By the same token, however, fully adequate care requires an element of justice. One of the dominant features of the care perspective is its focus on meeting the needs of concrete others (rather than, as the justice perspective does, emphasizing abstract equality for unspecified others). Recall the frequency with which children exclaim, "That's not fair!" Even given the invariant maternal reply, "Life is not fair," one of the great needs that individuals have is to be treated fairly.

Discussing the sense in which care and justice require each other should not, however, be taken as saying they are essentially the same thing. They are, indeed, distinct *orientations* to morality, involving different "primary moral commitments" (Friedman 1993: 268).

> The different perspectives which Gilligan called "care" and "justice" do point toward substantive differences in human interrelationship and commitment. From the standpoint of "care," self and other are conceptualized in their particularity rather than as instances for the application of generalized moral notions. This difference ramifies into what appears to be a major difference in the organization and focus of moral thought. (269)

The conclusion to be drawn from this is that we have (at least) two approaches to morality we need to take seriously on their own terms. Neither can be reduced to the other, and neither can adequately replace the other. One implication of this is that the notion of "moral maturity" becomes a more complex notion than had previously been assumed. Maturity must be understood in terms of the framework within which a person operates, and thus may look different from person to person.

Charity and Social Change

This same analysis can be applied to the charity/social justice debate within service-learning. Those more at home in the charity paradigm may feel as women did when male philosophers and psychologists defined women's inability/disinclination to adopt the justice perspective as moral inferiority. Conceptualizing service in terms of a single developmental continuum has in some cases led to a narrow view of what mature service should look like. For example, John Saltmarsh (1996) discusses the "limitation" of Dewey's approach to social change due to his hesitance to move from "a politics of mediation and gradualism" grounded in a faith in the power of positive association, to a politics of "confrontation and agitation" (19). According to Saltmarsh, the challenge for service-learning is "to foster the connection between the private and the public and *then to the political*" (19; my emphasis). The implication seems to be that mature service entails political activism, and that a nonpolitical approach to service is naïve.

In the preface to his treatise on ethics, the philosopher Levinas (1969) acknowledges the view that political activism is superior to "merely" moral modes of interaction.

> *Everyone will readily agree that it is of the highest importance to know whether we are not duped by morality. Does not lucidity, the mind's openness upon the true, consist in catching sight of the permanent possibility of war? . . . The art of foreseeing war and of winning it by every means — politics — is henceforth enjoined as the very exercise of reason. Politics is opposed to morality, as philosophy to naïveté. (21)*

This does not mean that political action is immoral. Rather, it means that politics is strategic — it seeks to understand oppositional power and to anticipate its use so as to be able to counter it effectively. Levinas speaks of politics in much the same way that Morton (1993) describes the social justice perspective.

> *Power . . . is a concept to be understood historically as a tool with which "ups" control "downs." Politics in this regard is viewed as a human system of distribution, or political economy, and the practical question, generally, is how to manage the redistribution of limited goods to achieve a just society. (6)*

In contrast to this, Levinas goes on to present an account of ethics that "does not consist in teaching the orientation of history" (22). He describes an ethic grounded in face-to-face encounter and dialogue, as "welcoming the Other, as hospitality" (27), and as characterized fundamentally by responsibility (1985). It was this sort of ethic that Morton (1995) found when he interviewed people who located themselves within the charity paradigm. Charity "begins with an individual grounded in community. . . . [It is] spiritually based service, outside of time and space, that bears witness to the worth of other persons" (26). This is the "different voice" of service, an approach neither based on political activism nor characterizable as condescending and ineffectual.

As with care and justice, however, neither charity nor social change can be understood adequately without incorporating elements of the other; indeed, "At their thickest, the paradigms seem to intersect" (Morton 1995: 28). Philip Hallie (1993) provides an example of what this intersection might look like. In the process of trying to understand the dynamics of cruelty, he observes that kindness is not the opposite of cruelty. *Kindness* is the term Hallie uses to denote what is often meant by *charity* when used disparagingly — superficial gestures that do nothing to change the situation causing the misery.

> *I found that kindness could be the ultimate cruelty, especially when it was given within that unbalanced power relationship. A kind . . . camp guard can exacerbate cruelty, can remind his victim that there are other relation-*

ships than the relationship of cruelty, and can make the victim deeply bit-
ter, especially when he sees the self-satisfied smile of his victimizer. (15)

Through his account of the actions of the French village of Le Chambon during World War II, Hallie illustrates what he claims is the opposite of cruelty:
hospitality.

During the course of the war, the people of this village in Nazi-occupied
France sheltered Jewish refugees in their own homes and in homes they set
up specifically for that purpose, and ultimately led some 6,000 Jews across
the mountains to safety in Switzerland. From Hallie's description, it is clear
that these people were operating out of a charity framework; nonetheless
their charity could not possibly be mistaken for (mere) kindness. "The people I have talked to who were once children in Le Chambon have more hope
for their species and more respect for themselves as human beings than
most other survivors I have met. The enduring hospitality they met in Le
Chambon helped them find realistic hope in a world of persisting cruelty"
(1993: 19-20). Two things distinguish the actions of the Chambonnais from
kindness: One is the deep and unwavering respect they showed to the Jews
they harbored, the other is that their hospitality took the form of changing
the circumstances faced by the Jews they encountered in order to remove
them beyond the reach of Nazi persecution. Thus thick charity includes an
element of social change.

By the same token, thick social change involves an element of charity, of
personal, not just social, engagement. Thus Morton (1995) quotes a community organizer: "Organizing is a fancy word for relationship building. No organizer ever organizes a community. . . . That's why we organize people around
their values — not just the issues" (28). Or, to put it another way, "To demand
justice for the other man, is this not to return to morality? . . . The seeking
out of the other man, however distant, is already a relationship with this
other man, a relationship in all its directness" (Levinas 1989: 242). As with
the care and justice orientations described above, however, none of this
implies that charity and social change are essentially the same thing; they
involve distinct ways of viewing the nature and role of service.

As Morton (1995) points out, the reason these issues are important is
that if we continue to approach service-learning from the perspective that
charity and social change exist on a continuum of types of service, we are
likely to be less effective than we could be.

> *While charity . . . and social change paradigms may lead ultimately to the*
> *transformation of the individual and the community, they suggest different*
> *ways of defining issues and understanding change over time. The irony of*
> *service, in service-learning, is enacted when we do not recognize these dif-*
> *ferences and teach accordingly. (29)*

When we replace the view that the goal of service-learning should be to move students away from a charity approach and toward a social change approach with the view that some students will be drawn to and most fulfilled by a charity approach and others by a social change approach, there is a concomitant change in the way we structure service placements. Presumably, the general goal has not changed: to move students toward more mature service. What has changed is our understanding of what constitutes mature service. The question now becomes, if mature service can take the form of either charity or social change, how can service-learning placements be structured to move students toward that maturity?

The Moral Self

Scholarship arising out of the justice/care debate can be helpful in addressing this question, just as it was for answering the question how charity and social change are related. In the earlier part of this paper I focused on the ways in which care and justice are compatible and mutually supportive. In this section I will focus on a significant difference in underlying assumptions between the two views: their views of the nature of the self.

The justice perspective has historically drawn its notion of the self from the Enlightenment view of humans as essentially rational, autonomous beings. The paradigm case is Immanuel Kant, who tells us that we should "never act except in such a way that I can also will that my maxim should become a universal law" (Kant 1981: 14). This formulation of his famous "categorical imperative" arises out of his discussion of the need for moral action to be motivated strictly by the thought of duty, by respect for the idea of law itself. "Now an action done from duty must altogether exclude the influence of inclination and therewith every object of the will. Hence there is nothing left that can influence the will except objectively the law and subjectively pure respect for this practical law" (13).

Rawls's veil of ignorance reflects this sense that one's true moral self can only be manifested apart from any contingent connections with concrete others and circumstances. The choices made behind the veil of ignorance reflect the deliberations of "free and rational persons" (Rawls 1971: 11). Several things follow from this way of thinking about the self. First, the force of moral obligation is from within. The advantage to such a notion of the self is that freely chosen actions do seem to have more moral worth than coerced actions. The second point that follows is that the self is self-defined. If the moral self is the true self, and morality is self-legislated, then we create our selves.

However, this notion that the self is undetermined and self-legislating has come under considerable fire over the past several years. A main source of the criticism has been the political theory of communitarianism. According to some communitarians, the concept of a completely unencumbered, self-creating self is entirely untenable. They would replace it with a situated self.

> *Open-ended though it be, the story of my life is always embedded in the story of those communities from which I derive my identity. . . . In the communitarian view, these stories make a moral difference. . . . They situate us in the world and give our lives their moral particularity. (Sandel 1992: 223)*

The situated self finds itself already in community, which, indeed, it does. The communitarian alternative seems both more realistic and more conducive to caring relationships and a sense of the whole person. However, the communitarian self finds itself not only *located* in community but, more to the point, *defined* by the community. The problem with this is that the force of moral obligation now comes from without, and not only the force but the content as well.

> *Although communitarians argue for a particularized, contextual approach to the constitution of morality, they fail to problematize the "community" they idealize. By assuming that only one moral discourse is extant in a community, they ignore the hegemonic forces that structure any community. (Hekman 1995: 61)*

Communitarianism improves on the Enlightenment self by providing it some contextualization, but it provides too much; the self defined by community can become overwhelmed.

The care perspective, by contrast, presents a self neither abstract and unencumbered nor determined from without, but relational. "As a framework for moral decision, care is grounded in the assumption that self and other are interdependent, an assumption reflected in a view of action as responsive, as arising in relationship" (Gilligan 1987: 24). The force of moral obligation for this self is neither from without nor entirely from within, but arises out of the relationship, out of reciprocity. The relational self is an improvement over the autonomous self of the justice perspective because it acknowledges and takes account of the reality that we *find* ourselves in relationship with others; we do not always choose these relationships, but their nonvoluntary nature does not absolve us of responsibility for them. The relational self of the care perspective is also an improvement over the communal self of communitarianism, insofar as it narrows the focus, taking each relationship individually. This focus on relationship rather than community decreases the tendency to define morality according to majority norms, empowering the individual without isolating her or him.

In service-learning programs one of the goals typically is to promote students' understanding of social problems and to foster a desire to become actively involved in addressing those problems. Moreover, the goal is that students develop an increasingly mature understanding and practice of their service. Morton's (1995) description of distinct orientations to service, involving differing views of the sort of action and type of outcome appropriate to a given problem, suggests that seeking to move students further along a continuum from charity to justice may be inappropriate. Although students may differ in the approach to service with which they are most comfortable, the relational self provides a common denominator. "Insisting on the humanity of another person in the face of sometimes overwhelming pressure to deny that humanity can be a motive for charity . . . [or] social change" (Morton 1995: 28). Unfortunately, at the practical level the preceding analysis raises more questions than it provides answers.

Research Questions

One reason to resist multiple paradigms of service is the fear of relativism. The existence of distinct paradigms, however, is consistent with the ability to establish criteria for evaluating progress toward mature service within the framework of a given paradigm, as Gilligan (1982) did for the care orientation. Gilligan's ability to articulate criteria for evaluating moral reasoning within the care orientation, however, was the result of extensive research, listening to and analyzing many personal accounts of moral decision making. Morton's (1995) interviews with community partners represent a good first step toward acquiring the data that would enable us to establish comparable criteria for service. More extensive qualitative studies could contribute significantly to our understanding of how best to encourage development toward mature service by describing the paradigms in greater detail and by analyzing the stages of development within each one. Furthermore, since there is currently considerable divergence in how the terms charity and justice — when used to designate approaches to service — are understood, more detailed descriptions would also improve the quality of discussion of these issues by providing shared definitions of the terms.

Once the different paradigms of service have been characterized, and the process of development within each one is delineated, there remain the practical questions of how to structure service-learning placements to maximize development. Here too research would need to be done. For instance, Morton (1995) observed that people change from one paradigm to another only rarely and with difficulty (24). Would this observation hold true for a larger research sample? If so, would the best strategy be to identify students'' preferred paradigm early on and funnel them into placements geared toward that paradigm? Or, on the contrary, would student development and community impact be positively affected if we consciously strove to "stretch" students beyond their preferred paradigm?

Another set of questions could be framed around this notion of a preferred paradigm. One of the major questions prompted by Gilligan's (1982) work was whether the care orientation is a "female" approach to ethics and the justice paradigm a "male" approach. By the same token, research could be done to determine whether there are specific demographic features (gender, economic class, religious background, etc.) that might predispose a student to prefer one or another paradigm of service. Finally, there is the question of how a student's view of relationships influences her or his approach to service. Does someone operating within the charity paradigm experience and interpret relationships the same way someone within the social change paradigm does? Do students actively engaged in any type of service perceive relationship differently from those who do no service? Are the differences (if any) between the paradigms as great as the differences (if any) between all students engaged in service and those who are not?

Conclusion

Throughout this paper I have identified similarities between Gilligan's (1982) analysis of the moral orientations of care and justice and Morton's (1995) analysis of paradigms of service, using some of Gilligan's insights to suggest ways in which the charity/social change discussion within service-learning might develop. Juxtaposing Morton's analysis to the work of Gilligan and others in the field of moral development highlights the significance of the former in at least two ways. One has to do with how we talk about service, charity, and social change, and the value judgments that adhere to those terms. The other has to do with practical questions surrounding how service-learning placements should be structured in order to encourage student development. Answers to the practical questions will require empirical research. The value question, however, is less a question of research than of vision.

The original impetus for this paper was the tremendous sense of empowerment I experienced upon reading Morton's (1995) analysis of the paradigms of service. Just as Gilligan's (1982) work helped legitimate an approach to moral problems and moral choice other than the dominant "justice" orientation, so too Morton's essay validates approaches to service other than the social change model. Gilligan noted:

The failure to see the different reality of women's lives and to hear the differences in their voices stems in part from the assumption that there is a single mode of social experience and interpretation. By positing instead two different modes, we arrive at a more complex rendition of human experience. (173-174)

Service-learning educators (and practitioners) should guard against the temptation to assume "there is a single mode of social experience and interpretation," lest a valuable voice be silenced and our understanding of service be impoverished.

Notes

1. An earlier version of this paper was presented at the 1997 annual meeting of the Association for Moral Education, Atlanta, GA. It also appeared in the Fall 1998 *Michigan Journal of Community Service Learning.*

2. Morton actually describes *three* paradigms: charity, social change, and what he calls "project." For the purpose of this paper I will discuss only the first two. The existence of a third paradigm in no way alters my argument, and the omission of the third paradigm from the discussion should not be interpreted as denigration of that paradigm.

3. The gender association of these two orientations is a complex and controversial matter. It is, however, not relevant to my argument. In the introduction to *In a Different Voice,* Gilligan notes that "the different voice I describe is characterized not by gender but by theme. Its association with women is an empirical observation. . . . But this association is not absolute, and the contrasts between male and female voices are presented here to highlight a distinction between two modes of thought and to focus a problem of interpretation rather than to represent a generalization about either sex" (1982: 2). It is these "two modes of thought" and the "problem of interpretation" that are of interest to me in this paper.

References

Friedman, M. (1993). "Beyond Caring: The De-Moralization of Gender." In *An Ethic of Care: Feminist and Interdisciplinary Perspectives,* edited by M. J. Larrabee, pp. 258-273. New York, NY: Routledge.

Gilligan, C. (1977). "In a Different Voice: Women's Conceptions of Self and Morality." *Harvard Educational Review* 47(4): 481-517.

––––––. (1982). *In a Different Voice: Psychological Theory and Women's Development.* Cambridge, MA: Harvard University Press.

––––––. (1987). "Moral Orientation and Moral Development." In *Women and Moral Theory,* edited by E. F. Kittay and D. T. Meyers, pp. 19-33. Totowa, NJ: Rowman & Littlefield.

Hallie, P. (1993). "From Cruelty to Goodness." In *Vice & Virtue in Everyday Life: Introductory Readings in Ethics,* edited by C. Sommers and F. Sommers, pp. 9-24. Fort Worth, TX: Harcourt Brace Jovanovich.

Hare, R.M. (1978). "Freedom and Reason." In *Moral Philosophy: Text and Readings,* edited by A. G. Oldenquist, pp. 338-356. Prospect Heights, IL: Waveland.

Hekman, S. (1995). *Moral Voices, Moral Selves: Carol Gilligan and Feminist Moral Theory.* University Park, PA: The Pennsylvania State University Press.

Kant, I. (1981). *Grounding for the Metaphysics of Morals,* translated by J. W. Ellington. Indianapolis, IN: Hackett.

Kohlberg, L. (1981). *The Philosophy of Moral Development.* San Francisco, CA: Harper and Row.

Levinas, E. (1969, orig. 1961). *Totality and Infinity,* translated by A. Lingis. Pittsburgh, PA: Duquesne University Press.

———. (1985, orig. 1982). *Ethics and Infinity: Conversations With Philippe Nemo,* translated by R. Cohen. Pittsburgh, PA: Duquesne University Press.

———. (1989). "Ideology and Idealism," translated by S. Ames and A. Lesley. In *The Levinas Reader,* edited by S. Hand, pp. 235-248. Oxford: Blackwell.

Morton, K. (1993). *Models of Service and Civic Education.* Providence, RI: Campus Compact.

———. (1995). "The Irony of Service: Charity, Project and Social Change in Service-Learning." *Michigan Journal of Community Service Learning* 2: 19-32.

Rawls, J. (1971). *A Theory of Justice.* Cambridge, MA: Harvard University Press.

Saltmarsh, J. (1996). "Education for Critical Citizenship: John Dewey's Contribution." *Michigan Journal of Community Service Learning* 3: 13-21.

Sandel, M. (1992). "Morality and the Liberal Ideal." In *Justice: Alternative Political Perspectives,* edited by J. P. Sterba, pp. 219-224. Belmont, CA: Wadsworth.

Varlotta, L. (1996). "Service-Learning: A Catalyst for Constructing Democratic Progressive Communities." *Michigan Journal of Community Service Learning* 3: 22-30.

P282, *Women in Philosophical Thought*
Spring 1999

Syllabus

Cathy Ludlum Foos
Whitewater Hall 266
973-8474
cludlum@indiana.edu

Tracy Knechel
Girls Incorporated of Wayne Co.
962-2362
tknechel.wayne@girls-inc.org

Course Description

This course is about the various ways society has thought about and portrayed women, and the impact these views have had on women's roles in society. The goal, however, is not merely passive acquisition of knowledge, but the development of authentic and well-informed responses to these philosophical views of women. Discussions will be loosely organized around three themes: ideas about and images of women's bodies, theories regarding women's rational abilities and the ways women gain knowledge, and opinions concerning women's ethical capacities. To help make the course content more meaningful, there will be an experiential component to the course--the opportunity to engage in service at Girls Incorporated of Wayne County--which will provide an occasion to develop relationships with, and learn from, future women. The course will be team-taught by Cathy Ludlum Foos of the philosophy department at IU East and Tracy Knechel, Executive Director of Girls Incorporated.

Course Objectives

Generally:
The Indiana University East Strategic Plan lays out seven learning objectives which, taken together, describe the conception of an educated person to which this institution is committed. This course contributes to **four** of them. They are:
- Educated persons should be exposed to a broad variety of academic fields traditionally known as the Liberal Arts . . . in order to develop a critical appreciation of a diversity of ideas and creative expression.
- Educated persons should be able to express themselves clearly, completely, and accurately.
- Educated persons should be expected to have some understanding of and experience in thinking about moral and ethical problems.
- Educated persons should have the ability to develop informed opinions, to comprehend, formulate, and critically evaluate ideas, and to identify problems and find solutions to those problems.

Specifically::
It is our goal that students in this course:
- be able to express informed opinions regarding ideas about and images of women and their role in society;
- live up to their potential to be **STRONG, SMART, & BOLD.***

* The motto of Girls Incorporated

By this we mean . . .

> **STRONG:** I am capable of thinking my own thoughts, feeling my own feelings, knowing what I know, being who I am.

> **SMART:** I can make an informed decision based on my thoughts, feelings, and knowledge along with other information I gather.

> **BOLD:** I can choose to take action based on my informed decision for the good of myself and others.

>   ***

Requirements (Summary--more details will be forthcoming)

Journal Entries -- alternating weekly between:
- First reactions--your own initial thoughts and feelings about the readings;
- Reflective, informed opinions--building upon your first reaction, but going beyond this to include knowledge acquired, and reasoned conclusions developed, through discussion in class and careful re-reading of the text.

Short Papers -- 3
- Synthesis of journal entries for *The Handmaid's Tale*
- Synthesis of journal entries for *Herland*
- "Strong, smart and bold" analysis of the course as a whole

Term Project
- Information gathering through **either**
  - a) Approximately 20 hours service at Girls Incorporated **OR**
  - b) a research project.
- Term paper

> *Details of the term project will be determined collaboratively by the class as a whole. To prepare for this discussion each student should spend a few hours at either Girls Inc. or the library gathering ideas before Jan. 26.*

Class Participation
- Attendance is required
- Students are expected to prepare for and contribute to class discussion

---

P282, *Women in Philosophical Thought*   **Spring 1999**

- **Respectful listening** is an important contribution to discussion
- Each student will make a brief presentation on a topic of her or his choice to supplement class discussion. The first few will be modeled by the instructors.

Grading

Paper on *The Handmaid's Tale*:	20%
Paper on *Herland:*	20%
Term paper:	20%
Final paper:	20%
Class participation & journals:	20%

Texts

Margaret Atwood, *The Handmaid's Tale*
Eve Browning Cole, *Philosophy and Feminist Criticism: An Introduction*
Charlotte Gilman Perkins, *Herland*

P282, *Women in Philosophical Thought*   **Spring 1999**

Schedule Of Assignments

Jan. 12:   Introduction to course

Jan. 19:   *Handmaid's Tale*, chs. 1-9--"First reactions" journal entry due

Jan. 26:   *Handmaid's Tale*, chs. 10-15--"First reactions" journal entry due

Feb. 2:   *Handmaid's Tale*, chs. 1-9--"Reflective" journal entry due

Feb. 9:   *Handmaid's Tale*, chs. 10-15--"Reflective" journal entry due

Feb. 16:   *Herland*, all--"First reactions" journal entry due

Feb. 23:   *Herland*, first half--"Reflective" journal entry due
                Handmaid's Tale paper due

Mar. 2:   *Herland*, second half--"Reflective" journal entry due

Mar. 9:   Open House at Girls Incorporated (display projects)

Mar. 16:   **SPRING BREAK**

Mar. 23:   Open House at IU East (display projects)
                Herland paper due

Mar. 30:   Cole, ch. 3--"First reactions" journal entry due

Apr. 6:   Cole, ch. 4--"First reactions" journal entry due

Apr. 13:   Cole, ch. 5--"First reactions" journal entry due
                Term paper due

Apr. 20:   Cole, chs. 3-5--"Smart" discussion over course as a whole

Apr. 27:   **Final paper due**

P282, *Women in Philosophical Thought*   **Spring 1999**

Learning Across Boundaries:
Women's Studies, Praxis, and Community Service

by Mary Trigg and Barbara J. Balliet

A central belief behind the national impetus toward placing service-learning in the curriculum is that it teaches college students what it means to be citizens in a democratic society. This concept emphasizes service as the responsibility of citizenship and argues that an educated and engaged citizenry is a prerequisite for a healthy democracy (Barber and Battistoni 1993). Advocates of service-learning hope it will contribute to creating new generations of citizens who understand the way government works, and who will feel and act on their sense of responsibility to their communities.

Women's studies is a particularly useful location from which to explore the contribution service-learning can make to American collegiate education. Women's studies has a double identity within the university. Programs seek to include their subject — women — in the traditional curriculum while recognizing the need for a separate location to develop new methods of inquiry more fully exploring the historical and contemporary position of women in society. The position of women's studies faculty as outsiders *within* the academy parallels the position of students as they enter communities from the university as part of service education courses (Collins 1986; Harding 1991). Even when students share ethnic, racial, and class identities with members of the communities they work with, their purpose as learners differentiates them. Students in service-learning courses are charged with empowering others while utilizing their experiences as a route to empower themselves. Similarly, women's studies faculty are engaged in transforming knowledge and questioning institutional power and hierarchy while benefiting from their position within the academy. The kind of learning that comes from reflecting on these contexts is the subject of feminist pedagogy.

In service-learning, students learn across boundaries as they move between communities and classrooms. In feminist service-learning courses, this movement occurs primarily in and among communities of women. Gender provides a special lens on the social issues students encounter in both their placements and readings. For example, students learn that poverty affects men and women differently. Ideas about community, hierarchy, and identity are both experienced and critically examined in a context that puts gender at the center of analysis.

Women students need to learn about American women's long and rich tradition of volunteering in their communities (Frankel and Dye 1991; Ginzberg 1991). The complicated history of women's community activism helps students forge an understanding of *their* location in this history and the different possibilities for female citizenship. The history of women's voluntarism also demonstrates the problems that can arise when women cross class, racial, and ethnic boundaries in the name of either service, democracy, or sisterhood. Historically, voluntarism and community building offered some women an avenue for gaining self-confidence and a socially acceptable way to develop leadership and political skills working with communities of less-privileged women. Women students today can utilize women's history to reflect on ways, both positive and negative, in which their voluntarism might impact the lives of those they serve in the community. They can gain a growing recognition of themselves as women and as citizen leaders from community service.

Rutgers University is a residential public research and undergraduate university, and is the state university of New Jersey. A large and at times impersonal institution, it enrolls about 40,000 students, has campuses in Newark, Camden, and New Brunswick and eight undergraduate colleges scattered across New Brunswick and Piscataway. Its student body is ethnically and racially diverse and the majority of Rutgers undergraduates come from New Jersey. Most of its students are from working-class to middle-class family backgrounds; many of them are the first persons in their families to have gone away to college (Moffat 1989).

The Women's Studies Program at Rutgers was founded in 1971 as an interdisciplinary certificate program. It became an interdisciplinary major in 1984. As one of the oldest of the more than 600 programs currently in existence in the United States, its form and its challenges cannot be detached from the movements that helped to create it, the civil rights movement and the second-wave feminist movement. (Aisenberg and Harrington 1988; DuBois et al. 1987). Women's studies remains shaped by its history, created in the years after black and ethnic studies had arrived on college campuses. Like most early programs, women's studies at Rutgers was originally molded by the passion (and largely volunteer labor) of women faculty. They discovered through the women's movement the androcentric bias of most of the traditional curriculum and resolved to reconstruct knowledge by describing and analyzing women's experiences. A proposal drafted in 1973 by a group of women faculty urging the establishment of a women's studies program at Rutgers defined the enterprise as a "center for research and teaching about women within the university" and as an "academic field concerned with the history, accomplishments, roles, status, and attributes of women; and with sex roles in American society and other cultures."

The program's beginnings in feminist politics and scholarship have left an indelible print on the curriculum and the program's relationship to the university. Faculty and students in the program struggle over the relationship between feminist theory and practice, advocacy and scholarship, and how much women's studies should emulate other academic departments and disciplines. Women's studies is valued by both faculty and students for putting gender as a social and intellectual category on the academic map, for its critique of institutional hierarchy and inequality, its openness to interdisciplinary scholarship, and as a site of intellectual experimentation and camaraderie.

These values, core to women's studies, represent a significant challenge to business as usual within the academy. Feminist scholarship and pedagogy reevaluate how knowledge is produced, stressing partnership and active participation in the classroom over competition and rote learning. Founded in absence, the absence of women from the traditional curriculum — women's studies fosters a critical perspective, examining the disciplines carefully for androcentricism and stressing the inseparability of gender from other social categories such as race, ethnicity, and sexuality. Women's studies was created in a context where disciplines organized in the late 19th and early 20th centuries claimed to represent objective knowledge but had manifestly ignored how gender, class, race, and sexuality shaped the knowledge they produced. This insight, central to feminist scholarship, remains a tension both within women's studies and between women's studies and older disciplines. Feminists in their effort to recover and analyze the experiences of women and reconstruct knowledge began trespassing on the disciplinary boundaries, borrowing methods and theories from other disciplines.

This epistemological challenge again owes much to the early history of women's studies. Faculty from different disciplines brought together by a mutual interest in feminism and their status as women in the academy, frequently facing hostility within their departments, began to build interdisciplinary networks and to teach cross-disciplinary courses. Faculty located in different departments eager to transform their disciplines offered courses such as Women and Literature, Sociology of Gender, Psychology of Women, and Women and Work. Women's studies developed its curriculum using both new courses developed within traditional areas of study and the interdisciplinary, explicitly feminist courses. This dual impulse to transform disciplines through the inclusion of women and gender perspectives and to create a separate arena for the study of women and gender continues to shape women's studies.

The seminar that accompanies the women's studies community service experience at Rutgers is entitled Community Activism: Women's Participation. It was inaugurated in the fall of 1992. Students receive a total of six credits: three for the seminar, and three for 10 to 12 hours of work at their site per week. The syllabus includes readings on feminist theory, which range from John Stuart Mill's *The Subjection of Women* to Diana M. Pearce's "The Feminization of Poverty," to bell hooks's *Feminist Theory: From Margin to Center*. It also includes readings on the history of women's community service and activism. Jane Addams's *Twenty Years at Hull House* is read alongside Ida B. Wells's *Struggle for Justice*. Students keep a journal in which they chronicle their daily experiences at their community sites and critically reflect on the connections or disjunctures between the feminist theories they are reading and the lives of the women with whom they are working. They also write a final paper in which they are asked to consider praxis, reframing their experiences using feminist theories.

The educational philosophy that shapes the course and serves as a framing idea for the program itself is drawn from feminist pedagogy. As it has developed over the last 25 years — often in tandem with women's studies programs throughout the country — feminist pedagogy has argued that the process of learning, and teaching, should be reconceptualized (Culley and Portuges 1985; Gabriel and Smithson 1991; Griffin 1993; Pagano 1990). Feminist teaching methods stress collaboration over competition, legitimize personal experience as an appropriate arena of intellectual inquiry, and raise questions about the authority of the instructor. As a pedagogy that strives to be nonhierarchical, it emphasizes interpreting knowledge rather than simply acquiring it, and promotes student respect for one another and for the differing experiences and beliefs each student brings into the classroom. In their 1994 book *The Feminist Classroom*, Frances Maher and Mary Kay Thompson Tetreault call it "a thoroughgoing revolution in curriculum content and pedagogy" that has "led to educational approaches that break the illusions and silences, and transform the visions of students."

Feminist pedagogy has something valuable to offer to service-learning courses. At its best, feminist pedagogy prepares students to reach out to community members with empathy and care. Participation in community service, like feminist pedagogy at an earlier moment, has been hailed as a potentially transformative educational experience for undergraduates (Guarasci and Cornwell 1993). In community service, students learn to dialogue with community residents, share personal histories and experiences, and respect differences. Effective community service is collaborative, nonhierarchical, nonjudgmental, respectful, and transformative, embracing the same goals as effective feminist teaching methods. It encourages students to consider the notion of community itself, and how people form and sustain communities. In a similar spirit, the feminist classroom empowers students to think of themselves as members of a community and to interact in ways that will stimulate shared learning and mutual respect. Both ways of learning may motivate students to create new definitions of leadership, ones that stress collective action rather than individualism, and suggest that everyone can, and should be, leaders.

The women's studies internship program at Rutgers views service-learning as an educational tool for our students, and approaches the community as a partner in education rather than as a set of clients in need of service. The same nonhierarchical, respectful, and nonjudgmental attitudes that the feminist teacher fosters in the classroom should be the ones that students take from the university out into the community with them. This approach seeks to avoid a charity-oriented, noblesse oblige philosophy, but instead encourages mutuality. Not only does this help to tear down the walls that often separate the university and the community in which the university resides; it also prepares students to enter a world in which the ability to reach across differences will be increasingly necessary.

An internship experience has been a part of the women's studies curriculum at Rutgers since 1973, reflecting its feminist commitment to linking theory and practice and the academy to the community. A seminar, Women and Contemporary Problems, was designed around community service to meet a program goal of combining scholarship with social involvement. During the late 1970s the program shifted its focus, downplaying community activism in favor of career preparation. Students resisted this move, arguing for the creation of a one-credit course in which they could actively participate in "a particular political experience" that could be "analyzed in relation to theoretical material studied in class." By the mid 1980s internships had again become a site for student initiative and experimentation. In 1992 under the auspices of the Rutgers Citizenship Education and Civic Leadership program (now Citizenship and Service Education) the internship became a course, adding a reading and writing curriculum, an instructor, and classroom experience.

The current women's studies internship program at Rutgers operates under the umbrella of the university-wide Citizenship and Service Education (CASE) program. This experiment in civic education and community service was launched at Rutgers in the spring of 1988, when President Edward Bloustein gave a commencement address in which he proposed a mandatory program of community service as a graduation requirement for all Rutgers students. His address called attention to the "pathologies of prejudice and radical individualism" manifest both in the nation and at Rutgers University (Barber and Battistoni 1993). He suggested the service requirement in response to what he perceived as a lack of connection and communication between the academic and local communities, the lives of students and their lives as citizens.

In 1990 the CASE program began to offer pilot courses integrating student community service into courses that are part of disciplinary majors. CASE is administered by the office of the vice president for undergraduate education, directed by a full-time faculty member. A staff member serves as an associate director. The program's larger goal is to link academic disciplines to general themes of community and citizenship through student service (Goldberg 1992). The success of the pilot program was recognized by President Clinton when he chose Rutgers University as the site to kick off his national service campaign in March 1993.

The Rutgers program currently offers more than a dozen courses that combine community service with classroom learning. The participating disciplines range from the social sciences (political science, psychology, and sociology) to humanities disciplines (English, French, Spanish, and Portuguese) and interdisciplinary programs including urban studies and women's studies. Although the intent is for each course to include the core civic education framework — which includes required readings and writing assignments on such topics as citizenship, diversity, and democracy — each course is adapted to the disciplinary concerns of the departments and programs that offer it. For example, a course cross-listed in political science and biology takes as its topic HIV and public policy, and offers students the opportunity to consider questions of public health, policy options, and social responsibility as they relate to issues surrounding HIV and AIDS. Students work in HIV-related community service placements, such as a hospital pediatric AIDS ward or delivering meals to people with AIDS (Barber and Battistoni 1993).

A community service course taught within the context of a women's studies program offers a site for students to move from feminist theory to practice. This is fueled by the idea that it's not enough to study feminist theory and writings in the classroom; the real goal is to improve women's lives. Students in a holistic learning experience such as this become practitioners of what they believe, or they recognize that for them, putting their theory into practice is an impossible task. A community service course can give students the opportunity to test, in a practical way, the kinds of classroom knowledge they may feel they have already learned. Striving for praxis is an advanced skill that may challenge both the ways that undergraduates have learned and the assumptions that they bring to their learning. It is a pedagogy rooted in a history that combines intellectual life with public citizenship developed by educational theorists, most prominently John Dewey. Service-learning courses provide a broader context through readings and discussion of the experiences students are having in the community. As one of our students wrote about her service with a transitional home for formerly homeless women: "My eyes were opened, unlike they could have been in any other way, to the circumstances that poor women are faced with. I was never before aware of how few of the needs of women in poverty are actually met by our 'welfare' system."

To more fully understand the unique problems of the women whom they serve in the community, it is important that students be taught, through feminist writings, the legacy of institutional sexism in the United States, and the impact that economic discrimination and exclusion from political participation have had on women's lives. It is also necessary that they learn the ways in which institutionalized racism has compounded these difficulties for women of color. The challenges faced by poor women, for example, who may be burdened with single motherhood along with wage discrimination, are different from the challenges faced by poor men. When confronted with real women with real problems, the women's studies student can begin to understand and use feminist theories as tools for improving women's condition, rather than as abstract sets of ideas.

Most of the community sites where students from the Rutgers women's studies program work focus on problems in which gender plays a defining role. The placements include Planned Parenthood Leagues, women's health and counseling centers, rape crisis centers, battered women's shelters, a transitional home for formerly homeless women, and a YWCA project for pregnant teenagers. Many of these organizations are primarily or exclusively female environments. One reflection of the program's success is the relatively high percentage of students who choose to continue to help after their internship ends. Some are even offered full-time positions with the organization after they graduate; for these students, the community service experience actually serves as a valuable entry into the work world. For others, who may find their experiences in the community placements negative or overwhelming, their 16 weeks of voluntarism helps them define what they do *not* want to do with their lives. This is an important lesson as well.

Feminist community service tests students' abilities to reach across boundaries of difference, and to move between the borders separating theory and practice, classroom and community, and their own conception of themselves as private individuals and public citizens. It also often coincides with their psychological and emotional movement from late adolescence into adulthood. For some students all of this comes together, and they are able to make these transitions with fluidity and grace; for others, the connections are far more difficult. As one student who took the course wrote, "Studying feminism in the classroom and applying and practicing it in the workplace is not an easy transition."

Through the community service experience, students come to understand differences more deeply. Many of the Rutgers students we taught self-consciously strove to cross differences of class, race, or age, to form bonds with the community women based on gender. One thoughtful student wrote:

> I know issues of diversity are important to explore within feminism
> because before we can demand equal rights and treatment based on gen-

der, we must first, or at least simultaneously, establish a community <u>with-</u>
<u>in</u> women. An important beginning is including women who have thus far
been considered "other" within the movement. It is therefore important for
me to learn about and to be able to relate to as diverse a group of women
as possible.

An important first step in understanding difference is to admit whatever feelings we might have about those we perceive as different. Some of the Rutgers students in the women's studies seminar honestly struggled with their feelings of prejudice and fear toward those they worked with in the community different from themselves. One such student, for example, worked at the New Jersey Women and AIDS Network, an advocacy and education organization for women with HIV or AIDS. For this middle-class African-American woman and senior, her struggle with difference, which she spoke about with self-reflection, had to do with the staff with whom she worked at her internship site, rather than with the community they served. She wrote in her final paper:

To the extent that four out of the seven people at NJWAN are lesbians, my
work here has forced me to confront my own homophobic attitudes. Here is
a journal entry I made after a discussion with my supervisor about her
bisexuality: ". . . I just know I feel (and have always felt) uncomfortable
around homosexuals, because I don't understand the whole phenomenon.
How can two men/women sleep together? It just boggles the mind. Since the
internship consists of 4 lesbians and 3 straights working in the office, I find
it necessary to confront my own homophobic attitudes and deal with them.
I'm sure it will be a difficult process, since I hate racists, sexists, and others
who can't accept difference. It's hard to realize I may be one of those people."

This student's willingness to confront her prejudices and make a commitment to "deal with them" is both honest and mature. As Audre Lorde has written, we cannot cross the boundaries that divide us if we do not first recognize our differences. "It is not our differences which separate women," Lorde writes, "but our reluctance to recognize those differences and to deal effectively with the distortions which have resulted from the ignoring and misnaming of those differences" (1984). If we recognize those different from us as our equals, she reminds us, we can then use those differences to enrich our visions and strengthen our joint struggles.

The borders that separate theory and practice, classroom and community, can be impassable for some students. One woman we taught who worked at a transitional housing development for formerly homeless women fluctuated between identifying with the women residents and firmly separating herself from them. Her job involved counseling the women in parenting, personal growth, health issues, and budgeting skills. The previous semester she had written a research paper on women and poverty; intellectually she understood the complex and interrelated systems of oppression that contribute to poverty and homelessness in America. She wrote:

> We have a tendency to look down on homeless people and poor people. We think that they are lazy people who just don't want to work. One thing that I learned while at Amandla Crossing is that anyone can become homeless. Some of these women at Amandla Crossing <u>were just like us</u> [our emphasis]. They had beautiful homes, nice cars and good jobs. A series of events occurred in their lives and they became homeless.

Yet this student, who had immigrated from Jamaica with her family when she was a child, and was slightly older than the average student (she was 25), was conflicted and found her experience at the transitional home depressing, stressful, and overwhelming. At times she judged the women at the shelter as people very different from herself, as Other. She wrote:

> This internship was very challenging and overwhelming at times. I was surprised to see how young the women were. The youngest woman at this shelter is 16 years, and the oldest woman is 30 years. This was really a shock for me. Some of the women are around my age, and many of these women have 3 or 4 children. I often look at my life and compare it with the lives of these women. I have accomplished so much. I am about to graduate from Rutgers University with a B.A. Many of these women have not even completed high school. I often wonder how they got to this point.

On the basis of her community service experience there, this student decided to give up her career goal of becoming a social worker. In fact, she recently requested a recommendation for a job in a bank.

Many students we taught drew on their own life experiences to try to find common ground with the community women. For example, the student described earlier, who wrestled with her feelings of homophobia about the staff of the organization, worked with a group of women who were HIV positive or had AIDS. At first, in class, this student (who was shy) had expressed feelings about not having "the right" to speak in front of these women, and being reluctant to present herself as someone who could talk about AIDS in front of this audience, since she herself did not carry the virus or suffer from the disease. "I had not experienced the same oppression as a woman living with AIDS," she remarked. As an African American, she knew what it was like to have people speak about her race without knowing anything about her life, or her experience, and she did not want to repeat this mistake.

But then, in mid-semester, this student herself had an illness that gave her the opportunity to try to understand what it feels like to have AIDS in our society: She caught the measles. Because measles is contagious, she was quarantined for four weeks along with other infected students, and the university launched a major immunization drive for all students, staff, and faculty, and even threatened to shut down if it became an epidemic. This student used her experience of illness — temporary though it was — to give her a bond and a basis for identification with the HIV-infected women. It also gave her a voice and the self-confidence to use it before this particular audience. She wrote in her final paper: "After listening to the stories of these women . . . I felt I could identify with them and offer support, based on my bout with the measles and the recollection of how I was treated. It was as if I myself had an incurable virus that someone could 'catch.'" At the end of the semester she described her community service as "a most empowering experience," which "I will carry . . . with me for the rest of my life."

Although her empathy was genuine, the student's need to stress similarities rather than the differences between her experience and the lives of the women she worked with reveals a complexity posed by community service and raises questions that proponents of service-learning must consider thoughtfully. Must differences be obliterated for empathy and understanding to flourish? Is commonality the only basis for connection? Or, does a student's attempt to see through another's lens and grasp the other's view, however briefly, provide a starting point for understanding? In emphasizing the value of knowledge gained through experience do we devalue other means by which we learn? Experiential learning situated within a feminist pedagogy becomes a place to raise these kinds of questions and deepen our conversations about the necessary relationship between experiential and other forms of learning.

Another young woman who used her life experiences differently to reach across difference was a white, middle-class, Jewish student who talked about the commonalities between anti-Semitism and racism with the African-American women with whom she worked. She wrote:

> I have become involved in some intense discussions about the reasons behind Racism between the residents at Amandla Crossing. Once my Judaism came up, and that was because the Black woman with whom I was talking said the prejudice she was subjected to was similar to anti-Semitism she had once witnessed. . . . The woman and I agreed that there were similarities between the oppression of Blacks and of Jews in this country. . . . I have been able to relate my own experience as a Jew to a lot of what some of the women have said about being African-American.

In having the conversation with women at her placement rather than in her journal or in the classroom, this student learned that a perspective she believed in was shared by women located very differently.

Students such as this one also used the community service experience as an opportunity to consider their own positions in social hierarchies and to recognize their privilege. For these exceptional students, voluntarism offered a new world view, one accompanied by a commitment to social change and community involvement. A student who worked at the American Civil Liberties Union of New Jersey described "a contradiction" she felt every time she went to the Newark office. She described this in her paper:

> I had to walk up to the third floor past Superior Cleaning. It is a temporary worker agency with a staff mainly made up of Latina and Black women (the rest are Latino and Black men). I was in stark contrast to them. There I was, a middle-class white student learning, thinking and working for credits. Not only was I not getting paid, but I was paying to be there. They showed up every morning looking for assignments that break their backs and do not pay well so they can feed themselves and their families. I am still trying to reconcile this situation. I am continually questioning how I am using the privilege I have to work on creating a society without racist and sexist institutions and without such economic disparity.

Noticing and reflecting on the differences between her position as a student and the position of female domestic workers, she is moved to consider how she can act to create a more just and humane society. A student who questions inequality with some knowledge is better educated and more likely to participate as a citizen.

It is clear to us that feminist community service, combined with a course that is academic in content yet allows class time for discussion of the service component, can be a powerful learning experience for students. It can encourage them to critically reflect on their cultural roots, to explore their values and emerging commitments, and to develop skills in collaboration and envisioning situations from a multiplicity of perspectives. Community service can help women find their voices as leaders and advocates, their position in the history of women's activism.

Faculty members can help students move successfully from the classroom to the community — and, by extension, from the university to their lives after graduation — by educating them to listen, to cultivate humility and acceptance of difference, and by themselves serving as role models. There are times, even in a democracy, when it is more important to listen than to speak. Students will best be able to forge intercultural partnerships with communities outside of campus by putting aside their preconceptions and by being willing to listen and learn.

This is also an important, and often overlooked, skill to foster in educating democratic citizens and community builders. In *The Call of Service*, child psychiatrist Robert Coles, who is white, says of his research in the

1960s with a 6-year-old black girl and her family who led the struggle for school desegregation in Boston: "I don't believe I could have understood Tessie and her family's capacity to live as they did, do as they did for so long, against such great odds, had I not begun to hear what *they* were saying and meaning, what *they* intended others to know about their reasons and values" (1993).

Women's studies faculty in particular have a unique role to play in fostering the development of community service initiatives in the academy. Because their discipline actually grew out of a social movement, their connections to the community should be strong and reciprocal, their commitments to activism and advocacy ongoing. As one theorist of women wrote, "It is senseless to study the situation of women without a concomitant commitment to do something about it" (Flax 1979: 81). A Rutgers graduate of the course Community Activism: Women's Participation reflected similarly on her learning:

> *I have, through this internship, realized the importance of inclusiveness and activism within feminism. . . . As a Women's Studies student, I think it is important to see the connection between community activism and feminism. You cannot be actively trying to educate and change things for the women of the world without being involved, hands-on, with women, and this internship has given me a good start.*

The historical development of women's studies and its continuing marginal position in the university, however, raise important issues for service-learning courses, which also question existing paradigms and traditional ways of learning. The challenges that women's studies represents to the academy are real and generate continued perplexity, even suspicion about its status as an intellectual rather than political location. Intellectual advocacy by women's studies of interdisciplinary scholarship, gender as a central analytic category, and its primarily female constituency can cause programs to appear anomalous and even separatist among older, more established or male-dominated departments. Like other area studies programs founded in the 1960s and 1970s (Africana, Puerto Rican, Hispanic, and Caribbean), whose intellectual roots grew out of political and social movements, women's studies is accused by its critics of confusing affirmative action with scholarship.

Despite the continuing emphasis within women's studies communities on their location as institutional homes for women's issues intellectually, programs continue to run into difficulties over where the line lies between the intellectual and the political (Kessler-Harris 1992). A recent controversy at Rutgers about the women's studies program reveals how complicated the heritage of advocacy and scholarship can become. In this debate the program's goal of building a feminist community with students and other groups, particularly racial and ethnic minorities traditionally underrepresented in governance within university hierarchies, ran up against a different set of assumptions about how to constitute departmental governance. Women's studies practitioners, as part of their effort to put the knowledge and insight gained from scholarship into practice, seek to put their many intellectual and political differences into the conversations that guide their programs. Feminist scholarship has explored the ways in which gender can provide a basis for commonalities among women. This shared identity as women does not, however, as women's history demonstrates, transcend differences among women produced by class, race, ethnicity, sexuality, religion, age, and nationality. Debate among differing perspectives is essential to build programs intellectually vital and responsive to their varied constituencies.

The program's by-laws seek to foster diversity within the women's studies community by ensuring the presence of underrepresented groups in the governance structure of the program. Goals (some might say quotas) for the representation of ethnic and racial minorities were specified for core women's studies committees. A senior university-wide faculty committee reviewing the program in 1995 perceived these aspirations as evidence that the program was a political rather than academic enterprise. One possible reading of the committee's conclusions locates them within the emerging nationwide debate about affirmative action, opposing the use of numerical targets for creating equality of opportunity for racial and ethnic minorities. This reading is plausible except that the committee made a surprising misreading of the by-laws that revealed its anxiety about women. The committee members, none of whom is among the 102 faculty affiliates of the program, read these provisions as including sexual orientation as a protected category (it isn't). How did this error arise? What does it signify? Possibly, a continuing misgiving that women in the academy organized apart from disciplinary structures are threatening because of their sexuality.

The error the committee made revealed a larger, underlying debate over which categories are appropriate to use in creating a community and building a curriculum. The committee had no difficulty with provisions that designated participation in the program by faculty rank. Even the presence of students on the committee went unremarked. The efforts of the women's studies program at Rutgers to create a teaching and learning community that reflected the program's broader democratic, feminist ideals put it into conflict with an alternative definition of community that recognized field, seniority, and status as the appropriate bases for representation. Both definitions are meritorious and each has a politics; but women's studies's tradition of advocacy makes its politics visible. Women's studies's efforts to give students and racial and ethnic minorities a place at the table still meet with resistance from established constituencies that rely on a different set of criteria for building a collegial community, educating students, and allocating power within the university.

Women's studies's location on the borders of the disciplines also speaks directly to what women's studies can offer students interested in service-learning. Alice Kessler-Harris has written:

> The institutional parallel to the outsider-within perspective, is the outsider status of women's studies within an institution that has its own rules and regulations. The outsider status simultaneously permits us to function with minimal attention to hierarchically and bureaucratically instituted norms and raises questions about how most effectively to relate to power. It thus forces us to negotiate between the competing values of community and hierarchy. (1992)

Women's studies is both self-conscious and made aware of its structural and philosophical differences with other disciplines. These differences can produce useful insights about the specificity and limitations of one's experience. Rather than universalizing from limited knowledge, women's studies teaches that in order to go beyond the specific conditions of one's life, a respectful and constant engagement with those differently situated is necessary. This is a profound and intellectually challenging position. Students learn that they must go outside the confines of their experience, imaginatively or actually, to learn. They must do this, however, without losing sight of how their own intellectual training and personal experience have shaped them. This kind of reflexivity is particularly useful when students engage in a learning experience that foregrounds citizenship and gender.

Women's studies historically has recognized the role education can play in transforming institutions and lives. The insight that the personal is political comes after all from the women's movement. Experiential learning can be a catalyst for students to act on insights gained from feminist theory about the ways gender differently constructs men's and women's social, economic, and political situations. Feminist interdisciplinary scholarship can enrich service-learning initiatives currently reliant on a literature about democracy and service derived largely from political science.

Service-learning and women's studies share an interest in educating students to take an active role in public life, expanding the categories of knowledge, and enlarging the community of learners. Despite these mutual interests, there have not been extensive discussions between women's studies and service-learning teachers. Women's studies's focus on gender and diversity and service-learning's emphasis on what community means in contemporary American society have the potential to enhance conversations about community, responsibility, citizenship, diversity, rights, and democracy (Barber and Battistoni 1993). Initiating a dialogue between women's studies practitioners and service-learning educators holds the promise of deepening each group's understanding of experiential learning, pedagogy, and citizenship.

Note

This essay appeared in *Democratic Education in an Age of Difference: Redefining Citizenship in Higher Education* (Jossey-Bass, 1997).

References

Aisenberg, Nadya, and Mona Harrington. (1988). *Women of Academe: Outsiders in the Sacred Grove.* Amherst, MA: University of Massachusetts Press.

Barber, Benjamin R., and Richard Battistoni. (June 1993). "A Season of Service: Introducing Service-Learning Into the Liberal Arts Curriculum." *PS: Political Science & Politics* 16(2): 235-240.

Coles, Robert. (1993). *The Call of Service.* Boston & New York: Houghton Mifflin.

Collins, Patricia Hill. (October/December 1986). "Learning From the Outsider Within: The Sociological Significance of Black Feminist Thought." *Social Problems,* pp. 14-32.

Culley, Margo, and Catherine Portuges. (1985). *Gendered Subjects; The Dynamics of Feminist Teaching.* Boston, MA: Routledge & Kegan Paul.

DuBois, Ellen, et al. (1987). *Feminist Scholarship; Kindling in the Groves of Academe.* Urbana & Chicago, IL: University of Illinois Press.

Flax, Jane. (Summer 1979). "Women Do Theory." In *Feminist Frameworks: Alternative Accounts of the Relations Between Men and Women,* edited by A. M. Jaggar and P. S. Rosenberg, pp. 80-83. New York, NY: McGraw Hill.

Frankel, Noralee, and Nancy Schrom Dye, eds. (1991). *Gender, Class, Race, and Reform in the Progressive Era.* Lexington, KY: University Press of Kentucky.

Gabriel, Susan L., and Isaiah Smithson. (1991). *Gender in the Classroom: Power and Pedagogy.* Urbana, IL: University of Illinois Press.

Ginzberg, Lori D. (1991). *Women and the Work of Benevolence; Morality, Politics, and Class in the Nineteenth-Century United States.* New Haven, CT: Yale University Press.

Goldberg, Vicki. (Sept. 27, 1992). "The Soup-Kitchen Classroom." *The New York Times Magazine,* p. 50.

Griffin, Gail B. (1993). *Calling; Essays on Teaching in the Mother Tongue.* Pasadena, CA: Trilogy Books.

Guarasci, Richard, and Grant Cornwell. (Spring 1993). "Democratic Education in an Age of Difference." *Perspectives* 23(1): 6-13.

Harding, Sandra. (1991). *Whose Science? Whose Knowledge? Thinking From Women's Lives.* Ithaca, NY: Cornell University Press.

Kessler-Harris, Alice. (Summer 1992). "The View From Women's Studies." *Signs* 17(4): 794-805.

Lorde, Audre. (1984). *Sister Outsider.* Freedom, CA: The Crossing Press.

Maher, Frances A., and Mary Kay Thompson Tetreault. (1994). *The Feminist Classroom.* New York, NY: Basic Books.

Moffat, Michael. (1989). *Coming of Age in New Jersey; College and American Culture.* New Brunswick, NJ: Rutgers University Press.

Pagano, Jo Anne. (1990). *Exiles and Communities: Teaching in the Patriarchal Wilderness.* Albany, NY: SUNY Press.

Van Dyne, Susan R. (1985). *Women's Place in The Academy: Transforming the Liberal Arts Curriculum.* Totowa, NJ: Rowman & Allanheld.

Women's Studies and Community-Based Service-Learning: A Natural Affinity

by Patricia A. Washington

Community-based service-learning is particularly useful to me as a black[1] lesbian teaching in a predominantly white university where many white students (as well as some students from racialized backgrounds) are often resistant to a feminism grounded in the critical analysis of the "intersectionality" of gender, race, sexual orientation, and class oppression (Crenshaw 1997; hooks 1994).

When I assumed my first full-time tenure-track position in women's studies, I was confident that my previous teaching experience would stand me in good stead. I already had significant experience designing course syllabi, selecting appropriate readings, lecturing and facilitating discussion, and using films and guest lecturers to augment class materials. Moreover, as a black lesbian, I was prepared for some of the white racism, homophobia, and internalized racism described by hooks (1994) and others who write about the difficulties that faculty of color and lesbian and gay faculty face in mainstream institutions of higher learning (Daufin 1995; James 1993; McNaron 1997; Vaz 1993). Despite my prior teaching successes, and despite what I learned from hooks and others regarding the potential for hostility because of my race, sex, and sexual orientation, I was nonetheless taken aback by the level of student resistance to the subject matter of my courses, my teaching methods, and — so it seemed — my very presence at the front of the classroom. One student, for instance, felt absolutely no compunction about telling me that my credibility as a scholar and teacher was suspect because I was "an affirmative action hire." Others expressed dismay that I did not exclusively privilege gender in my selection and interpretation of texts, complaining that the courses I taught were not really about women because we focused "too much" on race, class, sexual orientation, or other social markers — as if these categories were devoid of gender.

To say that my first semester as a new women's studies faculty member was difficult is an understatement. I learned from that difficulty, however, and I undertook a series of decisive measures that turned an arguably hostile teaching environment into a productive one. For immediate solace, I "took to the books" and grounded myself in written reminders that other faculty women of color had experienced similar situations and thrived despite early white student resistance (hooks 1994). I reviewed the writings of lesbian academics as well. In addition, I had been selected and trained to participate in a campus-wide prejudice-reduction initiative that began at my institution shortly after I arrived, and I gradually utilized aspects of that training within the classroom. I networked extensively with supportive university colleagues, who employed a wide variety of strategies for mentoring me through this difficult period. Last, but no less significant, I incorporated a community-based service-learning option into all of the classes I taught, and I found it to be a useful tool in overcoming student resistance to course objectives and teaching materials. It is the community-based service-learning component of my course offerings — specifically Sex, Power and Politics — that is the subject of this writing.[2]

Linkages Between Women's Studies and Community-Based Service-Learning

Prior to the advent of ethnic and women's studies centers, programs, and departments in the late 1960s and 1970s, mainstream academic disciplines were fixed on the notion that activism was something that occurred outside of the ivory tower. For these disciplines, *legitimate* intellectual inquiry was based on the pursuit of objective research, and *legitimate* teaching took the form of the learned professor dispensing knowledge to students conceived of as empty vessels eager to be filled.

In contrast, the feminist pedagogy embraced by women's studies fosters a learning environment that is woman-centered, interdisciplinary, and largely participatory in nature — meaning that it proceeds from an understanding that the educational process is a journey of interaction, rather than one of alienation and distancing, between the "knower" (professor, researcher) and the "learner" (student) or research subject matter (field of inquiry). This pedagogy can be defined as the interplay between feminist efficacy, scholarly inquiry, and human experience. It is the practice of connecting and integrating lived experience with the academic pursuit of knowledge for the ultimate goal of promoting positive social change. Not surprisingly, these women's studies' objectives bear a striking resemblance to the goals and objectives of community-based service-learning.

With the proliferation of programs advocating the view that academic excellence is very much grounded in enhancing the quality of human life, various forms of community-based service-learning gained inroads within colleges and universities. The community-based learning projects students undertake in the Sex, Power and Politics classes I teach are excellent examples of the synchrony between feminist pedagogy and community-based service-learning.

The Community-Based Service-Learning Component of Sex, Power and Politics

Student Population: Although there is often a smattering of racial–ethnic minority students enrolled in any given Sex, Power and Politics class, the students who sign up for the course are overwhelming white. Moreover, students who enroll in the class often do so not out of a particular passion for women's studies or because they are women studies majors or minors familiar with women's studies's pedagogical practices or perspectives but because the course satisfies a general-education requirement, meets at a day and time that fit within their schedule for that semester, and has a literally sexy title.

Many of the students who populate the Sex, Power and Politics classes I teach come to those classes firmly grounded in the banking concept of education addressed so well by hooks (1994). Such students believe that "all they need to do is consume information fed to them by a professor and be able to memorize and store it [and then regurgitate it]" (14). A number of the students begin the course fully expecting the class sessions to be composed of lectures from the professor, an exam or two, and perhaps a research paper as a final project. Some are alarmed at the prospect that they could conceivably be working in the field with community agencies. Thus, they tend to be suspicious of a participatory learning environment that includes sharing lectures among community partners and myself, intensive reading and writing components, and community-based course options. Safety, time requirements, concerns about the impact of this option on student grades, etc., all emerge as questions among students and faculty colleagues alike.

Course and Pedagogy: Sex, Power and Politics examines the social, economic, and political factors influencing the status of women in the United States and abroad. Topics include, but are not limited to, institutionalized systems of power and domination; media representation of women as political objects or agents; gender and sexuality socialization as they relate to political status; and women's individual and collective struggles for positive social change. Attention is steadily focused on the interrelationship of gender, race, sexual orientation, and class. Course materials are organized around four major objectives: (1) to understand historical and contemporary tensions between, and coalitions among, various strands of U.S. women's movements; (2) to examine some political issues addressed by contemporary feminists, especially as they intersect, or conflict, with (inter)national policies and practices; (3) to explore how institutionalized U.S. and international political attitudes and practices perpetuate systems of gender-based inequity here and abroad; (4) and to understand the role of individuals and groups in maintaining or dismantling these systems.

Procedures and Format: Students enrolled in Sex, Power and Politics receive course credit along several dimensions: oral class participation, completing electronic mail assignments, written course examinations, and a group research project or community service option aligned with course objectives. The community service option works as follows: (1) Placement options from which students may select are predetermined prior to the start of the semester; (2) representatives from the preselected organizations make class presentations during the first two or three weeks of the semester; (3) in consultation with me, individual students and their selected organizations draw up agreements committing the students to working on agency projects approximately three hours per week for 10 weeks; (4) agencies submit interim reports on student progress; and (5) students submit final reports critically analyzing the relationship between the community service performed and course objectives.

Central to the course's incorporating of community-based learning into the classroom are focused lectures by the community service providers who visit the class during the first few weeks of the semester. Providers lecture on the work their agencies do in the surrounding community and give detailed descriptions of what students will be doing to fulfill the service-learning requirement through their agencies. I immediately follow with additional lecture material (largely drawn from information covered in our course materials and additional research) that illuminates how these agencies' community work coincides with our course objectives, course readings, and other related materials (such as upcoming documentary material).

Regardless of whether students elect a community service option (and regardless of which agency they work with if they do opt for community service), they are required to integrate key issues raised in community service providers' lectures with other course materials throughout the semester. This ensures that all students treat the community service providers' presentations as integral parts of the classroom learning experience.

Class time is made available throughout the semester for students to discuss the ways in which their actual community-based learning experiences support or contradict other course materials. In addition, students are provided with written assignments throughout the semester that are conducive to helping them discover for themselves other connections between what they are doing in the community and what is happening in the classroom. We also periodically address tensions and concerns that emerge from being involved with community service agencies. Throughout the semester, I utilize various forms of evaluation, including participant observation, to ensure that students are on task, that concerns and problems are addressed efficiently, and that the amount of time students are devoting to the service project is appropriate. In addition, I confer periodically with the service providers to ensure that the benefits they derive from working with my students outweigh the time and energy they need to expend in monitoring student involvement.

Representative Community-Based Service-Learning Projects: Students are typically given a "menu" of three to four community-based service-learning options per semester. Projects have ranged from developing and conducting surveys on residents' responses to hate literature in their communities, to creating skits and games to teach children tolerance, to building a website to facilitate human service agency referrals, to helping children affected by domestic violence to use arts and crafts as a creative outlet for their emotions, to arranging and troubleshooting conferences, even to teaching art and creative writing to the homeless.

Student Learning Outcomes

It is my experience that the students who participate in community-based service make the best case for this form of experiential learning. Therefore, this section is largely devoted to student voices. For the sake of simplicity and consistency, I have selected for inclusion here only the remarks of students who chose to work with Harvest for the Hungry, a multiservice agency for the homeless founded by grass-roots activist and formerly homeless person Mary Mahy. Those remarks are ordered as follows: (1) why students elected to work with Harvest for the Hungry, (2) what students learned about themselves through community service, (3) lessons students learned about the homeless, and (4) the relationship between community service and course objectives, including the interplay between theory and application.

Why Students Elected to Work With Harvest for the Hungry: Reasons for electing to work with Mary Mahy's Harvest for the Hungry ranged from the pragmatic to the idealistic. Marcy chose to work with Harvest for the Hungry because it suited her career goals:

> Mary mentioned among the services she has coordinated for the homeless was a free medical clinic. As a premedical student, this especially appealed to me. I reasoned that it not only would be a rewarding experience for me but that it would also look good on my medical school applications.

James was moved by Mary Mahy's openness:

> What surprised me the most was that she held nothing back and revealed intimate details about herself and her life. The kind of details that most people would be afraid to share with their own friends. I decided that I would perform my service for Harvest for the Hungry, and I started the following Sunday.

Kelly had still another kind of reason:

> I elected to do this community service project because I realized that I had been socialized to believe many things about the homeless and had never found out if they were true. As a child, I was raised to believe that the homeless are that way because they're lazy and they don't want to work. They were a drain on society and added nothing back to it.

What Students Learned About Themselves Through Community Service: No matter what motivated students to select Harvest for the Hungry as their service option, most were surprised to learn how much the experience taught them about themselves. Ellen, who taught a creative writing class for the homeless, wrote:

> I have learned to love and accept the students that come to the class and I have also gained much respect for them. Many are hard working, highly intelligent and have taught me as much as I have taught them. They have taught me to push to be heard when I feel like retreating because I think no one is listening.

Tracy observed: "Working so closely with Harvest has taught me a lot about myself. It has taught me that nothing helps me build my perspective more than developing compassion for others."

Brian and Jolene also wrote eloquently about what they had discovered about themselves. In so doing, they revealed a newly awakened sense of social responsibility and accountability. Brian, for instance, stated: "Participating in this course and working with Mahy have helped me to at least recognize that I am wearing blinders. I have been confronted with issues that I would not normally have put myself in a position to deal with." In a related vein Jolene admitted:

> Before this semester I treated homeless people like they didn't exist. I simply thought if I ignored them openly enough and long enough, they would just go away. I now realize that before I could help anyone I had to first learn compassion and take a realistic look at the world.

Lessons Learned About the Homeless: In addition to increasing their self-awareness, participation in community service work with Harvest for the Hungry gave students insight into the depth, humanity, and multidimensionality of a group whom they had previously thought of only in monolithic, unidimensional terms. That the homeless had a community was a surprising lesson to some students. Tracy, for instance, wrote about an incident that was both distressing and encouraging:

> After interacting so closely with [the homeless] I can see how important

they all are to one another. They are always concerned with each other's safety and well-being. For example, one of the women in my work crew was badly beaten by her boyfriend. The others felt that they needed to take action so they reported to Mary that she was in the hospital. Immediately, taking care of Sharon became a priority to everyone. In fact, they all went and visited her in the hospital. Mary contacted a shelter for abused and battered women and asked if they could come and talk with Sharon. Sharon is currently receiving help from this shelter and has broken away from the constraints of her boyfriend. . . . Sometimes I think to myself that the only thing that is keeping some of the homeless alive is that fact that they have one another.

Other students talked about how their preconceived notions regarding the homeless had been challenged by their direct experiences. For instance, Brian wrote about his new ability to see and make distinctions:

While observing and interacting with members of the homeless community, I am struck by how many of these individuals do not resemble our society's stereotypes regarding the homeless. It is not always true that homeless people are passive with no motivation for self-improvement. While there are those who are mentally unstable, alcoholic, or addicted to drugs, a sizable majority of them appear as ordinary as you and I. Each has a different story. I will never again entertain the idea that homeless people are akin to lepers and societal outcasts, for it could happen to me just as it happened to Mahy and so many others.

One of the most powerful statements regarding lessons learned about the homeless came from Jolene. As I re-read this statement, I had to remind myself that the person who wrote it is only in her early 20s:

Seeing the families who came to meals regularly and speaking with them taught me that they were parents who cared but needed some help. The state welfare system labels the father as incompetent for not being able to support his family, and society feels that the mother shouldn't have brought the kids into the world if she couldn't take care of them. The reality is that they are people, they are not just providers and caretakers, and sometimes people come upon hard times. They need help. They do not need to be disregarded and cast away as outside of societal norms, therefore unworthy of participating in society.

Relationship Between Community Service and Course Objectives: As a black female teaching on a predominantly white campus, I have found community-based service-learning to be a remarkably powerful tool for helping me accomplish overarching pedagogical and course-specific goals.

As I noted in the opening remarks to this paper, students (including women's studies majors and minors) are often resistant to a feminist approach grounded in critical analysis of the intersectionality of gender, race, sexual orientation, and class oppression (Crenshaw 1997; hooks 1994). Community-based service-learning often diminishes — even eliminates — this resistance by moving students from a posture of so-called "objective" discourse to subjective, lived experience. This was the case with many of the students who participated in service-learning with Harvest for the Hungry. It did not take long, for instance, for Kelly to see the interconnection between class and gender when she first met a homeless woman who was battered by her husband: "Her face was black and blue and she could hardly open her left eye. I was horrified to find out that her husband had done this to her. [She] never returned to the group after going on that first day, but her image has not left me. She symbolizes to me the protected and sheltered life I have led."

Nikki began her final report on community service with Harvest for the Hungry with an explicit reference to one of the stated goals of the course:

> Throughout the semester it has been the goal of the class to break down the barriers, to diminish the stereotypes, and to disintegrate our biases so equality between all people can be achieved. I found that goal was not limited to gender-based discussions, but expanded also to race, class, sexual orientation, (dis)abilities, and age. This is important because if we one day hope to achieve gender equality, we must take into consideration these other elements.

In addition to exploring the interrelationship — or, to again invoke Crenshaw's term, "intersectionality" — of gender, race, class, sexual orientation, (dis)ability, and other social markers, another objective of Sex, Power and Politics is to understand the systemic nature of oppression, as well as to understand how systems of oppression are perpetuated and maintained. A number of students felt that this objective was clearly met through their work with Harvest for the Hungry. For instance, Tami concluded her observations with comments about the systemic nature of oppression: "Society contributes to the dehumanization of this group of people because it maintains the stereotypes people have." Jolene wrote similarly:

> Working with Mary Mahy has been a very enlightening experience for me. I admit in the past I have had some negative feelings toward the homeless, and have always been very quick to judge them. I have learned that many of the homeless are not lazy and there are specific reasons for their being homeless. I have learned that at any time in our lives, we too can become homeless. Our society often does not help those in need. Our system has been set up so it makes it difficult if not impossible for many homeless to get off the streets.

Cecilia applied a classroom lecture to her work with Harvest for the Hungry to illuminate her understanding of how systems of inequity are perpetuated and maintained:

> . . . the government perpetuates inequity. The immense paperwork one has to fill out in order to receive help, the long lines, along with the distant location of these places all play a part in discouraging an individual to even apply. How can they expect a homeless individual with no access to transportation to get to these places? Much less someone who has a physical disability. More often than not, when applying for a job, homeless people get rejected for not having an address or a phone number. . . . [Our] political system works to manipulate the lives of the less fortunate.

Still another example of how systems of oppression are perpetuated and maintained was provided by Marcy, the premedical student whose career goals led to her working at a barrio clinic:

> While the undocumented Latina immigrants often encounter the toughest problems with health care and other social services to which they have little access, documented immigrants, and even Chicanas who are American citizens, face sociopolitical challenges in these areas. For instance, we saw a documented immigrant woman whom we diagnosed with cervical cancer. Because she was uninsured, we referred her to County Medical Services (CMS). Because our clinic is a "clinic project," as opposed to a licensed clinic, our diagnosis was not sufficient to entitle her to the ongoing CMS benefits she would need to eradicate the cancer. She was given a two-week CMS entitlement, during which time she was to see a CMS physician to get an "official" diagnosis.

Illustrating the importance of grounding community-based service in academic learning, Marcy concluded her account of this patient's difficulty in navigating the health and social services systems by integrating her service materials with other course materials.

A final objective for the course is to understand the importance of individual and collective action in dismantling systems of oppression. Students involved in community service-learning with Harvest for the Hungry had no difficulty achieving this objective. The power of a single individual to effect change was borne out for them repeatedly through their interactions with grass-roots activist and formerly homeless person Mary Mahy. For instance, James wrote of Mary: "During the time that Mary struggled to survive on the street, she realized that those individuals who are homeless form a community amongst themselves. . . . Mary now strives to use her power as a viable, political entity to help soothe the plight of many others without homes." Brian wrote similarly:

The difficult issues associated with homelessness in America are largely being neglected by those in positions to effect change. At best, these problems are being overlooked by the majority of society and are most likely being perpetuated by our ignorance. Mahy is working to correct these problems through grass-roots activism in her community. . . . [She] is demonstrating that one individual can be effective in dismantling the systems of inequality in our society that most of us overlook and, therefore, preserve. I am fortunate to have witnessed the results of Mahy's activism. My participation in Harvest for the Hungry has been an eye-opening and meaningful experience.

Closing Comments About the Value of Community-Based Learning

Several students made direct statements about how the quality of their learning experiences in Sex, Power and Politics had been enhanced by community service. Brian noted that "it is useful to be able to make real-life connections with some of our course goals and readings through involvement in this program." James commented more extensively:

Reading about oppression is one way of gaining a perspective, but being able to observe the reality of its effects through community service gives the course an additional dimension. It is too easy to read about things and stay disconnected from them, but having it right in your face forces you to deal with it firsthand.

Jolene also noted:

This experience brought to life many of the topics and ideas that were discussed during the course of this semester. Oftentimes in an academic setting it is hard to really understand how the classroom discussions translate in the real world. Speaking of marginalized people and reading about them can only give one so much insight, but interacting with those same people and hearing their side of the story has really altered my perception of the issues and problems.

Related to such personal impact is a "hidden" goal of Sex, Power and Politics; namely, to foster higher levels of local, state, and national formal political participation on the part of students enrolled in the course. This is in keeping with the civic responsibility objective of both women's studies and community-based service-learning. It is also in keeping with Rothenberg's (1998) persuasive argument that faculty have an obligation to help students understand the fundamental importance of identifying race, sexual orientation, class, and gender as essential categories for analyzing our own lives and our nation's political, social, and economic institutions.

Turning now from student to faculty issues, I begin with the observation that as a women's studies faculty member, I am confronted with several realties very nearly on a daily basis. One reality is that women's studies full-time tenured and tenure-track faculty positions continue to be overwhelmingly held by white females. Another reality is that much of the women's studies curriculum is overwhelmingly based on white, middle-class, heterosexual women's interests, concerns, and experiences. Nearly 20 years of self-reflexivity among women's studies faculty — prodded and poked along by critiques from racialized women and other marginalized groups — has done little to systematically address these realities (hooks 1994). Comprehensive and systematic attention to the intersectionality of race, class, gender, sexuality orientation, (dis)ability status, and other issues in the lives of marginalized women (and some men) is still something of a novel enterprise within the women's studies environment.

And then there are the students who enter our classrooms steeped in the expectation that the instructor will be guiding them through an exclusive exploration of the gendered oppression of women and the obstacles women have overcome to prevail against sexism. Teaching from a feminist perspective that explores the intersectionality of multiple systems of oppression, as well as the independent nature of sexist oppression, is a challenge for any professor, but it is especially challenging for racialized faculty. Research shows that white students subject racial-ethnic minority female professors to a higher degree of intellectual resistance and negative behaviors or attitudes than they direct at white female professors or male professors of any race. My experiences are no exception to this general pattern. Informing students early in the semester — visually as well as verbally — that my pedagogy is grounded in understanding my social location as a black lesbian multi-issues feminist sometimes aggravates early student resistance to my presence at the front of the classroom, as well as any course content that discusses race or homosexuality. As I have already mentioned, I have found community-based service-learning to be extremely useful in overcoming such resistance.

As a tenure-track faculty member, I am increasingly aware that retention, tenure, and promotion committees often view community-based learning as tantamount to "giving" students grades for volunteer work. Therefore, I take great pains to distinguish carefully my use of community-based learning from voluntarism.[3] Some of the ways I have managed to offset these concerns include having a highly structured system of detailing the course objectives for Sex, Power and Politics; ensuring that the reading materials, documentaries, and course lectures all reinforce the learning objectives of the course; and working closely with a select group of community agencies whose mission and goals dovetail very closely with course objectives.

First and foremost, I work continually to safeguard the integrity of community partnerships and to be rigorous in my adherence to course objectives in the selection of community-based service projects. As a faculty member in a publish-or-perish teaching environment, I also seize every reasonable opportunity to refine and further develop my classroom work through research and participation in campus and system-wide endeavors dedicated to advancing the best aspects of community-based service-learning. I am also vigilant in pursuing opportunities to integrate community-based service-learning into conference presentations and articles for publication.

In conclusion, I would like to return to fundamentals: Intellectual pursuits within women's studies scholarship require an understanding of the civic, economic, political, cultural, social conditions of women. In a sense, then, women's studies is the study of the gendered "ways of life" that result in the reality that, world-wide, women are treated as inferior to men and are subjected to the decisions that men in power make about nearly every aspect of social life. Just as important, however, since not all women and not all men are similarly situated relative to power and privilege, the study of women's subservience within various systems of power also means understanding how some men are also subject to the power of other men, just as some women have power over the quality of life enjoyed by some other women and some men. Thus, women's studies has grown into a field of interdisciplinary intellectual inquiry that necessarily investigates the impact of race, sexual orientation, class, (dis)ability, and other social markers on the quality of life for women as well as men.

I have written elsewhere of the need for those of us in women's studies to "reinvigorate academic and community linkages in order to increase the likelihood that scholarly pursuits will benefit real lives in concrete ways" (Washington 1999: 178). Weaving community-based service-learning into the overall fabric of the women's studies curriculum helps promote teaching effectiveness and ultimately fosters civic responsibility among students and faculty alike, thus promoting the mission undergirding feminist pedagogy.

Acknowledgments

I wish to thank Kerrissa Heffernan for the invitation to submit this article; Edward Zlotkowski for sharing previous material on my use of community-based service-learning with the volume editors; and my life partner, Maggie Allington, for valuable feedback on the material included herein. I also wish to thank students enrolled in Sex, Power and Politics for their thoughtful and critical analysis of the community service-learning experiences they had, as well as their in-depth participation in the projects they undertook. Finally, I wish to acknowledge my gratitude to Terry Hauten and David Robertson for their support and encouragement of my scholarship and teaching.

Notes

1. I self-identify as black rather than African-American because being black allows me to embrace a broader population of people of African descent than is possible within an African-American framework based on tracing one's ancestry solely through the United States slave South and Africa.

2. I am particularly grateful for a course release provided by the Women's Studies Department and the College of Arts and Letters that facilitated my having the time to develop this article for publication.

3. This statement is not included to disparage voluntarism. Rather, it is meant to point out why it is imperative to distinguish between community-based service-learning grounded in the academic curriculum and volunteer service, which is often separate from the curriculum, though beneficial in its own right.

References

Crenshaw, Kimberly W. (1997). "Beyond Racism and Misogyny: Black Feminism and 2 Live Crew." In *Women Transforming Politics: An Alternative Reader,* edited by Cathy J. Cohen, Kathleen B. Jones, and Joan C. Tronto, pp. 549-568. New York, NY: New York University Press.

Daufin, E-K. (Winter 1995). "Confessions of a Womanist Professor." *Black Issues in Higher Education* 12(1): 34-35.

hooks, bell. (1994). *Teaching to Transgress: Education as the Practice of Freedom.* New York, NY: Routledge.

James, Joy. (1993). "Teaching Theory, Talking Community." In *Spirit, Space, and Survival: African American Women in (White) Academe,* edited by Joy James and Ruth Farmer, pp. 118-135. New York, NY: Routledge.

McNaron, Toni. (1997). *Poisoned Ivy: Lesbian and Gay Academics Confronting Homophobia.* Philadelphia, PA: Temple University Press.

Rothenberg, Paula. (1998). *Race, Class and Gender in the United States: An Integrated Study.* New York, NY: St. Martin's Press.

Vaz, Kim. (1993). "Making Room for Emancipatory Research in Psychology: A Multicultural Feminist Perspective." In *Spirit, Space, and Survival: African American Women in (White) Academe,* edited by Joy James and Ruth Farmer, pp. 83-98. New York, NY: Routledge.

Educated in Agency: Student Reflections on the Feminist Service-Learning Classroom

by Melissa Kesler Gilbert

In recent years, there has been a renewed call not only in women's studies but throughout higher education for learning that is community-based, socially responsible, and service-oriented. At our university we have taken up this call to activism and responded tangibly to our university mission, "Let Knowledge Serve the City." Five years ago, we implemented the requirement of a senior capstone course in which undergraduates would have the opportunity to work with an interdisciplinary team of students and community partners addressing a local problem or need in our city. Our women's studies department now offers 12 capstone courses each year serving the needs of local women's health activists and practitioners, family service agencies, teen girls, the city's feminist bookstore, a lesbian community project, women on welfare, incarcerated women, domestic violence survivors, and local women's history groups.

This essay is grounded in my feminist ethnography as an instructor in 10 of these capstone courses taught over the past three years. Students in these classes have worked with one of many types of agencies serving women and girls: (1) a family-based social service agency (Politics of Motherhood capstone), (2) a feminist women's health clinic (Narratives of Choice capstones), (3) our local nonprofit feminist bookstore (Pages Turning capstone), and (4) a variety of teen agencies and local high schools (Girltalk capstones). The projects have also taken on a variety of forms, but all of them have included a series of in-depth personal conversations with women and girls in the community as well as direct service experiences. Over the past three years, the students have conducted formal interviews with local policymakers and clients of a family-based social service agency. They have organized rap sessions with local teen girls, zine workshops, "girl radio" talk shows, city murals, leadership summits, theater workshops, and educational seminars. They have volunteered at the local feminist bookstore and abortion clinic, and have planned celebrations, art shows, and music festivals for women in our city. They have also edited collections of oral history narratives, quote books, and zines; and have written formal reports and informal chatbooks.

One of the primary objectives of our feminist service-learning work is to motivate students to apply feminist knowledge to social change in the community. Toward this goal we have combined the application of social movement strategies, feminist pedagogical practices, and feminist community-building processes to the service-learning experience. Many students respond to these processes by describing a new feminist consciousness, a renewed or clarified desire to become "active," and some even start to make plans to take part in a more global women's movement. However, what is more illuminating from a feminist community-building perspective is an insistent theme that emerges about the hopeful connections students now feel to their community and the women and girls who live there.

Our urban women's community serves our students by providing an epistemological site for a series of transformational shifts in the ways students come to know themselves and identify with their neighbors, see themselves as part of a collective, understand the role of an activist, and feel socially connected to the community in which they live. For some students this is a process of finding a new "place in the world" where they "fit in"; a place that differs significantly from a community in which they previously felt alienated or marginalized. For others, the capstone builds on social relationships already existing in their everyday lives. One student describes this shift toward connection as a metaphor of opening doors:

> I had not expected to feel more connected to community through this course. I felt pretty connected already and comfortable moving through some different forums that way. But . . . in less than two weeks, I feel bound to the world I live in a slightly different way. It's as if there has been a shift in how I think about what forums I have access to. . . . A shift is the best way I can describe it right now, like doors opening enough that it isn't so difficult to go on in to new rooms. (Girltalk, student journal)

In this essay, I weave together the voices of students and my interpretive voice, as well as excerpts from my own teaching journals. The essay takes us in and out of many rooms; however, much of what I discuss here are students' reflections about moments that occur within the walls of the feminist classroom. The student narratives that inform this piece are drawn primarily from my qualitative analyses of more than 1,000 weekly reflection journals written by 101 capstone students. While community-based experiences are certainly an integral part of service-learning, the students heard here consistently prioritize in their journals the interactive reflection, construction of knowledge, and mediation of multiple identities that take place back in their university "comfort zone."

Personal Identities of Sameness and Difference

During the first several weeks of the capstone course, student journals are usually filled with explorations about personal identity and situatedness in the world, probing the many contradictions students are facing in their lives and trying to figure out not only where they fit in but who the "new me" is that they may become. Most of the students describe experiencing some kind of "new awareness" about their identity through interacting with others. The following young woman recognizes that she is embarking on a somewhat painful process as she interacts both within and outside of the classroom:

> *Finding and being yourself is not as easy as it may seem to be. Listening to what happened [at sessions with teen girls] made me realize that not only is this experience a way for the teens to find and be themselves, but also the facilitator. . . . I know that I have yet to find myself in all the chaos of this world, but the journey can be exciting, yet sometimes painful. (Girltalk, student journal)*

Feminist Pedagogy

Some of these students' questions about personal identity may be motivated by specific feminist pedagogies designed to help students situate their learning and the project within the context of their everyday lives.

Consciousness-Raising. Students participate in consciousness-raising groups where they search for patterns in one another's personal experiences and observations. These groups begin with questions that emerge from readings related to an aspect of our community work (e.g., motherhood, women's health care, teen life). Students share either personal observations related to a chosen topic or, if they feel comfortable, a personal experience. A peer mentor then helps them uncover a number of similar themes that emerge through the sharing of stories. Together as a class we discuss these personal themes and situate them within local, national, and global political realities.

Personal Identity Narratives. Another series of classroom exercises take the students through a process of rethinking identities of sameness and difference. They begin by writing a Personal Identity Narrative in which they explore some aspect of their identity that simultaneously positions them as the same as members in one group and as different from members of another group. In each capstone, the identity narratives are directly related to the community project; for example, in the Narratives of Choice capstone students write about some aspect of their body identity. In the Politics of Motherhood capstone they write about their family identity, and in the Girltalk capstone they focus on aspects of their teen identity.

The Identity Circle. We follow the writing of the narratives with an Identity Circle activity and a discussion about the contradictory messages we receive and generate about others like us and others different from ourselves. We end the conversation by listing on the board all of the stereotypes that we have heard or hold about the women and girls we will be working with (e.g., feminists, women who perform abortions, women who have abortions, teenage girls).

Field Reflection Journal. The process of keeping a Field Reflection Journal throughout the course also necessitates that the students consciously and continually question and write about the relationship between themselves, the scholarship, and the project. These are due at the end of each week and are sent via email to both a peer mentor and me.

Gauges of the Self

These classroom activities, as well as both informal interactions among students and more formal interactions with community partners, begin a process of self-exploration that will continue for most students throughout the project. Students describe their classmates, community partners, and the women whose lives are told within their texts as new gauges for understanding themselves and their previous experiences.

What differentiates this experience of self-awareness from what occurs in more traditional classrooms is the immediate necessity to find commonalities and mediate differences in preparation for community work. Understanding, appreciation, and "tolerance" of diversity are often highly sought-after outcomes in classrooms where students are interacting with texts and teachers. But when students are about to move beyond their comfort zone and into a series of relationships with outsiders in an urban community, they usually feel an unnerving need to search for what they have in common with other people as well as what it is about them that may stand in the way of making a comfortable and meaningful connection. The "new me" that many students claim walks out of the feminist community-based classroom is one who has had to seriously reconsider how her or his own identity affects her or his being, thinking, and interacting in the world.

Digging Up Common Ground

For some students, exploring their identity means coming to a new awareness about what they unexpectedly have in common with others. The similarities they find between themselves and others may provide an immediate connection to the project and a comfort for future interactions and personal growth. At the beginning of the term, students quickly identify with women they are reading about or working with. They have had similar experiences in their family, academic, romantic, social, or work life, or they have made similar choices about abortion, health care, marriage, parenting, or politics. They, too, are women, mothers, teen rebels, patients, artists, homegirls, feminists, pageant winners, or boyfriends of women. Students often make choices about whom to work with based on these common identities. Some students choose to stay as close to the familiar as possible, to work in their own neighborhoods, interview women with similar political beliefs, or do rap sessions at their old high school.

Emotional Work. Finding commonalities between oneself and the project can often mean emotional work ahead. One woman who had an abortion when she was a teenager and who found herself in a capstone serving an abortion clinic felt the potential for self-discovery was positive because of the collective presence of other women who have been "in the same place":

> *I think this class will be good for me to challenge issues that I have buried deep down inside. It is good for me to be around other women that have been in the same place that I've been in. It will be a course that will open a window to more self-discovery. (Narratives of Choice, student journal)*

Other women feel that their prior experiences with abortion or motherhood, abuse, depression, violence, and oppression may help inform their projects but are scared of what bringing up the past might mean for them personally. For these students, uncovering similar experiences, commonalities, and like histories means taking an emotional and sometimes painful walk down a memory lane that they have tried very hard to forget.

Least-Expected Commonalities. For some students, the somewhat painful commonalities between themselves and others come where they least expect them. For one young man who was initially afraid of the impact his gender would have on an all-girl rap session, finding out that he shared with a teen girl the experience of racism helped him overcome his fears. By finding some familiarity within the intimate stories of girls' lives, he felt that he might now be able to envision himself in the teen's position.

> *Many of these stories made me examine my own childhood and experiences and how I felt in certain circumstances. A good example was the story about Asian stereotypes because I could relate in a very similar way, but through a guy's perspective. Many of these intimate stories are very important because when I head out into the field, it will be important for me to keep an open mind and envision myself in their positions by understanding their experiences. (Girltalk, student journal)*

Uncovering similar life histories, for this student, meant realizing the necessity of being open to new understandings, experiences, and ideas. For most students, unearthing a shared marginalized or privileged identity within a text or in the classroom means having to reexamine the social construction of the self. Although the following woman could relate to a definition that fit her, she had become acutely aware that she is part of a society that unfairly boxes others in.

> *I can see clearly that society's definition of mother is very heterosexual, white, female. Since I am that, I can relate to the definitions, though I may*

not agree with them all. But what troubles me is the diverse population we have, and the cultures that others share, and we are putting our standards and expectations on them. [Politics of Motherhood, student journal]

Finding common ground with someone that they perceive to be so different from themselves means having to reevaluate their perspectives and face stereotypes they have constructed.

Mediating Great Divides

For some students, searching for a way to connect personally to their projects seems very difficult. They do not immediately connect with other students, feminism, the community partner, the goals of the project, or the scholarship that informs our work. For example, several students with disabilities in the Girltalk capstone noted the lack of reading material relevant to their everyday lives. The lack of scholarship directly related to their experience reinforced their earlier feelings of being different from the others:

There is one thing that is really frustrating and that is the lack of material about teen girls with disabilities. We have read about just about every other group of teen girls. For me, as a young woman with a disability, I would have liked to read about that. Also if we are studying teens then we need to read about all the groups of teens. (Girltalk, student journal)

Students such as this young woman often feel that not being named in the project further alienates them from the class. Many of these students describe a marginalized identity that makes them feel misunderstood in their own community or by their classmates. Having been alienated in some way from other communities in the past, they now feel that this same part of their identity makes them feel disconnected from the team: "I guess what I'm trying to say is that sometimes in class I feel uncomfortable because I can feel that some people in the class are uncomfortable with my disability"(Girltalk, student journal).

Most of the men in these capstones (which have been 95 percent female overall) feel somewhat alienated, or decentered at the beginning. However, most of them also find some kind of connection with women in the class or with community partners early on and continue to build lasting alliances with women during the project. For a very few, however, feelings of alienation persist. For example, one man noted that the readings "make me feel like a minority" because of what he felt was an author's derogatory use of the word *man*.

Educating Others. For other students who feel marginalized from the group, the role they choose to take on is quite different from the subordinate one described above. As is the case with students who find themselves fitting in with project identities, students who feel less connected often base the choices they make about whom to interview, what groups of girls to do rap sessions with, and what agencies they might like to work with on an aspect of their identity that has marginalized them from others. Often students explain these choices as a need either to educate those different from them about their lives or to reach out and educate those who share similar backgrounds. The reflections of women living with disabilities illustrate these choices.

Similarly, most women and men of color identify their race and ethnicity as part of their primary identity, and sometimes associate their feelings, attitudes, experiences, and learning with their racial situatedness. One woman in the Politics of Motherhood capstone clearly identified a desire to educate others about the diversity of her upbringing:

> I had to reflect on my own upbringing. . . . I grew up in a family with two different cultures and it was important to my mother to find a balance between Chinese and American cultures to instill in me. In her country, communal mothering is an old concept. . . . I by no means was raised in what our society considers to be the nuclear family. If someone were observing my family they probably would have considered it to be dysfunctional just by the mere fact that my parents were divorced. This is where most of my concern lies within the framework of motherhood. I would like for people to know it is possible to be raised in a single parent family, with different cultural backgrounds and still come out as good as children who are raised in the traditional family. (Politics of Motherhood, student journal)

Different Worlds. Most students must negotiate many complex identities both in their personal lives and within the context of their work. But for some women mediating between drastically different communities is nothing new; it is part of their everyday life. The following narrative reveals how the process of living with multiple identities has cemented the idea that people's worlds are vastly different:

> Their [Girltalk students'] stories are informative and they take me into a world that I have never been to. . . . When I say world I mean that every group has its own little world where only the people who are like them can understand what their life is really like. For me I feel like I live in two worlds — the Able Bodied White Female American World and the Disabled World. (Girltalk, student journal)

Cliques

It is not uncommon for what one Girltalk student described as "cliques" to form in the classroom based on both commonalities and differences. In all the capstones, students quickly form groups based on identity. In one Girltalk classroom, for example, differences in group identity were clearly marked around the circle of seats. After several weeks of talking about high school identities and trying to work out the stereotypes we all have about teen girls in our city, the students fell gracefully back into the very groups they had previously identified with: *pretty, smart* girls, *disabled* girls, *minority* girls, the *boys*, the *freaks*, and the *hoodlums* (all of whom turned out to be the women's studies students). Almost always, women in the Narratives of Choice capstones who have been able to find other pro-life women sit beside each other throughout the term. If there is more than one token man in the room, the men also cluster in one corner of the classroom. Furthermore, such segregation is usually not confined within the walls of the classroom.

Community Presentation of the Self

Many of the students share fears about negotiating diversity beyond the classroom. They feel differences seep into classroom discussions about ethics, cultural messages, and stereotyping, and they are convinced that similar differences will make them even more uncomfortable out in the community. Indeed, out there the stakes seem higher: They might actually insult or hurt someone they are trying to help. Or they might get hurt themselves, in ways very similar to what they have experienced in the classroom, but without the "safety net" the classroom sometimes provides. Out in the community they might not have the time to "get to know people" in a way that allows for some mutual understanding about differences.

Thus, almost every student has some apprehension about the effect that being different could have on her or his community work. The students are nervous, anxious, and afraid to make preliminary phone calls, set up meetings, and make an initial site visit. One woman, about to do a rap session with girls who had been labeled at-risk by an alternative school, felt her own race and class might "show through" in her facilitation:

> I'm most nervous about presenting myself as a white, middle-class woman to a group of teenage girls who may be coming from very diverse experiences. What I feel most uncomfortable about is reflecting the same, institutionalized, class and race bias that I've been working a long time to combat. (Girltalk, student journal)

Collective Identities

Given the multiple identities that students are constantly negotiating among themselves (as well as between themselves and the community), "coming home" to the classroom can often mean a whole new series of negotiations, decisions, and what often feels like "family arguments." Forming a feminist collective takes time, and not everyone is ready and willing to participate. But most students recognize the importance of creating a space back at the university, their own "Fort Feminist," where they can reflect on the work they are doing in the city, "work out the frustrations," and coconstruct new knowledge about women's lives. Creating a community inside the classroom becomes almost as important to them as working with the community outside. Midway through the term the students have usually formed a cohesive group identity: They have begun to speak of themselves as a "collective" and a "team" instead of a just another university class. As one Girltalk student put it, "because of this project, I began to think of these people as teammates."

Feminist Pedagogy

Forming a collective, or what we call a "feminist advocacy team," usually takes an entire term to accomplish, but can be facilitated by a number of feminist pedagogical activities.

Creating a Common Language. We begin the capstone course by centering women's voices and experiences within a body of interdisciplinary feminist scholarship. The interdisciplinary nature of the scholarship helps to create a common language for us to use in the capstone, but leaves enough room for the students' own discipline-based analyses. We also do a series of readings that focus on feminist community building, feminist institution building, and case studies of feminist collectives that specifically relate to our work.

Personal Project Portfolios. Early in the term, students create a portfolio in which they address who they are as students and how they will contribute their ideas and skills to their projects. They look back on previous academic experiences and identify not only common themes but also the knowledge and skills they have acquired. From this assessment, they make a capstone plan that describes what they will personally contribute to their team. We spend part of a class session discussing each student's personal plan and drawing circles on the board that connect all the students' interests and expertise. By the time we are finished, there is an integrated chalk chain on the board that illustrates the intellectual connections among us and the knowledge that by term's end we will come to share.

A Collective of Our Own. During the second week of the course, we do an activity called A Collective of Our Own, in which students begin thinking about the ways in which they have worked in groups before. They usually note that they have been either leaders or followers, and describe situations where they have taken on too much work, not enough work, or have slacked off entirely. Over and over again women say that they often feel silenced in groups and "choose to sit back and let others make the decisions." Some say they just like to do the nitty-gritty tasks, whereas others hate to do them and only want to do the thinking and writing. Integrated into this discussion is usually a feminist analysis of gender differences in group interaction and a brief look at occupational segregation. Students begin to see the gendered aspects of their prior group work and decide that they want to do something different in the capstone. We end this activity by taking out a long piece of paper, taping it to the blackboard, and writing out our "Groundrules for the Collective." These usually include rules such as "Respect the experiences of others," "Trust other women," "Keep secrets," "Don't silence yourself," "Share all tasks equally," "Take responsibility for your actions," and "Negotiate authority."

Boundaries to Commitment. After we have exhausted our list, each student writes down all the barriers that she or he thinks might stand in the way of being able to stay committed to the group (e.g., other coursework, children's unplanned on needs). Together, we work out strategies for filling in for one another, shifting responsibility, and supporting one another through unplanned crises. We revisit the ground rules periodically over the term during rap sessions with teenagers, as part of guidelines for doing oral narrative interviews, and later in the course as students are compiling final products. We often rely on our phone trees, email lists, carpools, and classroom space for discussion when personal crises occur.

A Community of Individuals

Most community collectives gain strength and solidarity through recognizing the importance of the different individuals who make up the group. Within the capstone, it has been extremely important to help those who feel like outsiders to find their voice, a community partner to connect with, and in many cases their own "secondary project" to work on. Many of the students, even those who have at first felt alienated from the team, usually come to find that there is room for individuality in the collective. Indeed, for some students, seeing the importance of having different individuals all working toward the same goal results in a new understanding: "I could see how important we all were to the project on both the individual and the group level. It was a new understanding for me, so forgive me if this sounds a little dramatic, but I was just like, 'WOW!'" (Narratives of Choice, student journal). Frequently, students are able to apply this new knowledge about collective work to their community work.

The Classroom Comfort Zone

In order for students to process everything that is happening to them out in the community, they want and need a classroom space that feels safe, comfortable, and respectful. At the beginning of the course, they are looking for as many ways as possible to "get to know each other" and often are agitated if this process develops too slowly. They need a place where people and the real issues of everyday life, learning, and community can come together. For example, after an in- and after-class discussion about how many of us have coped with feelings of isolation, depression, and panic, a woman writes the following in an email message:

> I wanted to check in and say thank you to you for making space for all of that reality to seep into our work in class. We can never fully extract the rest of our lives from school work, and having room to let that happen sometimes is more valuable than anything else. (Girltalk, student journal)

Providing students with peer mentors is another way to help them feel more comfortable together. Having one other person in the room with whom they can make an initial connection, and whom they can trust and depend on provides an enormous amount of support. Even though some have argued that technological devices such as listservs create relational discomfort for students, many capstone students have felt that email conversations provide a useful way to connect. One of the class mentors even suggested that the technology created a "comfortable distance" that was an important step in getting students to open up.

Rethinking Authority and Co-Constructing Knowledge

Still another important aspect of moving toward a collective identity is taking the time to renegotiate authority, responsibility, and learning within the classroom. As a class instructor, I work carefully ahead of time to plan out specific community-based projects with our community partners. However, I still come to class the first day with all of the project materials marked DRAFT. This is a first step toward letting the students know that nothing is unchangeable; that they will be as responsible as I am for making our partnerships work.

For many of the students, having a voice in the creation of a project is an uncommon experience. As one student noted: "It is rare that a relationship is created where the student and teacher are working together to create the best possible learning environment." Codirecting a project is a first step toward that feeling of efficacy that will follow the student out into the community.

But while encouraging students to take chances, codirect our work, and create a team that replicates what community collective work might feel like, I am also honest about the university structure of which we are all a part. I explain the limits to negotiation and tell the students I will "take back the chalk" and exercise my university authority on a few rare occasions. Specifically, (1) I will not allow them to go into the community until they have carefully critiqued and understood appropriate methodological readings; (2) I will require that they uphold the ethical, social, and university responsibilities laid out, but not before debating them; and (3) after getting as much feedback as I can, I will be the one actually darkening in the circles next to an appropriate letter on the grade roster.

With all that said, most of the students move beyond me very quickly and look to one another and community partners for new insights, learning opportunities, and knowledge. When there is a perspective they do not understand, they usually ask each other, listen to the answers, and as one mentor puts it, engage in a mutual exchange of ideas.

They also are encouraged to bring to class articles that they have read in their disciplines to help inform our work. Indeed, when they have expertise specifically related to our project (e.g., graphic layout techniques, interruption skills, how to handle flashbacks, focus group strategies), they may even teach short in-class sessions. Finally, they are asked to bring to class literature from the agencies they work with so that the knowledge from our community partners can become a part of the learning experience as well.

Friends and Sisters

Forming close-knit relationships within the classroom has been one of the primary means of creating a community of both learners and activists. Like many of the most successful women's collectives, the formation of lasting friendships is one of the most important outcomes of the capstone experience. Prioritizing life over learning always seems to promote more learning.

For example, although we have a great deal of work to get through when we are together, we always begin class sessions sorting out frustrations and working through crises. We take the time to listen to stories about contacts that fell through, rap sessions that were painful, or in some cases personal issues that have surfaced as part of the project work. I have walked into class to find the students setting up for baby showers, engagement parties, and birthday celebrations; and I have signed numerous cards for young women who have lost their mothers, grandmothers, partners, and friends. One woman who lost her mother during the term sums up the feeling of personal support this way:

> My personal life has had its ups and downs in the past few weeks. When I think about the theme of working together, I think about . . . how they have been so sincere in their concern for my welfare and helping me make it through this term that I could never express it in words. If they had not worked with me I never could have completed any part of this term with a feeling of completeness. I could never have had this feeling without their openness in working with me to fulfill my needs. (Girltalk, student journal)

Consensus and Conflict

Even friends, families, and sisterhoods have to deal with conflicts and tough decisions. One of the criticisms of many leaderless feminist collectives has been their lack of ability to come to decisions, as well as the enormous amounts of time wasted in dialogue about minute details. The same sentiments are expressed by students in many of the capstones. Students feel that our sometimes endless but egalitarian discussions are a "waste of time," and that certainly "everyone can't be pleased."

> For the capstone collectives, passing authority around the room means having to come up with more innovative ways to make decisions. The students cannot rely on the instructor to tell them what to do next: they have to figure it out for themselves. They do not always agree on what they should do. Each collective has to come up with its own way to handle conflicts and make group decisions. Sometimes, usually out of frustration, a student might call for a vote. At other times, a consensus is just felt in the room and we move on.

Activist (and Sometimes Feminist) Identities

Grounding the learning and activism that take place during the quarter within continually negotiated personal and collective identities seems to be a necessary condition for understanding one's ability to revision the politics and permanency of women's lives. One student describes the relationship between her own self-awareness and the efficacy of our project this way:

> I think it will be interesting to work with teen girls to help them think about the process of becoming aware of who they are in this life. A similar process will also unfold for me as I become more aware of the role I play in my community and in my interactions with others. Self-awareness is a never-ending process, and I think it is important to convey to teens that we share similar experiences in our enlightenment. I want to help them understand that being stuck somewhere does not have to be permanent. (Girltalk, student journal)

Making connections between specific projects and a more global feminist ideology moves many students toward a new activist (and sometimes feminist) identity. Interactions both inside and outside the classroom help to raise students' awareness of oppression, diversity, and power inequities. Many students begin to question feminism more closely, others find a new sense of social responsibility toward women, or a sense of efficacy in the world. They come to understand how communities and action for social change work, and by the end of the term many self-identify as future volunteers and activists. For some students this process begins (and sometimes ends) with a new awareness, a new perspective, or at the very least a new way of seeing the world.

Feminist Pedagogy

Teaching toward activism through the service-learning classroom means continually relating the community work back to theories about inequity, social change, and personal agency. However, most students ground their learning about activism in the experiential part of the service-learning project. All of the projects that we have been involved in have been framed not as volunteer work but as social change work. We ask our community partners to situate the work we are doing within the context of social, economic, and political inequities, and we encourage students to think critically about the systems of interlocking oppressions at work in local communities.

Learning Conversations

While out in the community, students are usually required to have at least one if not an entire quarter's worth of learning conversations with women and girls who lead activist lives. These conversations range from an informal chat over a cup of coffee at a woman's workplace to a series of in-depth oral history sessions. In each case, the student and the woman are sharing stories and learning from each other. For example, if we are working on a Girltalk project, each student is usually paired with a community advocate who works toward educational, legal, or social changes for local youth. In the women's health clinic courses, students work closely with (and sometimes shadow) health movement activists, abortion providers, clinic escorts, and other women on the front lines of health-care reform. Students write about these conversations in their weekly journals, where they connect them to our overall project and their personal learning.

Open Minds

Students constantly talk about their projects as an experience that has opened up their minds in some way. They write about having "new" insights, perspectives, standpoints, and ways of thinking. Often they speak of the process as one that has also "broadened" their perspective, let them "take more in" or "widened" their vision. Some describe the process of grasping a new ideology as including "deconstruction of old ways of thinking": "Part of the process . . . is going through and examining past work and theories, even one's own, and using the dissection or acceptance as a means of moving forward" (Narratives of Choice, student journal).

A New Grasp on the Basics

Moving forward also means struggling with a basic understanding of diversity, power, and oppression.

Diversity. Many of the initial identity activities done in class as well as early course readings begin to help students understand and appreciate the diversity of women's experiences. But as they move out into the field, their feelings about the importance of negotiating diverse ideas and identities become more intense and applicable to their lives. One woman suggested that "diversity of experience, diversity of opinion, of life" was her "biggest lesson":

> I hope what I take from this course is one of greater understanding and empathy for all women and the circumstances they find themselves in. That is what I want from others in my life, and even though I try to be very understanding, I see that my perspectives can be biased. (Narratives of Choice, student journal)

Like this woman, almost all the students recognize the biases they have, and they leave the capstone with the goal of trying to break down stereotypes they have lived with their entire lives. Many students describe these stereotypes as embodied biases that are "close to the heart" or "something that was ingrained in me."

Power and Knowledge. A new understanding of the relationship between power and knowledge usually emerges through these capstone experiences as well. For example, many students discuss teen rap sessions as places where knowledge is shared, "voices are finally heard," and girls are "empowered." Students begin to understand that knowledge can be a source of power for women. One woman's insights into body knowledge and power come directly from a conversation she had with her narrator in the Narratives of Choice course:

> As I spoke with [the nurse practitioner] I asked her to describe empowerment because she talked about it frequently. She defined it as knowledge, or even knowledge from experience. The more I think about the term the stronger it gets. Empowering women means giving them the power of knowledge about their body and allows them to make informed decisions. (Narratives of Choice, student journal)

Most students also gain important insights into who has power and how it can be used against women. They begin to make connections between the power of the elite and the maintenance and perpetuation of systems of oppression (e.g., erasing women's history, creating public policy biased against mothers, silencing teen girl voices).

Gender Oppression. Even though most of the students elect the course because they believe that "something isn't right" about either women's reproductive rights, local family politics, or the way teen girls are treated, they do not at first identify these problems as forms of oppression. "It's funny, but I've lived all these years without giving real thought to the fact that our society is oppressively gender-based. I've been too accepting, unquestioning (but I was trained that way)" (Narratives of Choice, student journal). New understandings of the complexities of sexism, racism, ageism, classism, heterosexism, ableism, and other forms of oppression usually emerge in students' journals after debates in class about some of the inequities students are reading about or are facing for the first time directly in the field.

Thinking Specifically About Feminism

Although the capstones described here are offered by the women's studies program, the students come from a wide range of disciplines. Hence, it is not unusual to have sociologists, psychologists, accounting students, and biology students working side by side. Most of the students, except for the handful of women's studies majors who enroll, are surprised that they are learning about feminism. For some, this is a great new experience. They may not come to identify themselves as feminists, but they often identify with many of the ideas, beliefs, perspectives, and struggles of women they have met through the course:

> I never have been into the struggle of women before and am not a feminist, but I now feel a stronger connection to the beliefs [that] women who label themselves as feminists have. I think this is important for me to appreciate because their struggle has given me freedoms I did not have at first, the same way the civil rights advocates helped to give my race of people freedoms that were overlooked at one time. (Narratives of Choice, student journal)

Breaking Down Stereotypes About Feminists. Unlike the student just cited, other participants are *not* happy about the "feminist slant" that informs these capstones. Many students begin the course very resistant to the use of feminist jargon, feminist scholarship, and feminist methodologies. They write about feminism as "radical," "exclusive," "biased," and "reactionary."

For students new to women's studies, the road to activism is usually rocky, especially when it means breaking down stereotypes about feminist organizations, partners, potential teammates, and their teacher. One male from the Narratives of Choice project discussed how important it was for him to have "images" of real feminists he could use to deconstruct the "clichés" running around in his head.

I Am a Feminist. Though it is not an explicit goal of the capstone to turn students into feminists, many not only walk away from the course with a new feminist perspective on the world but also come to identify themselves as feminists. Sentiments such as the one expressed by this pro-life student below are not uncommon. Although she does not change her view on abortion, she finds herself within a definition of feminism with which she felt comfortable. "It is interesting that throughout this whole class experience I have come to realize that I am a feminist, where originally I would not have thought I was one. I am glad that I was able to learn the definitions of feminism and my perspective of feminism has changed" (Narratives of Choice, student journal). Other students come into the class with previously formed feminist identities. For these students, the capstone provides an opportunity to clarify ideas, opinions, and beliefs. They write about the course's work as "strengthening," "deepening," and "renewing" their commitment.

Understanding Social Change in the Community

For most students, new ideologies and feminist frameworks become the basis for a more complex understanding of feminist communities and the ways in which social change can take place.

Community Agendas. As students prepare for community work by making contacts, setting up site visits, and sending out information letters, they begin to learn "the way everything really works" out in the community. Agency contacts often take their time returning phone calls, and the students are surprised that the community seems to have its own "time." The real world is not on the academic clock, nor does it plan its projects for an academic calendar.

During Girltalk projects, students typically spend a great deal of the first part of the term doing outreach — making cold contacts to schools and agencies that work with teen girls. Many contacts refuse to work with the students because they claim a need to "protect" the girls in their charge. Some contacts say yes, but students are asked to present the project in front of a school board, an advisory board, an executive committee, or a parent group. Other contacts want the students to go through weeks of training before meeting any teens. Still other contacts attach strings to participation, insisting that students not talk about sex, "lesbian life-styles," drugs, or alcohol.

Thus, the students have to make important decisions about how to respond to what they believe are enormous barriers, "hoops," or "hypocrisy" in the community. They are surprised that communities are not ready to just "jump in" and get involved "for a good cause."

Many students become at least initially disheartened by the numbers of people who say no, whereas other students quickly take up the challenge of trying to find ways to build trust with community partners, educate the community, or "sidestep the system entirely." One Girltalk student decided it was her responsibility to educate a contact she identified as being homophobic and who refused to distribute our zine because of what the contact referred to as an "overemphasis on lesbians":

> I have to keep telling myself that people who are homophobic or racist or whatever are not bad people. They are just ignorant. My philosophy is that people are taught certain things as children and that can't be helped but, once a person becomes an adult, it is their responsibility to learn. Maybe that is an elitist attitude because I have had the tremendous opportunity to go to college and become educated. I feel it is my responsibility to teach what I have learned. Now that sounds patronizing, and I am not without my own prejudices and bias. I know that, and try to educate myself. (Girltalk, student journal)

Making Social Change Happen. Students who are on their way to thinking constructively about activism begin to consider carefully the many ways in which social change can occur. Certainly education is on the top of many students' lists. But many students also have broader notions of what social change can be, and almost all students come to believe that social advocacy and social change require certain kinds of people — "risk-takers," people who will "put themselves on the line for *anyone*." Only a handful of students characterize themselves as part of this group. Most prefer less risky, more subtle forms of advocacy.

In different capstones, students identify their projects with both individual and collective forms of social change. Students from the Narratives of Choice and Girltalk capstones usually come to think of the process of making "spaces in the community" for "learning conversations" and "diverse voices" as an important dimension of social change work. Other students contemplate more institutional forms of social change. In Politics of Motherhood, students work directly with a social service agency, and both shadow and interview local government policymakers. These students come to think about social change from a more liberal, distinctly feminist perspective.

Efficacy

One of the most powerful, consistent outcomes that students write about in their journals is a newfound sense of efficacy. For some students efficacy is the realization that their "voice is important." After finishing projects, most students feel like they have done something important for their community, have "made an impact" or a "difference" in someone's life:

> I have never felt as if my coursework was so important. Not only has the work been important for me in helping me deal with personal issues, but I feel what we have done might actually make a difference in other people's lives as well. I think that is what learning is all about. (Girltalk, student journal)

For many students, the capstone helps them to see that they can negotiate some of life's barriers and can move beyond society's narrow expectations. For one young woman who spent most of her teen years acting out an alternative self on stage, the Girltalk project helped her recognize that she has the power to widen her circle:

> I feel like I am not limited to what others want of me, but can expand the circumference to that circle and make it any shape and size I want. It is so easy to forget that life is more than doing the daily tasks. And it is so empowering to know that we have the ability to do so much more . . . and then to see it form before your very eyes. Maybe this is just one small insight on how to come to grips on what life really means to me. (Girltalk, student journal)

Finding an Activist Identity

Most of the time, students do not explicitly say that they plan to be full-time activists in the future. Instead, they describe futures where they will take on more social and civic responsibilities. They will be sure to vote, will volunteer when they can, will speak up against discrimination, and will be advocates for their friends when they go to the doctor. Some students plan on doing what they describe as the "little things," such as posting signs about feminist events on campus, stuffing envelopes, escorting women at the abortion clinic, or taking part in a Take Back the Night march.

With a new sense of efficacy, some understanding of the way things work "out there," and some grounding in the basics of feminist ideology, other students who had neither activist or feminist lives prior to their projects begin to think about more formal future activist roles. In order to take the next step forward, they say, they may need a bit more motivation. Or they might just need contacts, a women's network that they can hook into, or a phone number to call to volunteer. As one woman put it, "This whole class has really touched me, and is beginning to light a fire underneath me to do something. How can I participate in the women's health movement? I would really enjoy talking to someone about becoming active."

To be sure, we cannot attribute all the activism and feminism in the room at the end of the quarter to one capstone experience. Many students arrive that first day of class with activist experiences in other movements for social change. What they walk away with is a new feminist perspective on activism. Other young women and men come with a very deep and grounded commitment to feminism. They usually leave with a better sense of how to "get out there" and "do something about it."

Teaching toward activism is often very difficult. In a political climate where institutions have to answer public questions about the values we pass on to our students, feminist faculty who teach toward social change can face considerable backlash for the service-learning activism their students engage in (e.g., working with "welfare moms," abortion providers, lesbians, pregnant teens, gang girls). Some of us, who have seen friends persecuted or students die on behalf of a social movement, also face our own dissonance about teaching a new generation to do the kinds of work that may put their lives on the line for what they believe in. In the Narratives of Choice capstone, I have to inform students about the risks associated with working at the local women's health clinic because of letter bombs and death threats to the staff. In this context "choice" takes on a new meaning. Sometimes, I also share my hesitancy about educating another group of women who could go on to lose their lives working for reproductive rights. One night, after one of these disclosures, a young women's studies student beautifully framed for me my responsibility as a feminist teacher:

> What has happened is that I have finally become fine-tuned. And that is the greatest gift you could ever give. While I understand your sense of responsibility as a teacher, you must also remember that we students come to you because of what is inside us. And you have had the great fortune of getting to know, guide, and teach some amazing womyn [sic], who have gone out and done really brave things to better the lives of womyn. And for that, we all must be grateful. And, hey? Isn't that what teaching is all about . . . getting us out there, changing the world? Especially in womyn's studies. (Narratives of Choice, student journal)

Conclusion: Community Identities

Capstone students already belong to their local communities. They participate in community building in their neighborhoods by being parents, workers, friends, family members, students, and partners. Some of them have had direct activist experiences as volunteers, interns, grass-roots activists, and community leaders. They bring to their community-based learning identities and experiences that reflect multiple community relationships. However, when asked to describe their own community, they often write about it as very close to their immediate lives, describe only their "best friends" and their family as members; they do not relate to community problems that sometimes exist right in their own neighborhoods. One woman in the Politics of Motherhood class wrote: "I didn't have to worry about the community issues presented in class. As a matter of fact, I hadn't even thought of them. I have been home raising four children and involved in church, school, and family." However, as they move through the capstone course, they renegotiate these social locations and begin to reframe their experiences within the context of community work. Through their projects, they come to know themselves and their relationship to community differently.

Meeting Real Women and Girls

At the beginning of the term, when students describe the community, they write about something very abstract — although also something more "real" than the university. They have trouble finding ways to describe it that are not steeped in geographic, social, and economic stereotypes. As they then work their way through the scholarship and community-based projects, they come to see community as less abstract. Women become more than subjects of news broadcasts, stories in the paper, or urban myths. About midway through the term, the students begin to describe the women and girls they are working with as "whole" to them, and make statements such as "the women came alive to me" . . . the experience "gave me a visual person." Along with the faces and the real people who go with those faces comes a new sense of the complexities of these women and girls. These complexities deserve respect.

Finding a Place in the World

Not so far away, right down the street from our urban university, are local communities of women and girls who are feminist activists, health workers, homeless teens, and policymakers. Through connections with these women and girls and through extensive classroom teamwork and reflection, most of our students experience some combination of shifts in their personal, collective, and activist identities. But the identity that is the most striking, from a feminist and service-learning perspective, is the one that emerges through a sense of belonging to a community of women. Many students start the term already looking for a way to belong, relate, and fit in:

> Well, just remember, that many of the young womyn [sic] in your classes, like me for example, who have the fire in the belly and will (hopefully) get out there and work in the field, came to the class for clarity and guidance because the fire was already there, or was beginning. . . . I have always been active in the Pro-Choice mov't, but I wanted feminist guidance, feminist history, and I am looking for the place in the world where I fit. (Narratives of Choice, student journal)

The most passionate, painful, and powerful descriptions at the end of each term come from those students who have found a new place in the world where they feel they belong and that belongs in them. For some students, such as the capstone mentor below, a community identity also means recognizing not only that they have a place outside of the university but also that they might be able to affect that place as well:

> Before my experience with the WS department and my capstone experience I probably would have had a more difficult time stepping out into the real world. I have become comfortable in the University setting, but with the community experience I feel I have a place in the world outside of [the university]. I know I can make a difference and bring my individual skills and insights to a new place where I am not familiar with the communities. (Girltalk, mentor journal)

These students are telling us that what is really important to them in this process are the common bonds they find with others, collective experiences grounded in respect, trust, and friendship, a new sense of confidence and efficacy in the world, and communities where they now feel some sense of belonging. In the future, when I ask my students to let their feminist knowledge serve the city, I will also continue to ask myself, as a teacher, how knowledge from this amazing city of women can best serve our students.

The Urban Educational Initiative: Supporting Educational Partnerships With Young, Urban Girls

by Kimberly Farah and Kerrissa Heffernan

Education research has consistently noted minority girls' lack of readily accessible female mentors and role models in mathematics and the physical sciences. This dearth of positive role models creates a sense among many girls that science and engineering are gendered, male in nature. Piloted in 1996, the Mother Caroline Academy Seventh Grade Science Project was a service-learning initiative that utilized college women enrolled in upper-level math and science courses as role models and guides to young, urban girls through a community-based environmental science problem.

It was our hope in designing the project that the process of collecting data and verifying a hypothesis in the laboratory might increase young girls' competency and facilitate their perception of themselves as scientists. So engaged, they would also have an opportunity to discuss their interest in science and math with female mathematicians and scientists. Furthermore, participating faculty and students believed that designing a project relevant to both the school and the community might reinforce for the participating girls the connection between these two environments.

Finally, we saw the project as an epistemological site where diverse faculty and students could collaboratively explore and confront the gendered nature of knowledge. Within that space we could examine the intersections of feminist pedagogy; scholarly inquiry; and socioeconomic class, race, and ethnicity.

Background of the School-College Collaboration

Mother Caroline Academy: Mother Caroline Academy is an independent, urban school for low-income girls located in Dorchester, MA. Founded by the School Sisters of Notre Dame, Mother Caroline Academy began classes in the fall of 1993 and serves some 75 girls in Grades 4 through 8. The students at Mother Caroline Academy represent unique populations in that most are first-generation children of immigrant parents. As a group, Mother Caroline Academy's parents place a high value on education and are genuinely concerned with the educational success of their daughters.

Lasell College: Lasell College is a small, private, four-year college located approximately seven miles from Boston. It draws heavily from middle- and working-class public schools in New England. Approximately 24 percent of the student body are minority; 84 percent of the students receive need-based aid, and 70 percent are of the first generation in their family to attend college. Student demographics and the focus of study at Lasell (primarily professional programming and liberal arts) afford a base of student tutors with appropriate skills and a genuine sensitivity to the obstacles that young, urban children face. The science and math faculty at the college are predominantly female and are familiar with the literature regarding educational opportunities for minority students in math and the sciences.

Initially, the college sponsored a range of service-related initiatives at Mother Caroline Academy including:

- A twice-weekly evening tutoring program;
- A monthly kids-to-college program;
- A weekly after-school enrichment program;
- A monthly speakers series bringing prominent women of color to Mother Caroline Academy (called the Dreams Program);
- A guaranteed scholarship program.

Lasell chose Mother Caroline Academy as a partner because like the college, the Academy is a small, student-centered institution committed to educating women. (Lasell College has since gone coeducational, admitting the first men in the fall of 1998). Perhaps of equal importance, the Academy was an established community partner in need of assistance, and the proposed project offered an opportunity to further develop an innovative, comprehensive service-learning project.

Much of the strength of the Mother Caroline Academy–Lasell College partnership lay in the quality of the relationship and in the way in which it responded immediately and thoughtfully to feedback. For example, Academy faculty felt that the college's student tutors needed to model math efficacy for the Academy's students. This required the student tutors to reflect on and discuss the role of a tutor. Student tutors met with Academy faculty and discussed the ways they could model how to be a math and science student. As a result, the tutors transformed the evening study sessions into collective study sessions to which they brought their own coursework so they could study alongside the Academy students. During these study sessions, the Academy students were encouraged to rely on their peers as well as the college student tutors when they needed assistance and to reason through problems collectively. Academy faculty reported that these collective study sessions were extremely helpful to the schoolchildren and helped change those students' initial assumptions that intellectual pursuits were nonrelational, individual pursuits and that the role of a tutor was simply to provide answers. The children also articulated a sense of pride in the active role they played in the study sessions and began to think of themselves as scholars.

Project Rationale

In 1995, Lasell students participating in the evening tutoring program began to express concern that Academy students seemed to struggle more with math and the hard sciences than with other disciplines. They noted that the Academy students were at a special disadvantage in math and science courses because the school had limited manipulatives and no laboratory facilities. Furthermore, the girls repeatedly remarked to their tutors that math and science were not important or "appropriate" disciplines for them to pursue; from their perspective, math and science belonged to professions pursued by upper-middle-class white males. (The Dreams Program speakers series was the first opportunity any of the girls had had to meet and speak with a female scientist or mathematician).

Troubled by the girls' belief that math and science were inappropriate pursuits, the director of service-learning at Lasell worked with student tutors and faculty members at the college and the Academy to develop a proposal for a 10-week science project for seventh-grade girls. Though the director recognized the importance of helping all academy students address math and science stereotypes, the proposal chose to focus on seventh graders for a number of reasons.

• Research has shown that middle and junior high school girls exhibit a tremendous shift in their perceptions of math and science (Brunner 1996; Eccles 1989; Wellesley College 1992). After the sixth grade, girls are less likely than boys to continue with higher-level math and science courses. Rather, girls begin to express a dislike for math and science and often start to focus more on language arts and social studies (Sadker and Sadker 1994).

• Junior high seems to be the critical age at which career decisions are formed. Therefore, by the time girls reach high school age, it may be too late to impact their career choices to a significant degree (Dick and Rallis 1991). A variety of factors may contribute to this trend, including parents' perceptions and attitudes about their children's future career paths. For example, Yee and Eccles' (1988) research has shown that parents' perceptions of mathematics achievement are sex-linked. Mothers of girls think that girls in general are less talented in math than are boys. This discrepancy may account for the well-documented disparity in the number of college women and men who choose science and engineering fields (Friedman 1989; National Science Foundation 1990; Wellesley College 1992).

• Other research suggests that the use of female college students and faculty members might be effective in encouraging girls to value and pursue higher-level math and science courses. For example, Warren (1990) investigated the relationship between images of science careers and junior high school students' attitudes toward those images. His study of eight classes of students in Grades 6 to 8 indicated that male-biased illustrations of science careers have an effect on the children's attitudes. Similarly, Barman and Ostlund (1996) found that 170 fifth-grade students thought of scientists as white males who work in some type of laboratory.

Still another consideration was the fact that Lasell itself had a significant population of minority students. Hence, we felt we could convincingly introduce and educate young girls to the contributions of women of color in math and science. Studies have shown that both mentoring and educating students about the contributions of African Americans, Latinos, and females to mathematics and science are critical. In fact, an Urban Schools Science and Mathematics Program report (Archer 1993) emphatically stressed that students must be taught that there is a history of successful African Americans, Latinos, and females in science and engineering fields. In the late 1970s Koltnow (1980) developed a mentoring program called Expanding Your Horizons. Marlow and Marlow (1996) expanded on Koltnow's ideas and recently completed the third year of a mentorship program for middle schools girls. One especially significant factor that Marlow and Marlow have identified is the difficulty young girls encounter in accessing female role models as part of their daily routine.

In an effort to address the sexism and racism inherent in this academic area, national standards in science and mathematics have attempted to reevaluate both curriculum and instruction. Many school districts are attempting to increase both minority and female participation in science and mathematics at the upper grade levels. Hill (1997) has reported on one such effort (Project JUST) in an urban school district that has a minority population of 42 percent. Project JUST (Join Under-represented in Science and Technology) utilized problem-based learning, allowing students to tackle real-world problems while incorporating math and science skills. Barman and Ostlund (1996) have found that problem-based, experiential learning is an essential component of such programs, as most underrepresented students do not see a connection between what they learn in the sciences and how what they learn can be applied in everyday life.

Another initiative involving a real-world approach was conducted by the National Coalition of Girl's Schools, which developed the idea of "embedded assessments" (Pollina 1995). The authors describe these as activities such as performing experiments and discovering patterns to arrive at hypotheses. They suggest that, given the shift in middle school girls' interest in mathematics and science, it is critical that such girls have opportunities to work in a laboratory, develop experiments, and extend their thought processes in an encouraging atmosphere.

Project Goals and Objectives

As a new alternative school for girls from low-income families, Mother Caroline Academy had limited financial resources. Its teachers were young and dedicated but overwhelmingly inexperienced. The school had no laboratory space or equipment and limited manipulatives. The Lasell Center for Public Service included the Academy in grant submissions and fundraising efforts, and ultimately raised enough funds to install a modest lab at the school (the college also donated used lab equipment of its own). In addition to establishing a laboratory that the girls could use regularly, the faculty at both institutions felt it was important to bring them, together with their teachers, to the college whenever possible. Laboratory sessions at the college, it was hoped, would enable the girls to envision themselves as college students and scientists. At the same time, these sessions would allow their teachers to work with them and observe them in a different learning environment.

Faculty also felt that college lab sessions would help the Academy students better grasp the broad applications of the scientific method. Although the scientific method is often familiar to students from middle school through college levels, how one applies it to problem solving is not. This circumstance is often the result of expedience: Many available laboratory exercises are already completely structured. In other words, the theory the students study is discussed, procedures for an experiment are laid out, and the data to be collected are identified for the students in advance. When they are then asked to study a real-world problem, they lack experience in exploring and identifying the problem. However, applying scientific theory to a community-based problem could help address this challenge. Indeed, selecting problems the students themselves perceived as relevant might facilitate their ability to integrate knowledge and think analytically.

Lasell Tutors and Faculty

Lasell faculty were recruited by the community service director (a full-time faculty member) through "collegial discussions" on the value of service-learning or this particular project. Two senior faculty members, Dr. Kim Farah in chemistry and Professor Malini Pillai in mathematics, agreed to lead the project. Additional faculty in computer science, biology, mathematics, and library science agreed to teach sections of the curriculum that drew on their expertise. The faculty group was coordinated by Dr. Farah and a senior student assistant. The community service director coordinated the student tutors and served as liaison to the Academy. The community service director, Dr. Farah, and the senior student assistant met weekly to discuss logistical coordination of the project and to assess the curriculum. Three Lasell faculty members (the two lead faculty and a faculty member in biology) each identified one student from their course to serve as a project coordinator. After a thorough orientation to the project, the four students worked with participating faculty to create a job description for themselves. The job description included the following responsibilities:

- Meeting with the Academy girls and their teachers to discuss the project and its integration with the seventh-grade curriculum;
- Meeting weekly with Lasell faculty to discuss a proposed environmental science lesson plan;
- Serving weekly as a guide and laboratory assistant to the seventh-grade girls;
- Serving in a Monday evening tutoring program for Academy girls (fifth through seventh grades);
- Working with college and Academy faculty to evaluate and adjust the weekly schedule;
- Working with the Academy girls to determine the "products" (what will come of the research?);
- Facilitating group discussions with the girls;
- Facilitating a project-evaluation session with the girls;
- Organizing an event to showcase the work of the Academy students; and
- Maintaining a weekly reflective journal.

As the three project coordinators were already participating in the weekly tutoring program, they were familiar with the needs and strengths of many of the Academy participants. By providing continuity, competence, and connections, coordinators proved to be invaluable.

Additional student tutors were recruited through their college math and science courses. In some cases, faculty offered the option of service as an additional course credit or as part of a course requirement. Overall, students responded very positively. Since there were a limited number of tutoring positions, emphasis was placed on recruiting students skilled in math and science, students familiar with the Academy tutoring program, and students who were women of color.

Project Design

Prior to implementing the 10-week program, faculty at Lasell first assessed the current math and science curriculum at the Academy. Faculty felt that it was important to develop programming of continuity and coherence and to develop a curriculum that would not overlap with or overleap students' current coursework. Moreover, the program had to be able to maintain the interest of young, urban adolescent girls.

Collaborating faculty and administrators agreed to limit the program to 15 seventh-grade students. These students would attend one afternoon laboratory session at Lasell each week and one evening tutorial each week at the Academy. The weekly afternoon sessions would initially focus on helping the girls attain the laboratory and computer skills needed to address complex math and science problems. At the very least, faculty reasoned, the sessions would provide the children with an opportunity to become familiar with a laboratory setting under close, supportive supervision.

After evaluating the curriculum at the Academy and eliciting input from Academy faculty and students, the project leaders decided the work would initially focus on the field of environmental science, particularly urban environmental issues. Since the late 1970s, greater public attention has been paid to environmental issues, and the field of environmental science continues to grow as populations increase, resources become scarce, and pollution becomes more rampant. However, most secondary schools and post-secondary institutions do not require students to study environmental issues. Thus, introducing Academy students to environmental science would serve a twofold purpose: (1) they could increase their awareness of the environmental issues that directly affected them (e.g., siting a landfill near their homes) and (2) they would come to see the sciences as a worthwhile and relevant professional area to pursue.

During its first year (1996), the 10-week program focused on water and water quality. Over the course of several weeks, students tested water samples from the Dorchester community, from Lasell College, from a rural pond, from the Charles River, and from an industrial plant. Tests included identifying and determining phosphate, copper, hardness, cyanide, iron, sulfate, and zinc. The water was also examined for organisms.

In the spring of 1996, the 10-week program was evaluated and appropriate revisions were made for repeating it the following year. Overall, Academy students and faculty evaluated the project very highly. However, Lasell faculty and students identified needs for greater faculty collaboration, for a more comprehensive curriculum, and for providing venues for a more formal presentation of the Academy students' research. The student coordinators suggested that the project needed to be more overtly "relational" to encourage the girls to take a greater interest in its outcomes. The tutors felt the girls would be more inclined to participate in the exercise if the problems to be addressed were presented as a human drama.

The focus of the 1997 program was lead contamination. (A calendar of program topics is provided in the table *below*.) During its first week, Academy students were introduced to the scientific method and presented with a scientific mystery: "What made Carlos ill?" In order to reinforce the girls' understanding of the scientific method, teams of college and Academy stu-

dents designed and performed a laboratory experiment to study the photo-toxic response in earthworms. Then, after completing the experiment, they discussed how the scientific method could be used to research the issue of lead toxicity in their environment.

The second week of the project involved discussion of the environmental causes of lead contamination, the environmental effects of lead, and the toxicity of lead to the body. Some students were already aware of the dangers of lead as a result of their living situations: for example, lead paint in their buildings and the need to use filtration systems to clean contaminated water. During the third, fourth, and fifth weeks of the project, Academy students were given a sampling budget of $150 and access to testing materials for lead in both water and solids. Students had the option of performing tests themselves or sending samples to an EPA-approved laboratory. For qualitative analyses, lead swab kits from local hardware stores were used. Testing for lead in water could be done in the lab at the college, and there students learned that water would give positive results for lead if concentrations of it were in the parts-per-million range (ppm or mg/mL). The EPA laboratory was able to report lead levels in water in the parts-per-billion range (ppb or mg/L) and in soil in the parts-per-million range (mg/kg).

Some groups chose to test only water, some groups performed only qualitative tests, and other groups performed a combination of tests. Each group developed a set of hypotheses to structure its project.

During the sixth week of the project, the mathematics faculty member from the college presented the students with ideas on how to analyze their data. Students were then provided with calculators, and the faculty member and student coordinator spent time introducing their use and assisting the students in analyzing the data the children had obtained from their experiments. For example, students learned to plot data on both line and bar graphs, and were taught to work with concentration terms of *ppm* and *ppb*.

The students' final task was to develop ways to disseminate the information they had gathered by preparing a community pamphlet. The pamphlet would describe their test results and provide information about the dangers of lead contamination. Library faculty at the college worked with Academy students to conduct searches for any additional information they needed by using both the Internet and online databases in the library. The students learned how to download articles from the Internet and how to access articles not available in their local network.

As part of the overall project, students were given a tour of the public health laboratories in Boston. The Board of Health also provided them with a large data set that included lead levels in children 0-5 years of age in the Boston area. Zip codes were included as part of the data set so that students could perform graphical and numerical analyses by age and location. The students also worked in the campus computer laboratories to gain a greater understanding of the data presented. The last two weeks of the project involved discussing the results, preparing the pamphlet, examining surveys, and holding a pizza party.

Although most of the test results were negative, some of the student groups did find significant levels of contamination in the drinking water they investigated. The owners of the sites where the contamination was found were contacted in writing and were asked to contact the Department of Public Health for more information regarding testing and cleanup.

Evaluation

Program evaluation has been and remains an area of concern. Though the feedback from all participants has been overwhelmingly positive, the program has relied exclusively on written participant evaluations as well as focus groups with participating faculty, students, and student tutors to measure success. Recognizing the need to provide greater statistical support for the program, faculty are currently designing a pre- and posttest assessment tool. Faculty at both institutions are curious as to the long-term effects of participation, and are currently discussing ways to track Academy participants once they enter high school.

A written survey given to the Academy students during the last week of the project has provided some interesting insight into their experiences. Many of the girls indicated they had a newfound interest in chemistry and noted that the math they did during the project was far more interesting than their classroom math. Discussions with Academy faculty and Lasell tutors confirmed this increased interest among participating students in both math and science.

Students from both institutions also noted that they had enjoyed best the collaborative, hands-on components of the project. Those who had done water and soil testing spoke with enthusiasm about the trials and tribulations of attaining samples. They indicated they had enjoyed analyzing water samples from home and from school and had been very eager to find out the lead levels contained in their samples.

Both written and oral evaluations showed that the students wanted to do more laboratory work and fieldwork. The Academy girls were enthusiastic about working in the Lasell chemistry lab with college women and faculty, and also mentioned how they enjoyed the opportunity to plot their own sets of data in the computer labs. They now saw that, far from living isolated lives in distant laboratories, scientists and mathematicians could be vibrant agents for community change.

For their part, the Lasell participants rated the service experience very highly. The student coordinators spoke with great enthusiasm about the ways in which the experience helped them to reconceptualize their interest in math and science. They suggested that prior to this experience they had experienced both math and the physical sciences as dry and pedantic. The 10-week service experience allowed them to examine the possibilities math and science held for solving community problems and for engaging a range of community members. They also expressed a renewed interest in and respect for the teaching and learning process. As one student coordinator noted in her journal, "Prior to participating in this project I always believed that math was a gift you were born with. . . . Now I see that it can be taught and it can be learned."

Academy and Lasell faculty and administrators rated the project a success on a number of levels, yet also recognized that it remains a work in progress. Faculty felt they had accomplished the modest goal of introducing the girls to broad applications of the scientific method and were pleased with the enthusiasm all the students expressed for the subject matter throughout the 10-week period. Faculty also felt as if they had been successful in helping young, low-income, minority girls envision themselves as college students, scientists, and contributing members of their communities. (Indeed, the Academy students produced a valuable product for their community — an educational pamphlet on the dangers of lead poisoning.)

But perhaps most important, faculty and students both felt they had reflected seriously throughout the semester on the ways in which race, ethnicity, socioeconomic status, and gender affect educational access. Many of the faculty and tutors articulated a powerful sense of responsibility to the Academy girls — a sense of responsibility framed by the commonality of gender, ethnicity, socioeconomic status, and race. As one tutor participating in the evening study program noted:

> When I work with the Academy girls I am reminded that I have a responsibility to try and better the chances of other blacks and other women. I think service is more personal in the black community. They are not just helping this community but they are helping themselves and each other. . . . It's more of a shared thing. I think with a lot of service . . . and the way I hear people talk about service, it's like we're helping this foreign, different community and for a lot of black organizations, it's not us and them — it's we — and we are helping each other and this is our obligation to each other.

References

Archer, E. (1993). *New Equations: The Urban Schools Science and Mathematics Program.* New York, NY: Academy for Educational Development, Inc.

Barman, C.R., and K.T. Ostlund. (1996). "Protocol to Investigate Students' Perceptions About Scientists and Relevancy of Science to Students' Daily Lives." *Research on Curriculum, Teaching, and Learning* 7(4): 16-21.

Brunner, R. (1996). "Reflections on an Awareness Program to Encourage Seventh and Eighth Grade Girls in Mathematics." *Focus on Learning Problems in Mathematics* 18(1-3): 155-163.

Dick, T.P., and S.F. Rallis. (1991). "Factors and Influences on High School Students' Career Choices." *Journal of Research in Mathematics Education* 22: 281-292.

Eccles, J.S. (1989). "Bringing Young Women to Math and Science." In *Gender and Thought*, edited by M. Crawford and M. Gentry, pp. 36-58. New York, NY: Springer.

Friedman, L. (1989). "Mathematics and the Gender Gap: A Meta-Analysis of Recent Studies on Sex Differences in Math Tools." *Review of Education Research* 59(2): 185-213.

Hill, S. (February 1997). "Encouraging Equitable Enrollment." *The Science Teacher,* pp. 18-21.

Koltnow, J. (1980). *Expanding Your Horizons in Science and Mathematics. Conferences for Young Women Interested in New Career Options: A Handbook for Planners.* Washington, DC: Office of Education, ERIC Document Reproduction Service, ED191700.

Marlow, S.E., and M.P. Marlow. (1996). "Sharing Voices of Experience in Mathematics and Science: Beginning a Mentorship Program for Middle School Girls." *Focus on Learning Problems in Mathematics* 18(1-3): 146-154.

National Science Foundation. (1990). *Women and Minorities in Science and Engineering.* (NSF No. 90-301). Washington, DC: NSF.

Pollina, A. (September 1995). "Gender Balance: Lessons From Girls in Science and Mathematics." *Educational Leadership* 53(1): 30-33.

Sadker, M., and D. Sadker. (1994). *Failing at Fairness: How America's Schools Cheat Girls.* New York, NY: Charles Scribner's and Sons.

Warren, C.R. (1990). "An Exploration of Factors Influencing the Career Preferences of Junior High Students." Paper presented at the Annual Meeting of the National Science Teacher's Association, Atlanta, GA.

Wellesley College Center for Research on Women. (1992). "The AAUW Report: How Schools Shortchange Girls." Washington, DC: American Association of University Women Educational Foundation.

Yee, D.K., and J.S. Eccles. (1988). "Parent Perceptions and Attributions for Children's Math Achievement." *Sex Roles* 19(D-6): 317-333.

Women, AIDS, and Social Justice:
An Autobiography of Activism and Academia

by Sally Zierler

I begin first by giving you some context of what my work is now, and then begin again, to tell you a version of how I came to do this work. Along the way, I had many teachers and guides, too many to name . . . and some I cannot, because I never knew their names.

As an epidemiologist, the goal of my work is to describe population patterns of disease, health, and well-being, and from these patterns, investigate what explains their differences. The framework that I use recognizes that social and biologic experiences are interactive and inseparable, and thus, how and where people live happens within bodies that are, by definition, engaged in society. But beyond this, beyond the individual interactions that people have as social beings, are the structures that loom large and too often invisibly, structures that support and sustain positions of wealth and poverty, and of dominance and subordination. How these inequalities in economic, social, and political power, and how acts of resistance to injustice show up in people's bodies, is the focus of my work.

For the past 10 years, my work has focused on women and HIV infection. To tell you why, I offer some stories of my life.

As I ask my students to introduce themselves, let me begin by telling you that I am a white woman and a Jew, born and raised in a family of seven with a single wage earner until the kids were teens and we got our own jobs. The wage earner was my father, and he loved his job as a scientist in academic medicine, but with a salary that he and my mother always described as "not enough." My mother said we were middle-class. Her father was a salesman, and sometimes they had money, and sometimes they were poor. My great-grandparents were immigrants from Austria, Russia, and Poland, although my father's mother said she had Spanish lineage.

My father's lab was on the fifth floor of a research unit of Johns Hopkins Hospital, located in the midst of one of Baltimore's urban ghettos. The surrounding neighborhood housed, inadequately, the destitute poor, most of whom were African-American families. Walking into the hospital, I crossed the threshold from these streets of social ills to their biologic expression inside. The elevator that took me to the research lab was amidst densely populated patient care units, so the faces of sickness were everywhere.

I loved being in that hospital. The workers everywhere bustled about with a great sense of purpose, human drama painfully played out in the hallways and clinics, in the steel trays filled with medicines and needles. I thought that the workers never left because the hospital was always open. This was a comfort to me, actually: to know that the doors would never lock and that people were awake and tending to the sick somehow made me feel more secure, particularly late at night when I couldn't sleep and feared I was the only person awake in the entire world.

That was my sense as a child. The drama and dedication of the hospital brought me back again and again. I began working there as soon as I was old enough, which was at the age of 14, child labor laws notwithstanding. I worked in the outpatient clinics, registering patients. I saw the first trans-sexual operations in the 1960s; I greeted people as they came into the clinic, and I was the first person to meet them and ask them for their names. I had the medical records of everyone scheduled for visits, and my job was to fill out the paperwork indicating that they had arrived, and later, after their visit procedures had been recorded, to complete the billing form. When people couldn't pay, I would tear up the bills. Since most of the people had Medicaid coverage, this didn't happen too often. But sometimes it did.

Where I wanted to work the most, and finally did, was in the emergency room. I often elected to work double shifts on weekends. Since the hospital was in the poorest part of the city, I saw a lot of people wounded and sick because of conditions of poverty. One time an African-American woman came in carrying her young child. Despite the fact that she had been blinded by lye thrown at her face, she walked to the hospital to get care for herself and her son. He had burned the soles of his feet walking on the floor where the lye had fallen. The mother died. I held the baby while the doctor treated his burns. I remember the woman telling us that the child's father had thrown the lye at her, and no, she didn't want to call the police, although they were everywhere in that emergency room. Years later, I recalled this woman's insistence on not involving the police when Shannon, another African-American woman but one who had survived violence, said this to me as we talked in the prison where she was incarcerated: "I am a proud African-American woman who has survived violence, drug wars, and black on black crime." Having spent her life in foster homes where she was sexually and physically abused repeatedly, she finally escaped, and both stole and worked as a prostitute to survive. The man she had to protect her on the streets turned out to be for her the most dangerous of all. But she said, "In Roxbury, you don't turn your man over to the white man."

Also, years later, I found words of the poet and essayist June Jordan that spoke to the powerful and painful wisdom handed down to me from people in struggle attending that hospital:

I am entering my soul into a struggle that will most certainly transform the experience of all the peoples of the earth, as no other movement can, in fact, hope to claim: This movement explicitly demands the testing of the viability of a moral idea: that the health, the legitimacy of any status quo, any governing force, must be measured according to the experiences of those who are, comparatively, powerless. (Jordan 1981)

What was the context of that Hopkins emergency room when I was growing up? Baltimore in the 1950s was a city at war. Racial war. I didn't really understand this until I was in high school. Before then, I remember my sister Linda bringing home a placard that had large letters on it reading "Fair Housing." She asked me to march with her as she carried the placard with other people. Around this time there was a white man running for governor. His campaign included distributing pencils that had the slogan on it: "A man's home is his castle." I knew that outside of the amusement park, there were no castles in Baltimore. But I knew that men ruled homes.

My neighborhood was full of kids, and it was, I later learned, what was called an integrated neighborhood. I didn't have a conscious concept of race at that time, but then, being white, I didn't have to, although I was living in a city entrenched in Jim Crow and signs of segregation everywhere. But my immediate area was full of families that we did not distinguish as colored or white. At least not among us, the children. But one day, my mother's brother from Virginia came to visit. I remember we were outside, sitting on our brick steps, when my uncle asked: "Do you have any Negroes in your classes?" "Negroes?" I thought, not understanding the term. Not being able to come up with anything close to making sense, I asked him, as I lifted my leg and rubbed my hand over my knee: "What is it about growing knees that I would have in my class?" He laughed and said, "No, no . . . colored kids. Do you have colored kids in your school?" Something about the way he asked this made a distinction that disturbed me. I became very uncomfortable, but I couldn't put my finger on what had just happened. I saw the faces of my friends — Arlene, Toby, Willy, Evelyn and Eva, who were identical twins — and for the first time, I realized that they were "colored." With our various differences in skin color, it just had not occurred to me that these were categories for grouping people. The way I grouped kids was if they were boys or girls, if they were smart or dumb, and if their mothers made them lunches with special treats like potato chips or Twinkies so I could sit near them and trade.

It was soon after that, when I was 10, that my brother was born and we moved. Our new house was on the edge of the neighborhood . . . big old houses with spreading lawns. I learned that we were the first Jewish family, learned that we had neighbors who said we were personally responsible for the death of Christ, felt my own isolation thanks to rejection by my peers, and a lot of confusion about this since I didn't have much of a sense what a

Jew was anyway.

My parents didn't talk much about our Judaism. Our home was secular, for the most part, and we belonged to no organized religious experience where prayer was a collective event. My parents seemed uncomfortable acknowledging openly that we were Jews, and so I didn't identify myself this way until many years later, when I lived in Israel for that very reason — to claim this part of my life. As a child, what I knew about the Jews was the Holocaust, and I knew quite a bit about this.

For when I was a small child, maybe 4 or 5 years old, I discovered in our attic an old army trunk used by my father when he was in Europe during World War II. Inside was my father's army cap, his gun, and a pile of photographs. Amidst the pictures of U.S. soldiers posing in groups was one of a pile — a high hideous pile — of extremely thin bodies. Another photo had rows of steel boxes with round doors in the front that I later learned were ovens. I didn't know what I had discovered, but I knew it was horrible. I asked my father what the photos were about, and I asked him whether he had ever used his gun. "Once," he said. But he wouldn't say more, and in fact, he said very little for the ensuing 35 years or so about those camps, and his role, as an army physician, in examining the survivors as U.S. troops liberated the camps from Nazi control.

I had stories from my parents about their political activism, but not about their experiences with anti-Semitism, not until much later. My parents were afraid of the McCarthy witch hunts. Being Jews made anyone suspect of subversive activity. My mother, in fact, said that being Jewish meant knowing who your friends were by sensing who would hide you under their floorboards and who would not when SS troops came to the door. My mother believed in the power of the vote, and this is where she put her energy. Taking me by the hand, we walked door to door to campaign for Adlai Stevenson in the 1950s. She wore a pin in the shape of an old shoe, a hole in its sole to indicate solidarity with the poor. This was a symbol of Stevenson's campaign, my oldest sister reminded me during our mother's 80th birthday party.

In 1963, at the age of 14, the year of the civil rights protest known as the March on Washington, the year of Martin Luther King's "I Have a Dream" speech, the year of the assassinations of Medgar Evers of the NAACP and JFK, I got a job as a research assistant in a study to investigate the usefulness of Head Start programs in preparing children from poor communities for school. This was my first job involving scientific research, and it was noteworthy that its purpose was to demonstrate that intelligence tests were culturally biased; that is, biased toward privilege of race and class; and related to this, that social and educational stimulation, along with good meals, would raise scores on these tests, thus providing evidence that intelligence was not a simple biologic and genetic construct. I observed teachers in classes of kids ages 3 to 5 years old, mostly black and always poor, and recorded in great detail their interactions. I saw lots in those classrooms. I tested the children during their first week of school, and then again many weeks later to measure their gains. And there were many gains, not just in their learning, and in those silly but very powerful IQ tests, but also in their spirits and strengthening bodies. I remember one class in particular: The teacher had taken the kids the day before on a field trip to the Baltimore suburbs. The next day, when I was observing, she instructed the students to gather in the middle of the classroom where there was a large open space. "Show our visitors with your bodies what the neighborhoods you saw yesterday looked like," she said. The kids spontaneously spread out their arms and danced in wider and wider circles around the room — open and spacious — in celebration of freedom of movement. Then, the teacher said: "Now show with your bodies your neighborhoods." The children rushed to the center of the room, squished themselves together into one dense mass of bodies, and didn't move at all.

I had, by that time, entered high school. In 1965, a few months after Malcolm X's assassination, our student body elected a black student for the first time as president of the student council. I was elected vice president.

One day I got a note to see the vice principal, an older white man. He told me that the local TV stations were asking selected schools to send a student representative to interview the mayor of Baltimore before a live audience — a time to tell the mayor about issues facing youth in 1965. I asked him why the school wasn't sending Marcia, the president of the student council. "Because," he said, as if he were telling me something that should have been obvious to me, "she's Negro."

"Marcia should be our representative," I said. He shook his head and I shook mine. "No, I won't do it," I told him. "Marcia goes or nobody goes."

I don't remember how it all ended, this particular incident. But I do remember that I learned something about the risk of taking a stand: Soon after this incident I had a meeting about college applications with my high school guidance counselor. I was pretty much an A student then, at least in math and science. So anyway, my guidance counselor, Mrs. Wheeler, said to me: "Sally, you get good grades here because you are an overachiever. You will only be a C student in college. Of course I have to let them know that."

Now, between that guidance counselor's unenthusiastic recommendations on the college admission forms and my membership in just about every student activist group that had local chapters in Baltimore, I didn't get accepted to a single college, including Pembroke College, the former women's college of Brown University. But, never mind. I did eventually get a Brown degree, an honorary one as a result of my tenure promotion in 1991.

I finally found a place that would let me in — a woman's college near the Finger Lakes in upstate New York. I turned 17 a week before my mother

dropped me off. Apart from attending my math class (the others didn't interest me too much) and doing my calculus homework, I spent my time at a
nearby migrant workers camp, taking care of the children in a place called
the "sugar shack" while their parents picked fruit for $1 a bushel. When the
winter winds started coming through in early November, the migrants
moved south and I left college and returned to Baltimore.

But after a year or so of working full-time and attending night classes, I
returned to college life, missing the community of learning that had always
been a place of safety and nourishment for me. And in the 1960s, college
campuses were seething with moral passion. At Goucher College, I found my
community in the New University Committee, or NUC, an organization of
students and faculty. I don't think college staff were among us, although I
suspect that would have been fine. Our work was to organize the campus as
a part of three larger U.S. campus-based movements: (1) ending the war in
Indochina, and the larger issues of ending the U.S. military-industrial complex that was supporting and controlling dictatorships throughout the
world; (2) fighting for civil rights, particularly in relation to racial equality;
and (3) the free speech movement, which overlapped with the first two by
challenging fundamental assumptions about the responsibilities of universities and what they should be teaching.

I had intended to major in math, but not for any career goals. I had
wanted to go to medical school but assumed that this was not an option for
me because I was female, and because I had no money; but I took math
courses because I loved math. The department, however, was full of hawk-
ish faculty, a term that applied to supporters of the Vietnam War, and in general, of U.S. imperialist goals, and I didn't want to be affiliated with such a
department. I turned to courses that would help me locate the times in
which I was a student historically, politically, and spiritually. My heroes then
were Angela Davis, William Kuntsler — a white lawyer for New Left activists
— and a group of Catholic Jesuit and Josephite priests and nuns and their
friends, known collectively as the Catonsville Nine because their nonviolent
antiwar efforts took them, in 1968, to the military induction center in
Catonsville, just outside of Baltimore. Here they burned draft records with
napalm they had manufactured themselves from a recipe in the U.S. government's *Special Forces Handbook,* and then they were arrested. As part of the
larger Catholic peace movement, these activists represented a moral framework that I wanted. And some of them lived right there in Baltimore, so I met
with them from time to time. I was missing spiritual community and
thought that I might find a place for myself if I studied various religious
texts. My favorite course was on the Catholic Peace Movement, and we had
two texts for that course: one, a book by theologian Michael Novak called *A
Theory for Radical Politics;* the other, the New Testament. It was my first read-

ing of this part of the Bible, and it represented a great introduction, since my professor taught us to read the New Testament as a collection of political documents. A major theme in that class was: "Granted that I must die, how shall I live?" (Novak 1969). It was 1970 and the federal troops had shot and killed students gathered on the campus at Kent State. Living mattered.

In my campus activism, I also learned other lessons. One, I had certainly noticed that women were not leaders in the New Left movement. We were relegated to positions of running the mimeograph machines, ripping up black cloth to make armbands, and being pretty props for the men in charge. And I learned another lesson when I spray painted graffiti all over the campus demanding an end to the war in Southeast Asia, freedom for Angela Davis, and racial equality. The lesson actually came the following day when I learned about the janitor who had to scrub out my words — letter by letter — and I felt the perverse irony of it all: I leave a mess of self-expressed indignation about injustice in the world for someone whose life was severely structured by that injustice to clean up.

How, then, was I to live? As a woman, I believed my options were limited. I was raised in a home ruled by my father; my mother was not a wage earner until my brother, the last born, was 10 years old. I was not encouraged to seek a career. But I was encouraged to learn. When I expressed an interest in going to medical school, my mother responded incredulously. We were not raised to believe that we could do whatever we wanted. In college, our vocational guidance was essentially that the job market was tight, and that bookkeeping and secretarial jobs were our best bet. I was actually thinking about law school after witnessing civil rights lawyers in the various Black Power and New Left trials. Instead, after graduating with a degree in history, I returned to Hopkins Hospital, gained more skills in psychometrics, and moved to Boston, where I became involved in the (mostly white) women's movement.

When I left for Boston, it was 10 years before evidence of AIDS first appeared. I worked for a few years saving money for graduate school tuition, then entered a graduate program in education that emphasized a theory of moral development. This theory posited that children and adolescents pass through stages of reasoning about moral issues, and the ultimate stage was one of social justice. This meant that people made decisions based on the common good, even if that meant having to give up their own privilege so that others could participate fully in activities of labor and love with dignity. Justice implied fair distribution for living well. For the first time I saw ways of combining activism with academia. I applied my training to the education of adolescents, in particular, to developing curricula that would stimulate the moral reasoning of teenage girls so that they would make decisions about their bodies that went beyond obeying socially constructed gender rules. Most of the theory had been developed without regard to gender (and certainly not with race or class distinctions); nonetheless, I found the framework a useful one for developing curricula intended to develop human connectedness and collective responsibility.

For the next few years I taught groups of young adolescent girls in the United States, and later, in Israel, in a course I called the Psychological and Physical Experience of Puberty. With other women, I went around the Boston area delivering a disposable speculum with an illustrated instruction sheet on how to use it. Teaching groups of women how to examine their reproductive tract and to perform pelvic exams on each other, I began to realize that a speculum was not sufficient for redistributing gender-based power in our society. I was disturbed as well that particular strategies for empowerment seemed inattentive to women who were not white. Most of the women's movement's visible leaders were women with financial resources. The civil rights movement and actions against the military-industrial complex had clearer links to the women's health movement. As Audre Lorde (1984) has written: "Once you live any piece of your vision, it opens you to a constant onslaught. Of necessities, of horrors, but of wonders too, of possibilities."

And so I returned to school, this time in public health. I knew I wanted a methodology and a language. I wanted skills to work inside the powerful biomedical system, that complexity of social phenomena that exercised largely unchallenged authority over the production of medical and scientific knowledge, and the profitable free market of drug and technology development. I wanted to influence creation of a system that was more participatory and holistic in response to how and what health care was available and for whom. And I wanted to apply methods that I could glean from my graduate training to challenge what counts as knowledge. This meant I had to challenge assumptions about the biomedical framework, which narrowly focuses on biological determinants of and medical solutions to disease.

I had applied to a Department of Maternal and Child Health at Harvard, but within a month of attending, I realized it was really a "department of womb and child health." Since I was concerned about the lives of women not only as reproductive organisms but also as people in all their complexity, living in bodies as social beings, I left the department to join epidemiology, an area I hadn't ever thought about before I started there. But the required course turned me on to a methodology and mission, and also, to an opportunity to make a great deal of noise about what is accountable for disease and well-being in the world, noise in a language that had considerable authority and credibility. And it turned out that the department was full of faculty whose research was about women's diseases. But the biomedical model still ruled there, and along with it, a legacy of scientific racism. We were taught that race is a meaningful biologic construct, and that social class was generally something to control for, not to study. *Gender* and biologic *sex* were terms used interchangeably as if they referred to the same phenomenon.

I behaved pretty well during my training. Doing so was relatively easy because the intellectual challenges were fascinating. I was completely seduced by the methodology and the logic of scientific thinking applied to a mission of producing knowledge in the name of reducing suffering in the world. I just had to find ways of replacing the biomedical model with theories that explained population patterns of disease in terms of where people are positioned in society, and it was gender positioning that I was particularly interested in. As I began teaching physicians who had returned to graduate school to receive public health degrees, I realized that I could teach epidemiology using sexual assault examples to illustrate principles of research. I taught measures of incidence and prevalence using data on sexual assaults of women and children; our class imagined long-term biologic effects of these assaults, inviting theoretical discussion of social and physiologic interactions over time.

So it was in the midst of my doctoral training that the Centers for Disease Control announced the first cases of AIDS. I remember reading the June 5, 1981, story in the *Morbidity and Mortality Weekly Report*. It wasn't on the first page, and I was drawn to it because it was about gay men. I was concerned for my friends, and because the disease touched on issues that were important to me.

As I have come to learn in my subsequent research on women and HIV, the Centers for Disease Control eventually did, that year, identify six women in the United States who had unexplained underlying cellular immune deficiency. And later, many more. But because the afflictions of these women were happening within lives already fraught with the social ills of poverty and racism, the phenomenon of women with AIDS was hardly noticed. For these were women — if they could get work, they were rarely earning wages sufficient to meet basic needs for food, child care, clothing, and shelter; mostly they depended on public assistance and men for economic survival — for the most part African-American, Latina, Haitian, American Indian, raising young children. Unlike white gay men diagnosed with AIDS, sickness among these women was not unexpected. It was just a part of the ongoing, typically excessive morbidity and mortality that prevailed among the poor and racially oppressed.

There is injustice here, and AIDS holds up a mirror to this social reality. And so I ask, teach, and write about this question: Why is it that economic deprivation and membership in groups defined, in part, by discrimination, are so interwoven with risk of AIDS among women? How is it that women's relations with power in personal and public life shape their susceptibility to HIV infection?

To begin to answer these questions, I speak with you today about love and action. "Love should be put into action!" yells the hermit in Elizabeth Bishop's (1993) poem "The Hermit's Scream." In response to this poem, another great poet, Adrienne Rich (1993), asks:

> What would it take to put love into action in the face of lovelessness, aban-
> donment, or violation? Where do we find, in or around us, love — the imag-
> ination that can subvert despair or the futile firing of a gun? What teach-
> es us to convert lethal anger into steady, serious attention to our own lives
> and those of others?

What teaches us? I draw on the writings of social commentator Parker Palmer when I say that classic spiritual values of humility, love, and community are epistemological values as well. It takes humility "to hear the truth of others," and yet, this humility "must stand in creative tension with the faith that empowers us to speak our own" (Palmer 1983). A spirituality of education and scholarship comes down to facing the fear of teaching and learning, of naming as Truth an eternal conversation about things that matter, conducted with passion and discipline; a conversation where the conclusions keep changing.

Doing work in a context that holds the teacher and scholar accountable to people most affected by this knowledge reduces the likelihood that our ideas will become distorted and our moral posture deformed. To meet this responsibility we need to work within a "communitarian epistemology" (Novak 1969). In fact, wrote biologist Richard Levins (1996) decades later:

> The optimal condition for science is with one foot in the university and one
> in the communities in struggle. . . . We should not pretend or aspire to a
> bland neutrality but proclaim as our working hypothesis: all theories are
> wrong which promote, justify, or tolerate injustice.

As a scientist, my approach has been to keep in the forefront of my mind a vision of women capable of passion and playfulness, of hard work and creativity, of loving parenting and strong kinship, people who desire full participation in society, to be generative and to make a difference in the world. Pushing against such a vital possibility are social, economic, and political history and practice that threaten and often take women's lives and the lives of their loved ones. Women's struggles with and resistance to social and economic subordination include strategies for survival that bear the burden of drug use, violence, hunger, and social disintegration. And then, recognizing how dynamics of subordination and resistance simultaneously play out at multiple levels over the course of a life, we ask how women embody the risk of HIV infection in relation to these powerful social forces.

And we do so drawing on a kind of knowledge of which Parker Palmer speaks. It is a way of knowing that begins with love . . . or compassion.

> *The goal of knowledge arising from love is the reunification and recon-struction of broken selves and worlds. A knowledge born of compassion aims not at exploiting and manipulating creation but at reconciling the world to itself . . . a knowledge that springs from love will implicate us in the web of life; it will wrap the knower and the known in compassion, in a bond of awesome responsibility as well as transforming joy; it will call us to involvement, mutuality, accountability. (Palmer 1983)*

So this is some version of how I came to do this work, and why. But don't be fooled if the path I described seems neat and sure-footed. Much of the time, I was doing legwork toward some goal that wound up being in a very different place than where I thought I was going. And lots of times, I didn't have a particular place to go. The intrinsic process itself was compelling, and I trusted an encounter when I felt deeply my own capacity to love. When this didn't come through easily, I moved on. Thomas Merton has written about the "hidden wholeness" in ourselves and our world, and I believe in this, believe that we touch one another whether we mean to or not. More than touch . . . penetrate in ways that move and shift our social and biologic expe-rience, responding, resisting, remembering.

Note

Adapted from a talk for the Brown University Convocation Series, December 5, 1996.

References

Jordan, June. (1981). "Where Is the Love?" In *Civil Wars*. Boston, MA: Beacon Press.

Levins, Richard. (1996). "Ten Propositions on Science and Antiscience." *Social Text* 14: 101-111.

Lorde, Audre. (1984). *Sister Outsider: Essays and Speeches*. Trumansberg, NY: The Crossing Press.

Novak, Michael. (1969). *A Theology for Radical Politics*. New York, NY: Herder and Herder.

Palmer, Parker J. (1983). *To Know as We Are Known: A Spirituality of Education*. San Francisco, CA: Harper and Row.

Rich, Adrienne. (1993). *What Is Found There: Notebooks on Poetry and Politics*. New York, NY: W.W. Norton and Co.

TCBY in Limón, Costa Rica: Women's Studies and the (Re)construction of Identity in International Service-Learning

by Debra J. Liebowitz

For weeks we walked through town watching construction workers put the final touches on the new store, a building that seemed strangely out of place in Limón, a relatively impoverished city located on Costa Rica's Atlantic coast. More than two weeks before the store's opening in June 1998, the building's bright crisp colors and corporate-style marque were visible blocks away. It was unlike any other city establishment.

Anticipation of the store's opening day was so intense that when the day finally arrived, more than 70 Costa Ricans, mostly teenagers, lined up outside. My group of 13 college undergraduates who were in Limón to participate in Rutgers University's Community Service and Study Abroad Program also eagerly awaited the store's opening. Although they were not standing in line on that day, they nonetheless waited impatiently for their taste of home.

When the doors finally opened, the crowd found a store unlike any other in the Atlantic Coast region of Costa Rica. Limón's stifling heat, often upwards of 100 degrees and 90 percent humidity, was cooled by high-powered air conditioners. This made the new store the only establishment (beside the banks) that regulated the area's hot, humid, tropical climate. In addition, the inside was bright and shiny: new tiles, new tables and chairs, new cooking equipment, and a full sound system including a large-screen television. Limón had never seen anything like this. TCBY (The *Country's* Best Yogurt [my emphasis]) was the first U.S. retail franchise to open its doors in Limón. The response of locals was so enthusiastic that strict crowd control was necessary as the store's capacity was easily overwhelmed by the hundreds of people muscling their way in. "I can't believe how excited people are about frozen yogurt," said one of my students in a discussion just after the store's grand opening.

At first, the Rutgers group was just as excited as the mobs waiting nightly on long lines to eat their frozen yogurt. However, the students entered the store, carrying (figuratively speaking) the conceptual premises of women's studies on their shoulders. While in Limón, participating in this Community Service and Study Abroad Program, students took my class Theorizing Race, Class, Gender, Nation: Afro-Caribbean Culture and History — A View From Limón, Costa Rica. The course met twice weekly for two to three hours and traced the cultural, political, and social history of Costa Ricans of African descent as a framework for understanding present-day Limón. It also focused on analyzing Costa Rica's national social structure and the country's historical and current role in Central America. (The syllabus follows this essay.)

The purpose of the course and the program itself was twofold. First, the course was designed to help program participants make sense of the environment in which they were living. To do so meant focusing on the intersections of race, gender, class, and nation in constructing the identities of those living in the area. Second, the course was designed to stimulate students to think about the intersections of identity — race, ethnicity, gender, and class — with international economics, history, nationalism, language, culture, and politics in the context of Limón. Throughout the program's six weeks, the students struggled to understand the confusing ways in which experiences in Limón seemed to destabilize their own racial, national, class, and gender identities. The course sought to accentuate their discomfort while providing the analytical skills and space for them to grapple with their confusing roles both as outsiders/insiders in Limón and as *gringos* (of racially diverse backgrounds) in Central America. Their community service work in Limón created a dynamic where the group was not simply a collection of outsiders living and working in Costa Rica. Even though we were obviously outsiders, our work at the St. Marks school, an important center of the Afro-Caribbean community in Limón, gave us a partial and temporary insider status. The Rutgers group worked closely with community members, and our arrival was eagerly anticipated. Once in Limón, we were visible in the community at large, both because we were obviously outsiders, and also because we were important community guests — in this way we were temporary insiders. Theorizing this outsider/insider status proved critical to the students' learning. The attention in women's studies to issues of identity facilitated this process of discovery.

I began this article with the opening of TCBY in Limón because it helps to illustrate the power of bringing women's studies concepts and methodologies into community service programs. Indeed, the general goals of women's studies analyses and community service programs can fit well together. Both, I would argue, are aimed at transgressing "those boundaries that would confine each pupil to a rote, assembly-line approach to learning" (hooks 1994: 13). Moreover, women's studies acknowledges a "connection between ideas learned in the classroom and those ideas learned in life practices" (hooks 1994: 15) — precisely the goal of service-learning.

Defining Our Role in Limón

Using experience as a means of understanding the (re)production of identity and the politics of its construction was critical to the goals of the Study

Community Service and Abroad Program that I directed in Limón in the summer of 1998. The program brought 13 undergraduate students (nine from Rutgers and four from other schools in the Northeast) to Limón to teach English at the St. Marks ("San Marcos," in Spanish) school.

Puerto Limón is the geographical and cultural center of the country's Afro-Caribbean community. Afro-Caribbean immigrants came primarily from Jamaica, although smaller numbers emigrated from Barbados, St. Lucia, and St. Kitts. The Afro-Caribbean migration to Limón began in the late 19th century.

For many years, because of the intense overt discrimination against Afro-Caribbean peoples, the town of Limón remained segregated. West Indians in Costa Rica were not granted citizenship until the adoption of the 1949 Constitution. Moreover, until 1949 it was illegal to employ blacks in other parts of the country, and they were frequently rounded up in the country's center and deposited back on the Atlantic coast. So, for instance, when the railroad from Limón reached the outskirts of San José, the nation's capital, the train was stopped and the black crew would have to be replaced with a white crew who conducted the train into the country's heartland (Purcell 1993). In addition, the train carried only cargo — there was no passenger train.

In response to these conditions, Afro-Caribbean immigrants and their descendants have worked hard to preserve their English-speaking Caribbean identity. Maintaining and valuing their identity, culture, language, and religion have been critical survival mechanisms within this historically racist environment. Existing within the larger Costa Rican culture, Afro-Caribbean Costa Ricans, or Afro-Costarricenses, created institutions that preserved and valued a separate identity. This helped them to maintain their cultural ties with their countries of origin while sustaining a positive ethnic identity in the face of prejudice. Yet, the removal of overtly discriminatory laws in the past few decades has meant that preserving a separate identity within the greater Costa Rican culture has become increasingly complex.

Fear of losing a separate and distinct identity has centered on the role that the English language plays in the Afro-Costarricense community. Once nearly exclusively English-speaking, today fewer and fewer Afro-Costarricenses use English as their primary household language.[1] Historically, the ability to speak English enabled West Indians to communicate with the owners and managers of U.S.-owned banana plantations. Although the ability to speak English "helped" people of Afro-Caribbean descent in the banana industry, their inability to speak Spanish ultimately proved to be a liability. This grew increasingly pronounced as overtly discriminatory practices and national legislation were weakened or repealed. It was difficult for Afro-Costarricenses to participate in national life without mastery of Spanish, we were told by Marjorie Maxwell, principal of St. Marks.

In response to these conflicting language needs, the Anglican church in Limón started a school in the early 1970s with the explicit purpose of providing quality instruction in both English and Spanish to children in the community. The St. Marks school began with just a few students and has grown tremendously over the past 25 years. Today, this private school has approximately 600 students and includes kindergarten through 12th-grade classes. In recent years, the school has been ranked as one of the best in the region and prides itself on providing a very good education for very low tuition.[2]

For the past five summers, students in the Rutgers Community Service and Study Abroad Program have assisted in the school's English program. They work with the school's English teachers to promote conversation, interest in, and comfort with speaking English. Working at St. Marks was a critical part of the learning experience provided by the Rutgers study abroad program. As I mentioned above, working in the community creates a situation where the group traverses the line between outsider and insider.

Women's studies analytic tools were able to highlight the significance of this outsider/insider positioning to demonstrate the ways in which identity and experience are deeply situated and historically contingent constructs. In this program, questions about the construction of identity and difference were used to interrogate the subject matter of international economic and political relations, particularly questions of globalization, neocolonialism, and foreign policy. At the same time, attention to international political and economic dynamics helped to challenge an understanding of identity that did not include questions of nation and colonial relations.

The rest of this essay uses the students' outsider/insider status to explore how attention to their position in the community challenged them to rethink and reassess fundamental assumptions about the meaning(s) of identity. This status allowed the group to be "shocked" by the familiar — to see events, people, and themselves in a new light. In the following pages I will trace a process of outrage, destabilization, and discovery as the students grappled with living and working in Limón, trying to make sense of their experiences in the community and with others in the Rutgers group.

Outrage

In many ways, the course the students took while in Limón capitalized on their unique status as outsiders/insiders in this community. Indeed, their particular location in this community made them more willing to recognize and indict prejudice and systemic discrimination.

Complex and contradictory facets of oppression and discrimination became evident early on. The program began in San José, where the group spent a few days before heading by bus to the Atlantic coast. Even in those first few days the students realized that Limón was a much-derided place. Relatedly, students were struck by the resource inequities between Limón and other parts of Costa Rica, particularly Cartago and the central valley. The "shocking differences" between the development status of Limón and San José were particularly interesting, because many of the students were incensed that a group of people would be treated so unjustly simply due to race. So, right from the beginning, the connection between the analytic concepts of women's studies and the students' involvement in the community meant that they were outraged by the racism and classism that seem to structure Costa Rican society.

Destabilization

Students were outraged by the ways that power and privilege based on particular constructions of identity affected the lives of those who lived in Limón. The options of people with whom they worked at St. Marks school were constrained by systemic manifestations of this system of values, and students believed this to be unjust. Why was it that the public school system in Limón province was among the poorest in the country? And, what were the implications of this discrimination and oppression on people in the community? As we addressed these issues in class, our discussions of the constructedness of identity and systems of value were critical. Students began to come to terms with what it meant that identity was constructed and was historically and contextually contingent. Their service at St. Marks school provided data for theorizing about the (re)construction of identity, while the conceptual tools of women's studies made it possible for students to begin to understand the destabilizing challenges with which they were presented.

In one of our class discussions about the students' community service experience, a Rutgers student described a situation at St. Mark's, in which she was working with a group of English-as-a-first-language students. Students at St. Marks school were divided into two groups for their elementary English courses — those who spoke English at home and those who did not. In reality, this division was a racial one, since all of the kids of Afro-Caribbean descent were in the English-as-a-first-language group, and all of the kids of Hispanic and Chinese descent were in the other group. When the Rutgers student was with the former group, the kids suggested that she go and work with the "white" students in the other room. At first she was completely baffled, since she hadn't seen a "white" kid the whole time she had been working at the school. But when she questioned those who had made the suggestions, she realized that they were referring to the Hispanic kids as white. Her reflections on this experience generated an important discussion about what it meant that Hispanic people in Limón were regarded as white — with all of the attendant power and resource implications that being white has in the United States.

This complex and often counterintuitive construction of racialized categories was especially perplexing for the Latino students. They were the first to begin to let their experiences in Limón destabilize the fixity of their own identities. They were white? How could they be white in Limón and Latino in the United States? What were the implications of this? As they grappled with unfamiliar meanings assigned to race, they confronted the fluidity of identity categories. In concrete terms they were faced with what they had been reading about in our course: Categories of identity are culturally, historically, and contextually determined rather than fixed and immutable in the way that they had generally assumed. Suddenly, this was not such an abstract idea, but could be seen to have real implications in people's lives. These revelations were a result of the theorization of the group's outsider/insider status. It was the connection between their work at the St. Marks school and the analytic concepts of women's studies that provided this opportunity for reconsidering assumptions they had thought were unassailable.

Questions about the intersections of identity and class continued to get raised as students participated in work assignments at St. Marks school. Slowly they came to realize that even their own perceptions of wealth and poverty were culturally, economically, and geographically situated. As a result, they were compelled to think about the privilege of their backgrounds. Mark, for instance, a white student from a wealthy, predominantly white suburban area of New Jersey, wrote in his journal:

> Last night I had the great experience of eating dinner with Dunia . . . [a kindergarten teacher at St. Marks] and Heather [another Rutgers program participant]. One of the first things that struck me was the size of her [Dunia's] house. I think her entire house could fit into my house's living room. Now normally seeing this poverty wouldn't seem weird to me. When I went to my church's workcamps we worked to fix up houses that were very similar to Dunia's. The difference was that in the U.S. the people who have houses similar to Dunia's are considered very poor. They are on welfare, probably are unemployed and are often women with young children. . . . Here Dunia, an employed professional working two jobs [one as head of the English program at St. Marks school] . . . lives in the same poverty. The difference is that poverty takes on a new meaning down here. I am starting to realize that what is middle class here is like the poor in the U.S. I am realizing that you actually don't need all that much money to live and to live happily.

These revelations proved quite powerful and Mark continued to address issues such as these when responding to some of the course readings.[3] In particular, he struggled to understand the connections between gender, race, and class. "Were the people in the village [in the novel by Paule Marshal] oppressed because they were black or because they were poor? . . . Are women singled out for harsher treatment because they are poorer or because they are women or because they are black?" In many ways, Mark's connections to the people at St. Marks, combined with an emphasis on the construction of identity and systems of power and privilege in the course, served to destabilize his sense of himself and what he "knew" about the world. Just as important, he was also challenged to think about what he really "needed" to survive. He began to recognize that stereotypes and cross-cultural generalizations are not accurate because the world we see isn't objective, but is instead always interpreted through our own lenses.

Thus, students began to move from simply being outraged at the injustices they perceived to having injustice destabilize or challenge what they knew and how they understood who they were. In large part, this process of destabilization was profound because the students' outsider/insider status in Limón connected them to the lives of those with whom they worked.

Discovery

As the group settled in to life in their community service placement and became more comfortable with the materials assigned for the course, they also began to let their experiences lead them through a process of discovery. They started to realize the ways that systems of oppression constrain and affect their own lives. In particular, their status as "outside" of a system of oppression was challenged by differences within the group. The 13 students who participated in the program came from very diverse backgrounds. Of three men and 10 women, seven were white and the remaining group members identified themselves in a wide variety of ways: Native American, Latino, Salvadoran, black, and Caribbean.

As the Rutgers group used the conceptual tools from women's studies to examine and explain issues of power, discrimination, privilege, and identity construction, they came to recognize that their individual experiences of their outsider/insider position differed among themselves. Indeed, feelings of outrage about discrimination and privilege as well as fear about the destabilizing effect of conflicts around issues of race, class, and gender were evident in dynamics within the group. These differences were brought to the surface in the interaction between the course materials and the students' community service experiences.

During one class, a white student was talking about her teaching at St. Marks and referred, a number of times, to the "bad English" spoken by most of the students there. Others then picked up the label "bad." After several moments in which a number of students (both white and Latino) used this term, Caren, another student, challenged the group to think about what they were saying. Born in Antigua, but having lived in New Jersey since she was 8 years old, Caren talked about how she had grown up speaking "bad English" — the same "bad English" her mother still spoke. She was quite angry and suggested that others in the group think about why they labeled a dialect of English *bad* or *incorrect*. Indeed, we engaged in a very productive examination of how these labels express power, racism, and privilege. The group then had to grapple with the meaning and impact of these labels. Was labeling West Indian English "bad English" a product of their own biases, the biases of the school administration, or both? Using women's studies analyses about the construction of norms and systems of power and privilege, we were able to broadly interrogate the students' service experience at St. Marks school. Questions arose about how standards are set and why it is so difficult to diverge from those norms. Students had to confront the fact that they represented the value of speaking "standard" or "American" English as opposed to the patois that is traditional in the community. Could teaching standard English as opposed to patois actually be seen as a means to preserve Afro-Caribbean culture? Or, as bell hooks suggests, is standard English the "language of conquest and domination . . . which hides the loss of so many tongues?" (hooks 1994: 168).

The final aspect of the process of discovery came when group members realized that they themselves had internalized many of the values and norms that we had been examining in our analysis of course materials and discussions about working in Limón. However much they wanted to view manifestations of discrimination and oppression from the perspective of an outsider, they now had to confront the ways in which they too had been affected by gendered and racialized norms of value and worth, and thus were implicated in the system. In part, their temporary insider status, which came from working in the community, had made it impossible to keep an outsider's distance.

Conclusion

Although it is difficult to statistically or objectively assess the impact of any experiential learning program, anecdotal evidence made it clear that combining the analytic concepts of women's studies with community service in the Rutgers study abroad program led to productive learning. This combination provided an opportunity to apply women's studies insights about systems of domination and oppression and the construction of identity to real-life work experiences. In addition, the integration of women's studies and community service provided a method for exploring the group's outsider/insider position in Limón. It made them aware of their role in this community and the ways in which they themselves were part and parcel of the same system of power and privilege that defined the lives of those who lived there. All of the students who participated in the program commented on the significance of working in Limón in their final evaluations. They felt connected to the issues facing Limón and individual community members as a result of their role at the St. Marks school. Clearly they were challenged by what they learned from working there. Indeed, without their service at St. Marks school, there would have been no way for the group to even begin learning so much about Costa Rica, Limón, and themselves. In her final program evaluation, one student wrote:

> The best way to describe how I felt throughout these six weeks was challenged. And I honestly love to be challenged. I was challenged to explore a new city and find interesting hidden places in it. I was challenged to meet and understand a people/culture that has a rather complicated history that is still subtly played out today. I was challenged to use another language. . . . I was challenged to learn about our group and to work and live with them. And most definitely, I was challenged at [St. Marks] school.

A number of the program participants had previously had other study abroad experiences. Two of them, one who had spent seven months in South Africa and another who had spent a year in Mexico, talked about how they had learned more in six weeks in Costa Rica than they did while on their other, longer programs. In large part, they attributed this difference to the Costa Rica program having pushed them to "theorize" their role at the St. Marks school. From my perspective, the success of this program lay in the ways that mixing women's studies and community service brought questions about the construction of identity, power, and privilege to the analytic surface.

Notes

1. Three main languages are used in Limón province: Spanish (the official language); Standard Limón English; and Limón Creole (a derivative of Jamaican Creole). The majority of Afro-Costarricenses speak Spanish (80 percent) and some combination of Standard Limón English and Limón Creole. For greater detail about the politics of language in Costa Rica, see Purcell 1993.

2. At this point, the tuition is approximately $30 per month, which is both a significant amount of money for most of the parents who pay and considerably cheaper than other private schools in Limón.

3. Mark was responding to Paule Marshall's *The Chosen Place, The Timeless People* (Vintage Contemporaries, 1992).

Theorizing Race, Class, Gender, Nation:
Afro-Caribbean Culture and History a View from Limón, Costa Rica

Interdisciplinary Studies 556:300
Instructor: Debra J. Liebowitz
Summer 1998

TEXTS

The following books must be purchased and brought with you to Costa Rica. They have been ordered and are available at Recto/Verso Books, New Brunswick, NJ 08901. Their phone number is 732-247-2324.

Fanon, Frantz. 1967. *Black Skin, White Masks*. New York: Grove Press.
Lamming, George. 1991 [1970]. *In the Castle of My Skin*. Ann Arbor: University of Michigan Press.
Marshal, Paule. 1992 [1969]. *The Chosen Place, The Timeless People*. New York: Vintage Contemporaries.
Purcell, Trevor W. 1993. *Banana Fallout: Class, Color, and Culture Among West Indians in Costa Rica*. Los Angeles: Center for Afro-American Studies Publications, University of California.

An additional book is needed but must be purchased in San Jose, Costa Rica:

Palmer, Paula. *What Happen: A Folk-History of Costa Rica's Talmanca Coast*.

The rest of the readings are available in a packet which must be purchased and brought to Costa Rica. The packet is available at Pequod Copy Center at 119 Somerset Street in New Brunswick. Their phone number is 732-214-8787.

EXPECTATIONS AND ASSIGNMENTS

Your final grade for the 6 credit course will be based on the following:

Fulfillment of responsibilities at the St. Marks School, plus
- ▸   Class participation   15%
- ▸   Class presentation   15%
- ▸   Journal   30%
- ▸   Final paper   40%

Seminar Grade:

<u>Attendance and Participation:</u> This course will be run as a seminar and its success is consequently dependent upon your level of commitment and preparedness. Therefore, you are required to attend each seminar meeting and come prepared to analytically discuss the readings and relate them to your experiences in Limón.

<u>Discussion Leading:</u> Each class, one or more class members will help lead class discussion by preparing discussion questions for the group as well as facilitating the class discussion. (see "Guidelines for

---

Interdisciplinary Studies 556:300   1

Discussion Leading" sheet for more detail on my expectations). A sign up sheet will be passed around during our first class meeting. You will be graded on your presentation, the outline that you hand in, materials that you hand out to the class, and your meeting with me at least two days before you are the discussion leader.

Journals: One of the central requirements of the seminar is that you keep a reading and teaching journal. You should make entries as often as you can, but at a minimum, twice a week. Each week you should have two types of entries. First, you should thoughtfully reflect on each of the assigned readings for the week. Second, you should reflect on what is happening in your work at the school. See "Guidelines for Journal Writing" sheet for more details.

Final Paper: The assignment for your final paper will be discussed in detail in class. The paper is due on August 3rd. You may either write a traditional academic essay or an essay of informed reflection, in which you draw both on the texts we read and on your experiences and research in Limón. The paper is a major essay and should be approximately 10-15 typed, double-space pages in length.

A note about your grade in this course: Please note that although your teaching at the St. Mark's school is not graded, you are required to work there at least two hours per day, five days per week. Students who do not fulfill this requirement will not pass the course.

COURSE SCHEDULE

May 24: Meet at airport in Costa Rica. Group orientation and dinner.

May 25: Tour San Jose

May 26: Travel to Limón.

SECTION I: COSTA RICA IN CONTEXT

PART A: Costa Rica / Central America

Wednesday, May 27: Welcome to St. Mark's School. Observation period at school begins.
Assigned Reading:
   Skidmore, Thomas E., and Peter H. Smith. 1997. "Chapter Ten - Central America: Colonialism, Dictatorship, and Revolution." In *Modern Latin America*, 4th ed. New York: Oxford University Press, pp. 321-358.
   Barry, Tom. 1987. "Chapters 2, 3, 4 and pp. 148-153." In *Roots of Rebellion: Land & Hunger in Central America*. Boston: South End Press, pp. 21-90 & 148-153.
   González-Vega, Claudio, and Víctor Hugo Céspedes. 1993. "Costa Rica: Basic Information." In *The Political Economy of Poverty, Equity, and Growth: Costa Rica and Uruguay*, ed. Simon Rottenberg. New York: Oxford University Press, pp. 15-27.

PART B: Costa Rica: Historical Overview

Friday, May 29: Observation period at school ends.
Assigned Reading:

The Costa Rica Reader. 1989. Ed. Marc Edelman and Joanne Kenen. New York: Grove Weidenfeld. Pp. ix; xv-28; 83-111; 161-169.

Calabrese, Cora Ferro, and Ana María Quirós Rojas. 1997. "Women in Colonial Costa Rica: A Significant Presence." In *The Costa Rican Women's Movement: A Reader*, ed. Ilse Abshagen Leitinger. Pittsburgh, PA: University of Pittsburgh Press, pp. 39-51.

Anonymous. 1997. "Central America." *Economist*, January 11, 42-43. This article say "Citation 70" at the top.

Clinton, William J. 1997. "Remarks at the Welcoming Ceremony at the Central American Summit in San Jose, Costa Rica." *Weekly Compilation of Presidential Documents* 33(19, May 12): 673-674. This article says "Citation 33" at the top.

SECTION II: THEORIZING IDENTITIES IN LIMÓN

PART A: Cultural Theory

Tuesday, June 2:
Assigned Reading:

Hall, Stuart. 1994. "Cultural Identity and Diaspora." In *Colonial Discourse and Post-Colonial Theory: A Reader*, ed. Patrick Williams and Laura Chrisman. New York: Columbia University Press, 392-403.

Featherstone, Mike. 1990. "Global Culture: An Introduction." In *Global Culture*, ed. Mike Featherstone. London: Sage, 1-13.

PART B: Intersections of Race, Culture and Class

Thursday, June 4:
Assigned Reading:

Purcell, Trevor W. 1993. *Banana Fallout: Class, Color, and Culture Among West Indians in Costa Rica*. Los Angeles: Center for Afro-American Studies Publications, University of California. [BOOK]

June 9:
Assigned Reading:

Palmer, Paula. *What Happen: A Folk-History of Costa Rica's Talmanca Coast*. [BOOK]

June 11:
Assigned Reading:

Fanon, Frantz. 1967. *Black Skin, White Masks*. New York: Grove Press. [BOOK]

Brewer, Rose M. "Theorizing Race, Class and Gender: The New Scholarship of Black Feminist Intellectuals and Black Women's Labor." In *Theorizing Black Feminisms: The Visionary Pragmatism of Black Women*, edited by Stanlie M. James and Abena P.A. Busia, 13-30. New York, Routledge, 1993.

June 16:
Assigned Reading:

Fanon, Frantz. 1967. *Black Skin, White Masks*. New York: Grove Press. [BOOK]

PART C: Theorizing the Intersections of Gender, Race, Class in Feminist Organizing

---

Interdisciplinary Studies 556:300   3

June 18:
Assigned Reading:
>Fajardo, Yadira Calvo. 1997. "Different Times, Women, Visions: The Deep Roots of Costa Rican Feminism." In *The Costa Rican Women's Movement: A Reader*, ed. Ilse Abshagen Leitinger. Pittsburgh, PA: University of Pittsburgh Press, pp. 5-12.
>López-Casas, Eugenia. 1997. "Women Heads of Household in Costa Rica's Limón Province: The Effects of Class Modified by Race and Gender." In *The Costa Rican Women's Movement: A Reader*, ed. Ilse Abshagen Leitinger. Pittsburgh, PA: University of Pittsburgh Press, pp. 141-146.

PART D: Race, Identity, Nation

June 20-21: Trip to Cahuita
Assigned Reading:
>Bourgois, Philippe I. 1989. *Ethnicity at Work: Divided Labor on a Central American Banana Plantation*. Baltimore: The Johns Hopkins University Press, pp. xi-110.

June 23:
Assigned Reading:
>Lamming, George. 1991 [1970]. *In the Castle of My Skin*. Ann Arbor: University of Michigan Press. [BOOK]

PART E: The Politics of Religion, Race and Gender

June 25:
Assigned Reading:
>Harpelle, Ronald N. 1994. "Ethnicity, Religion and Repression: The Denial of African Heritage in Costa Rica." *Canadian Journal of History* XXIX(1, April): 95-112.
>Martin, David. 1990. *Tongues of Fire: The Explosion of Protestantism in Latin America*: Basil Blackwell, pp. 185-202.

PART F: The "North" in the "South": Identity and Location

June 30:
Assigned Reading:
>:Marshal, Paule. 1992 [1969]. *The Chosen Place, The Timeless People*. New York: Vintage Contemporaries. [BOOK]

SECTION III: ECOTOURISM

July 1-3: Trip to Tortuguero
Assigned Reading:
>Place, Susan. 1995. "Ecotourism for Sustainable Development: Oxymoron or Plausible Strategy?" *GeoJournal* 35(2): 161-173.
>Norris, Ruth. 1994. "Ecotourism in the National Parks of Latin America." *National Parks* 68(1-2, January): 32-37. This article says "Citation 219" at the top.

July 4: Travel to San Jose

July 5: Flight back to U.S. End of Program

August 3: Final papers due

Interdisciplinary Studies 556:300   4

"Civic Character" Engaged:
Adult Learners and Service-Learning

by Eve Allegra Raimon and Jan L. Hitchcock

In its summer/fall 1997 issue, *The Educational Record* published a special double issue on the topic of "College and Character: Preparing Students for Lives of Civic Responsibility." This particular edition of the American Council on Education's journal included contributions by former U.S. Cabinet members, college presidents, vice presidents, deans, and endowed full professors — in short, voices of authority in the academy in general as well as in the increasingly popular arena of service-learning. Assuming, then, that this volume is illustrative of the orthodox vocabulary of the field at this stage in its history, we begin this essay by interrogating the usefulness of that vocabulary in relation to a growing segment of the total population of U.S. college students: adult student learners, the majority of whom are women.[1] Our aim is to examine who the imagined subjects are of influential academic discourse about service-learning, and to question how applicable and productive the tenets of such discussions are for the less-visible yet sizable number of older undergraduate students.

Moreover, if, as we maintain, the academic rhetoric that dominates the national service-learning conversation does indeed lose some of its value when the subject of study shifts significantly from traditional-age students, then several important and related questions must be addressed. First, what conceptual or rhetorical barriers has the academy — unwittingly or not — erected that impede such students from benefiting fully from service-learning programs? Second, how does the face of service-learning change when a high percentage of the students enrolled in such programs are older and bring with them well-established foundations of civic involvement and character? Finally, how do we at institutions that serve nontraditional students constructively reconceptualize service-learning programs to best serve adult learners?

Examining the Record

Before considering these questions, however, let us take a closer look at the language of several of the essays collected in that "College and Character" issue of *The Educational Record*. A good place to begin is with the prefatory remarks of ACE president Stanley O. Ikenberry. In one passage he extols the transformative effects of programs that require students to ponder their place in civic life, and makes the following clarion call:

> *The time has come for higher education to expand its role in equipping students to live productive lives through and beyond their careers — to be civic-minded, to take on leadership roles, and to exercise personal, professional, and ethical judgments that are based on values. (1997: 9)*

Several problems arise in this formulation, not the least of which is that such rhetorical use of philosophical abstractions allows for the avoidance of more thorny issues concerning what public policy direction might effect the kind of social change such "values" reflect. However, more relevant to our present concerns is the issue of prior life experience. A plausible (if definitely debatable) argument can be advanced that traditional-age students — that is, young people — simply by virtue of their youth have had fewer opportunities by and large to take part meaningfully in civic life or to be asked to take on leadership roles. However, that portrait changes undeniably when instead of teenagers the classroom is filled with 15 adults, three quarters of whom are women with children ranging in age from infants right up to those in college themselves. Indeed, Ikenberry's assumptions need to be revised yet again when we consider that most of those mothers have in fact been directly involved in civic life through their involvement in the public school system at a minimum.

Let us turn to the title of the first essay, "Character for What? Higher Education & Public Life," written by David Mathews, a former secretary of the Department of Health, Education, and Welfare and a past president of the University of Alabama. This reference to character marks the second titular use of the term in as many articles. Indeed, *character,* by itself or preceded by the adjective *civic* is employed repeatedly in these essays, as it is throughout the academic literature on service-learning.[2] The singular claim about such programs is that they build "civic character" and "social responsibility." Here, for example, Mathews celebrates the establishment on a growing number of college and university campuses of National Issues Forums designed to encourage citizen groups to deliberate key issues facing local communities. About such forums, he effuses, "What a marvelous setting for students to learn the practices of democratic citizenship. What an excellent set of practices for building civic character!" (1997: 17).

Our objection is not to the abstract goal of furthering a sense of civic involvement, which service-learning programs most assuredly do accomplish. Rather, our concern lies with the large set of assumptions embedded in the phrase "building civic character" when applied to older students. The phrase implies mistaken assumptions about students' lack of experience and maturity in the civic arena that may also ultimately betray a sense of class privilege. In other words, to extend the phrase's construction metaphor, the figure suggests that the service-learning instructor has an opportunity to design and shape the building in question from the foundation up. In this way, the student/structure can be seen as a moral/social tabula rasa whose sense of civic virtue is molded and nurtured by the intervention of the teacher and the program.

But what happens when the student/structure the program is engaged in constructing is already in place? Not only that, but is already firmly grounded in an existing community full of heterogeneous groups organized along axes of age, physical condition, and economic status? Given such a different student/architectural demographic, how useful is the metaphor of civic virtue as moral/social construction site? It seems to us that the trope can only retain its persuasive force if it remains deeply invested in a nostalgic vision of undergraduate education when such an experience was the exclusive domain of late adolescents and young adults. This desire to envision only the young as students in higher education is evident in Mathews's reporting of a study on the political life of college students:

> Despite charges that undergraduates are preoccupied with personal self-interest, the study revealed that the underlined{younger generation} is no more uncaring than the underlined{older generation} is apathetic. In fact, underlined{students care} a great deal. Even so, they are more cynical than underlined{their elders} about the way the political system operates — and far more pessimistic about their ability to reform it. (15) [emphasis added]

There appears to be a palpable need here to maintain binary categories based on age, whereas in actuality such rigid distinctions have been applicable over recent decades to an ever smaller and highly privileged sector of the undergraduate population. As if to underscore the point, this textual polarization is rendered visual in the title page to the next essay, "The Power of Peer Culture" (Dalton and Petrie 1997: 18). Here, in a full-page color photo, we are presented with a representative sampling of the "peers" in question: the smooth faces and strong shoulders of 11 grinning college students — all decidedly young adults and all hamming it up for the camera. Any suggestion that student peers might be older than 21 is entirely absent from the scene.

Such an alternate vision of higher education is equally lacking in "Character and Civic Education: What Does it Take?," another article from *The Educational Record*. The piece, the third to include the term *character* in its title, was written by Patricia M. King, professor and chair of the Department of Higher Education and Student Affairs at Bowling Green State University. It is explicitly concerned with "the development of morality" (1997: 90) in students through institutions' "character and civic education programs" (89). Working from a model of moral development formulated by John Rest, King asserts, "Many college students interpret fairness in terms of possible negative impact *on themselves*, without showing empathy toward or understanding of others" (90). Here again, such an assertion makes assumptions that are no longer tenable — if they ever were. First, as with previous examples, it presumes a college population composed of young adults exclusively. Second, and perhaps more disturbing, it suggests a sexist gendering of the category "undergraduate." That is, the typical college student is imagined to be both young and male. Otherwise, how credible would a claim to such self-absorption be if we took into account the growing numbers of women of all ages who are returning to school after having and raising children — a period during which practically *all* they have been asked to do is to show "empathy toward or understanding of others"?

Adults and Service-Learning

Having presented examples of the extent to which youth is the predominant imagined subject of current literature on service-learning, we will consider in more detail the experiences and challenges of such programs for older, nontraditional, community-based, and most often female, students.[3] Our experience with service-learning has been on a small campus of a public university. The mission of the Lewiston-Auburn College campus of the University of Southern Maine is interdisciplinary and encourages bridging the liberal arts and professional applications, community and college. Our own degree programs are arts and humanities (Raimon) and social and behavioral sciences (Hitchcock). Our students are predominantly nontraditional (average age 32), and women (more than 75 percent). Many are the first in their families to attend college; most have significant family or work responsibilities. Although there is support — in fact, a call — from the academic administration for the integration of service-learning into the curriculum, until the last few years most service-learning projects on our campus had taken place in the context of one degree program that combined management and public policy perspectives.

When the administration decided to make extension of service-learning across the curriculum a priority, initially we hesitated. We wondered aloud whether our particular student population would be best served by this new initiative. After all, as we've indicated, many of our students have already spent the majority of their adult lives responding to the needs of others in their families, churches, and communities. Indeed, might their college experience provide perhaps their sole opportunity to focus on the development of the self and its potential for genuine intellectual inquiry? Would the much-celebrated benefits of service-learning for younger students be as marked for students in their early and mid adult years?

Indeed, we have observed that though nontraditional students have often interrupted their school or work histories to care for children, many adult women learners *have also already* engaged in service activities before enrolling in college, even if they probably would not identify those activities as such prior to taking a course with a service-learning component. Take Gail, for example, a student in her 40s in a recent arts and humanities service-learning course. She reported that as a mother she "was involved in the public schools until my kids told me to go away," though she never thought of herself as "doing service."[4] Given the benefit of reflecting on that first experience, Gail now believes that even though it went untheorized at the time, her earlier work in schools nonetheless helped shape the direction of her career: "I was always attracted to the bad kid," she recalls. "I was trying to [mediate] for the kid who was the target for both other kids and the teacher." Gail is now in a master's degree program in education and plans to teach troubled youth.

Or there is Michelline, another arts and humanities service-learning student who, years before returning to college, took it upon herself to start a creative writing program at an area nursing home. She would read her own poetry to the residents, encourage them to write, and discuss what they had written. Yet, when the issue of prior service came up in class, initially Michelline did not have the conceptual framework to categorize her activity as service. The class only learned of her endeavors weeks later when she "remembered" them.

The experiences of these quite typical adult learners underscore two crucial shortcomings in the way service-learning programs currently function. The first is the relative invisibility of this student population, as we have seen in the literature. If nontraditional students somehow are not considered a valid category in conceptualizing service-learning programs, then clearly the value of their previous service experience will be diminished. As important, however, is the degree to which *the programs themselves will be impoverished* by failing to take advantage of the special backgrounds of such students. Unlike traditional undergraduates, these students have a range of relevant experience up to and including expertise in many of the same activities that often constitute service-learning projects. Considered in this light, then, far from being marginalized or omitted altogether from the discourse, these returning or adult students might be recognized as offering particular advantages to such academic programs. Moreover, unlike traditional-age students at prestigious private schools, these adult learners are often a part of the same community that the service-learning projects are intended to serve. As such, they are in a position not to be overlooked but rather to serve as resources to administrators, faculty, and students engaged in service-learning endeavors.

Of course, we do not mean to imply by the foregoing that older students have nothing to learn from service-learning initiatives. On the contrary, in implementing our service-learning projects, we have found that nontraditional students — like their younger cohorts — have a great deal to gain from opportunities that allow them to reflect on and integrate their community experiences with newly gained academic skills and theoretical perspectives. The experience of Paul, enrolled in an interdisciplinary service-learning class in our social and behavioral sciences program, provides an example of this process of educational and professional growth. In transition between employment in the construction trades and identifying new career goals, Paul commented that his experience with service-learning gave him more "control" over his education: "I found that service-learning allowed me to have a sense of control over my education that regular classes have not provided." The autonomy and responsibility involved in working with a community agency to design and implement a survey study of local environmental issues helped Paul recognize and integrate old and new competencies. In addition, the experience confirmed for him the relevance of the policy-related course readings and the importance of the writing and public presentation skills he was in the process of refining.

For many older students, entry into college studies entails risks, movement into unfamiliar domains where success and failure appear defined in new, sometimes arbitrary ways. It would make sense that adults, accustomed to exercising autonomy and responsibility in many areas in their lives, would find service projects a congenial setting for bridging formal academic experiences with desired directions for their careers. Another student, Catherine, offers a good example. She was involved in a project intended to allow school children to have input into municipal environmental discussions and priority setting. Already employed full-time in another school system, she commented that she had learned more from her service-learning project than she had in any of her other classes. She explained that her project entailed a different level of interaction with school personnel and students than her daily work responsibilities required, and it presented challenges that, once surmounted, yielded a high degree of satisfaction and confidence. Interested in advancing her work with children, she was led to reflect more fully on school administrations, the classroom experience, and the perspectives of children in judging environmental risks facing the community. She concluded:

> What I had conceived of as a simple case of gathering the views of school children I had taught had turned out to be an exercise in interpersonal relations. Never again would I take for granted an assignment as challenging as this. . . . Next, it was amazing to discern the passion reflected in the responses, coming, as they did, from mere youngsters. I had assumed, from

working with this age group over the past couple of years, that teenagers were too self-engrossed to care about the environment. After reading through their responses, I learned to revise my opinion of teenagers.

Here again, Catherine's acquaintance with the service-learning model as an older student enriched her present experience. At the same time, the project substantially helped her better integrate course and field experience and increased her readiness to take on additional independent projects.

A final example we observed of the potential benefits of service-learning to older learners occurred when students involved in environmentally focused projects had the opportunity to present their work to knowledgeable community members in decision-making positions. This workshop experience highlighted for the students the extent to which their coursework and education could matter in their community and to people they knew and respected. The audience for student presentations on games designed to enhance children's environmental awareness, for instance, included two individuals with extensive environmental education experience. Student recommendations concerning techniques for increasing public involvement in community discussions of environmental issues were presented to a city planner and leaders from business and economic development organizations who had considerable experience in conducting such public meetings. In both examples, workshop audience members were in a position to make well-informed evaluations of the strengths and weaknesses of the students' projects. One student summarized the workshop experience in this way:

> *It was a great forum and the guests from the community added a great dimension that is so important to the service aspect of this type of endeavor.*
>
> *These feelings were further amplified by my own experience at the [environmental fair for children]. It was great to have an opportunity to talk with other students from other colleges, people from the community, various agencies, and the like about environmental issues and what we have been studying. Service-learning and the opportunities it affords offer students a chance to do "something real," to interact with the community, and do something useful.*

Having students implement service-learning projects in their own communities can, however, pose ethical issues different from issues likely to arise with projects involving more traditional-age students, many of whom are from localities at a significant distance from their college or university. Specifically, preexisting relationships may create some complications in roles. For instance, students researching patterns of pollution may find themselves "investigating" neighbors — or their employers. One student who elected to withdraw from an environmentally focused course was a resident of a neighborhood identified as likely to receive specific scrutiny throughout the semester.

To more systematically assess our students' experiences, we conducted a survey during the final class meeting of three recent service-learning courses. Forty-two students, or 82 percent of the total, completed the survey. Their demographics were consistent with our college-wide statistics: their average age was approximately 30, 83 percent were women, and the majority were residents of nearby communities. Thirty-eight percent were employed full-time, and 52 percent were parents with children residing at home. Consistent with our claim that such a student body already demonstrates the values and activities associated with "civic character," 50 percent of our students were also undertaking volunteer work in the community during that same semester, independent of any and all academic service-learning activities.

In addition, 57 percent of the respondents "strongly agreed" and another 33 percent "somewhat agreed" that they were satisfied with the service-learning component of the course. In total, 86 percent "strongly" or "somewhat" agreed that the experience significantly added to their understanding of the course concepts. The questionnaire also documented students' intent to continue to contribute to the community through related projects: 55 percent thought they "definitely" would become involved in other community-based projects in the future, and 38 percent thought that "maybe" they would. Generally, therefore, we received decidedly positive student reactions.

However, the questionnaire results and student comments also revealed that service-learning experiences were not without some challenges. Students suggested that scheduling limitations should be taken into consideration for older, nontraditional students who are employed full-time: Twelve percent of the respondents reported that it was "very difficult" to coordinate their schedules to meet service-learning responsibilities, and a total of 59 percent found scheduling at least "somewhat of a challenge." For example, in one evening class, two students were employed full-time during the day at companies with firm policies against personal calls, the category to which any course-related calls to service-learning community contacts would have been designated. One student commented that though she certainly expected to spend time outside of class studying and completing assignments, there were many limits on when she could schedule those hours. However, though students experienced scheduling demands as challenging, they *did* accomplish the required tasks.

Recommendations

Our contention, then, is that higher education's dominant mode of understanding who benefits from service-learning and how it is implemented necessarily changes once we recognize the value of the substantial numbers of adult learners on campuses across the country. Many of today's classrooms include a mix of adolescents and adults of varying ages. The issue then becomes how prepared faculty and programs will be to acknowledge and adjust to these demographic and structural contingencies. As we have suggested, the field can best serve the needs of older students by modifying its youth-directed rhetoric of universal values in favor of a less lofty vocabulary that nonetheless embraces the potential of such programs to forge stronger bonds between students and their social and political environments. Beyond its vocabulary, however, academic service programs can become more responsive to older students by tailoring their curriculum accordingly. In his essay "Linking Service-Learning and the Academy," Edward Zlotkowski argues similarly — though for different reasons — for a more context-specific view of service-learning, advocating that schools move from "one-size-fits-all service-learning to service-learning as a pedagogy carefully modulated to specific disciplinary and interdisciplinary goals" (1996: 27). To apply Zlotkowski's notion to our concerns, we foresee programs taking students' vastly different backgrounds and skills into greater account in both design and practice.

For instance, on the concrete level, an instructor offering a service-learning class to a group of older, nontraditional students must inventory students' prior professional and service backgrounds in order both to make use of such student resources and to identify new learning opportunities. Perhaps a student with significant prior experience in a given area can be paired with another — perhaps younger — student in a kind of peer-mentoring arrangement. Additionally, as reflected in our survey results, students need to know, ideally before — or at least upon — registering for a course that there may be extra scheduling demands associated with a given project. Finally, the instructor needs to make explicit the goal of connecting and integrating real-world service experiences with other more abstract course material. These links are what will make the project more than a mere add-on, and will lead to a more vital experience of learning.

In following this approach, however, we must make sure that we meet the goals of *both* the institution *and* the students enrolled. To be sure, these will overlap significantly, but they may not be identical. For example, adult students may place more importance on activities that have some bearing — however indirect — on their professional objectives. Even though service-learning should not be confused with professional internships, programs that attract nontraditional students should expect that adults may have a more developed sense of direction with respect to their interests in community service, and such programs should be prepared to accommodate this sharper individual focus. In our experience, the reason many returning students demonstrate a clearer sense of purpose about what projects they want to pursue has everything to do with students' sense of rootedness in the community that the institution has dedicated itself to serving. Older learners, as we've pointed out, have years of engagement in one form or another with the problems and assets of their hometown, and therefore are in a unique position to contribute materially to its social, cultural, and educational advancement. Given this context, it is possible that the content and range of what typically constitutes a service-learning project may need to coincide more closely with individual community needs. Rather than volunteering in a soup kitchen, for instance, some adults may have a greater investment in contributing their services to an entirely different sort of undertaking — yet one that would prove equally valuable to their town or city.

A case in point is the service work engaged in by Ann, a nontraditional student in an arts and humanities service-learning course taught by one of us. Herself Franco-American, Ann chose to work for the Franco-American Oral History project, an effort by an archive on campus to record and preserve the storehouse of history represented by many elders in Lewiston, a Franco-American cultural center that has begun to undergo a renaissance in its ethnic and cultural heritage. A musician and music teacher herself, Ann decided to conduct a series of oral histories with seniors who had been influential in the regional Franco-American music scene. This excerpt from her final assessment of the project reveals her sense of connection to her subject and her significant stake in its success:

> As Lewiston is experiencing a renaissance in Franco-American cultural affirmation, this project could not be more timely. As the population with direct knowledge of our cultural beginnings in Maine decreases year by year, the significance of this project is underscored. As a way to gain experiential knowledge and its incorporation into the classroom, this project was again valuable.

Though not a typical project, Ann's offers an example of a student engaging in activities that are highly relevant and meaningful both to her sense of professional identity and to her daily life in her family and community. Also manifest is perhaps a heightened level of reciprocity, as compared with the traditional model, in the degree to which older undergraduates become both learners and resources in the course of their interaction with the community.

However, these meaningful exchanges can only succeed if programs and instructors can broaden customary understandings of service-learning, and if the necessary preparation is undertaken to anticipate adult students' different backgrounds, skills, and expectations. That is, to borrow from

Zlotkowski, if service-learning is reenvisioned as a "pedagogy carefully modulated" to meet the changing demands of a more varied student population. In addition, we have found that part of any such successful "modulation" will entail a significant element of formal academic inquiry, both in the form of students' written and oral self-reflection about their work and in readings and discussions of more abstract theoretical issues in the field of service-learning itself. Older learners with greater life experience are perhaps better prepared to consider not only questions about how their service and their academic studies correlate but also more advanced — and thorny — topics about, say, the relation between charity and service-learning. To illustrate, students in one of our courses wrestled with the sophisticated issues raised by Joseph Kahne and Joel Westheimer's "In the Service of What? The Politics of Service-Learning," which outlines *charity* versus *change* models. The essay compares two service-learning courses: Mr. Johnson's, based on traditional altruistic ideals and practices, and Ms. Adams's more innovative method, in which students are encouraged to engage in "a systematic and critical analysis of the causes of homelessness and of the strategies employed to prevent it" (1996: 594). Kahne and Westheimer clearly favor the latter approach and argue for the "need to clarify the ideological perspectives that underlie service-learning programs" (594). Students in Raimon's course, however, imagined the two instructors developing a synthesized pedagogy that would combine the empathetic and engaged qualities of Mr. Johnson's course with the analytic rigor and depth of Ms. Adams's.

Naturally, class discussion on such a meta level perforce entails explicitly political considerations that might be avoided given a less prominent component of self-reflexivity. Just as older students are likely to have a clearer fix on their professional interests, so they also tend to have a more highly formulated sense of where they situate themselves politically. Whereas this might at first glance be viewed as a potential peril of teaching adults, it can, in fact, become one of the most compelling and provocative aspects of a course. Students' political worldviews can be challenged or confirmed in perhaps more concrete and striking ways than in any other setting in the university, but not unless the political realm is made an explicit and important consideration in class.

If, as we suggest, programs need to recognize better that adult students comprise a vital constituency in service-learning, and if, as we also advocate, proponents would profit by modulating their rhetorical use of such abstract values as "civic character," what then can be said to remain as the core principles of service-learning? It would seem to us important to view academic service work in the context of a continuing commitment by higher education to the notion of civic *engagement* while recognizing that some students will already have prior community experience. This engagement can and does take an infinite number of forms, both in and beyond service-learning activities. In addition, the valuable combination of experiential work together with a rigorous academic component must continue to be a central feature of service programs. Indeed, one student coined the apt phrase "ethics in action" to describe her experience of such a course. Although it can be argued that "ethics" itself requires further scrutiny and explication, the student felt that the formulation captures the unique admixture of theory and practice that distinguishes the best of service-learning pedagogy.

Even though our focus has been on a subset of adult students who have been relatively neglected in the service-learning literature, we hope that these discussions will be relevant for the field of service-learning as a whole. At the same time that we advance recommendations to facilitate effective service-learning initiatives with nontraditional students, we propose that lessons learned from service-learning with these students may also be relevant for those educators working primarily with younger students. As has already been noted, the potentially patronizing tone of the all-too-frequent reference to "building character" is conveyed particularly clearly when it is addressed to midlife adults already managing the multiple responsibilities of family, workplace, and community. Thus, we suggest that administrators and faculty would do well not to dismiss or minimize the extent of character formation, experience, and civic engagement that *all* students — older *and* younger — may already be able to bring to service-learning opportunities. Our experiences with adult learners, together with descriptions of service-learning undertaken with traditional-age college populations, support the position that for all students, younger and older, male and female, there exists here the potential for a vital connection and integration of different types of learning — real-world with more formally academic, prior life experience with new accomplishments and aspirations.

Acknowledgments

The authors wish to acknowledge support received from a Lewiston-Auburn College/University of Southern Maine summer faculty stipend to Raimon. In addition, a Learn and Serve America: Higher Education project grant to Lewiston-Auburn College, awarded by the Maine Campus Compact, supported the service-learning initiative of Hitchcock. The contributions of our students — in terms of both their service and their reflections on the experience — are also gratefully acknowledged. Finally, thanks to John Bay and Penny Hilton, who read the manuscript and made helpful comments.

Notes

1. In 1995, individuals age 25 and above made up 43 percent of all students attending institutions of higher education, either full- or part-time; 19 percent of the total student population was age 35 and above. "Older" students made up a comparable percentage of students in 1990; these levels represent the culmination of a steady trend of greater participation by older students over the previous two decades. Since 1970, the percentage of students 35 and older has more than doubled, and the absolute number of students in that age category has more than tripled. This trend of increasing participation in higher education by older students has recently reached a plateau, with projections for 2008 suggesting a slight decline to come in the percentage of older students (NCES 1998, 1999).

Populations of older students are likely to include high percentages of women: Fifty-nine percent of all full- and part-time students enrolled Fall 1995 of age 25 and above were women. Sixty-four percent of the students 35 and older were women (NCES 1998). These demographic trends are important contexts for our linkage of issues around age and gender in service-learning projects and higher education.

2. Another recent example of the sort of rhetoric we interrogate here in the context of adult students is a November 1998 announcement by the national Campus Compact concerning a Templeton Fellows program that seeks to encourage student leaders to interview college presidents about "the role of higher education in civic renewal." A primary purpose of these discussions, according to the announcement, is to discuss "the relationship between community service and character development."

3. We use the term "community-based" to mean students who reside within the greater geographical region that surrounds the institution. We intend to distinguish such students from a residential college campus, where a majority of students reside outside the region or state where they attend college.

4. This quotation from a student and all others that follow were drawn from either student papers or written student commentaries and evaluations in our service-learning classes. Individual students who are identified have reviewed their quotations and have given their permission for publication.

References

Dalton, J.C., and A.M. Petrie. (Summer/Fall 1997). "The Power of Peer Culture." *The Educational Record* 78(3): 18-24.

Ikenberry, S.O. (Summer/Fall 1997). "President's Note." *The Educational Record* 78(3): 7-9.

Kahne, J., and J. Westheimer. (1996). "In the Service of What? The Politics of Service Learning." *Phi Delta Kappan* 77(9): 592-600.

King, P.M. (Summer/Fall 1997). "Character and Civic Education: What Does It Take?" *The Educational Record* 78(3): 87-94.

Mathews, D. (Summer/Fall 1997). "Character for What? Higher Education and Public Life." *The Educational Record* 78(3): 10-17.

National Center for Education Statistics. (1998). *Digest of Education Statistics 1997*. Pub No. NCES 98-015. Washington, DC: U.S. Dept. of Education.

———. (1999). *Projections of Education Statistics to 2008*. Accessed at <http://nces.ed.gov/pub09/pj2008>.

Zlotkowski, E. (Jan./Feb. 1996). "Linking Service-Learning and the Academy: A New Voice at the Table?" *Change* 28(1): 20-27.

Resolving a Conundrum: Incorporating Service-Learning Into a Women and the Law Course

by Mary Pat Treuthart

A decade ago, I began teaching an upper-class elective law school course on Women and the Law at Gonzaga University in Spokane, WA. I have since taught a variation of this course at two other law schools and as an adjunct instructor in the Gonzaga undergraduate Political Science Department.

Initially, I focused on gathering appropriate teaching materials that would combine the theoretical and the practical. I wanted all students to be familiar with the philosophical underpinnings of feminist political and jurisprudential theory. At the same time, I believed it was critical that the law students have some ability to appreciate the concrete problems of their future clients. The first section of the course included readings from feminists with contrasting theoretical approaches. The remaining two thirds of the course highlighted legal and public policy issues of significance to women such as discrimination in education, the workplace, and the public entitlement systems; violence against women (rape, pornography, prostitution, and intimate partner abuse); reproductive freedom; and mothering and family life.

The composition of the class varied from year to year in sex, age, race, ethnicity, and sexual orientation. The course was purposely designed to be flexible, and it allowed maximum student input. I established the parameters for the initial phase of the course that explored feminist theory; the students selected the topics for discussion during the rest of the semester. Every student was expected to cofacilitate the class discussion with me at least once during the semester in a topic area chosen by the student. One of the three graded assignments was a collaborative project. These teaching methodologies comported with my perception of good feminist pedagogy (Combs 1990; Rhode 1993; Torrey, Casey, and Olsen 1990).

The emphasis of the course also varied greatly from year to year. Sometimes it seemed as though our perspective were removed and detached; other semesters, our enterprise resembled something decidedly unlawyerlike. I knew that additional focus — if not structure — was warranted when I overheard one of my students ask a colleague in reference to the class, "Are you going to 'group' today?" Though I recognize the value of group therapy, I had clearly lost my way as a legal educator.

Abandoning the photocopied materials that I had carefully compiled, I adopted a newly published textbook.[1] I used film excerpts to make specific points. I asked speakers with certain areas of expertise to make presentations to the class. The stories of battered women in particular were very powerful in helping students gain greater insight into the problem of violence against women. I retained student input on the course design but established a more limited universe of choices. Although these changes brought greater structure to the course, I sensed that it still lacked context. Knowing that many women law students feel alienated in the typical large classroom setting where casebooks place the review of legal concepts in a context ostensibly devoid of the reality of people's lives (Guinier et al. 1994; Weiss and Melling 1988), I wanted students to gain more of a real-world understanding of the difficulties faced by many women. As a former legal services program director, I had some awareness of the day-to-day problems confronting low-income women and women in transition. I realized that many law students had few opportunities to deal directly with people whose life experiences differed dramatically from their own.

I was not interested in duplicating the work of the law school's existing clinical program, where students have the opportunity to give advice and serve as legal counsel on behalf of clients. Previously, a female colleague who is now a judge and I had established a clinical program to provide advocacy and legal representation to battered women at their civil protection order hearings. Such work from a faculty point of view is labor-intensive, because close supervision is required to promote a beneficial learning experience for the students, to ensure competent and zealous representation to the clients, and to comply with professional ethical obligations (Critchlow 1990-91). The low faculty-student ratio necessary to achieve clinical program objectives is prohibitive in a classroom setting (Shalleck 1993-94). I kept thinking there must be a mechanism to achieve my objective of infusing a dose of the real world into the classroom of "paper people" and "paper cases," but I was stumped as to what that mechanism might be.

The Epiphany

As I was struggling to find an answer to this ostensibly intractable problem, fate intervened in the form of a professor from the business school. Acting as an emissary on behalf of the university's service-learning committee, he informed the law school faculty of the benefits of service-learning. Law faculty are often cordoned off, geographically and psychologically, from the mainstream of campus life. Despite the existence of institutionalized service-learning programs at the college level for more than 20 years, the concept of service-learning was novel for us. It was more than that for me; it was an epiphany. Eschewing the caution of my colleagues, who were reluctant to get involved in a new venture three months prior to the beginning of the new semester, I decided to go ahead and incorporate a service-learning component into my fall semester Women and the Law course.

Fortunately, law faculty have a primary role in the governance of the law school and almost unfettered discretion and autonomy in the classroom. There was no recalcitrant or skeptical department chair for me to persuade of the wisdom of my plan. At least one faculty member friend questioned my judgment in experimenting with an unfamiliar teaching methodology — unfamiliar at least by law school standards — just as I was applying for tenure. My student course evaluations in Women and the Law, both numerical and narrative, had been consistently superior from year to year despite all the other variables, so she wondered why I was inclined to jeopardize that success. But I had the fervor of the newly converted and would not be deterred.

The Preparation

Through my work as a community volunteer, I had developed contacts with agencies that I thought might be willing to act as community partners for my students. I concentrated on organizations that provided services to women and girls. I made a few phone calls and the process was under way. Shortly before the semester began, the university volunteer services office (now named the Center for Community Action and Service-Learning, or CCASL) was responsible for arranging appropriate placements for my students. I worked in conjunction with the service-learning coordinator to determine the suitability of the community partners.

Although a few students had undoubtedly been exposed to service-learning as undergraduates, I assumed many students would be unfamiliar with the concept. Prospective class members were not aware that service-learning would be an integral course component at the time they registered because at that point I *myself* hadn't known. I wanted to differentiate service-learning not only from the aforementioned clinical program but also from the law school's externship program, which placed students in law offices, public service/government agencies, and public interest organizations to perform legal work. From my reading about service-learning, I gathered that one distinguishing feature is the emphasis service-learning places on the reciprocal nature of the endeavor: giving to the clients, the organization, and the community as well as reaping the benefits of enhanced knowledge (Kendall and Associates 1990; Mintz and Hesser 1996). I trusted my ability to set the stage for this aspect of the experience.

Another difference is that most externship programs are connected to a student's primary field of study — in our case, the law. Although my intuitive sense was to separate service-learning from doing legal work, I was conflicted about this for two reasons. First, public interest legal organizations were desperate for assistance, and their orientation was on serving the needs of the client community, albeit with a specific legal focus. Second, even if I were to require the commitment of only a minimal number of hours throughout the 14-week semester, I was uncertain whether busy law students would be willing to juggle studying, paid employment, and other obligations with service-learning.

I approached the first dilemma by reaching a compromise. A few of the community partners would be organizations that provided legal services, although most of the suggested placements would be nonlegal. In addition to ensuring demarcation from the externship program, justifications for encouraging the selection of a non-legal placement included: (1) allowing students to recognize that social justice is broader than legal justice; (2) fostering a sense of service in students apart from their identity as lawyers; (3) providing a broader linkage with the community in which students live; (4) enabling students to value the professionalism of nonlawyers who staff nonprofit and public agencies; and (5) avoiding infringement of rules governing the practice of law by students.

The mission statement of our university emphasizes justice, although the meaning of that term has been vigorously debated. To many faculty members, it clearly implies social justice. An ad hoc committee of faculty and administrators began exploring precisely that issue in 1998 in preparation for a regional conference of Jesuit colleges and universities on social justice. When Gonzaga students university-wide were polled, they defined justice more narrowly by focusing on the legal system and notions of procedural justice, regardless of their field of study. Committee members were chagrined that the students made virtually no connection with other issues such as peace and justice, gender/race equity and justice, or poverty and justice. It was my hope that service-learning would aid students in understanding some of these interrelationships.

When teaching the Legal Ethics course, I tell my students that their legal proficiency will be in demand in the future on a pro bono basis. The term pro bono is the common shorthand for the Latin term *pro bono publico*, which means "for the public good." Although the Model Rules of Professional Conduct for lawyers does not require lawyers to offer pro bono legal services, the language of the applicable rule and the accompanying comments indicate that it is strongly encouraged (American Bar Association 1996: 465-469). Even though providing service in their area of professional expertise might be the best way to give back to the community, I want students to understand that it is not the *only* way.

Students are often temporary residents in the localities where their schools are situated. Many have been active volunteers in their home communities. But even interested students are deterred from making new com-

munity connections due to barriers that should be readily surmountable —
barriers such as uncertainty about the needs of service providers or lack of
transportation. Service-learning might prompt those students already
inclined to participate in community work because an organized program
would remove a few of these logistical hurdles.

Lawyers and law students sometimes develop a sense of elitism about
the importance of the work that they do. Legal and analytical skills are
essential in certain circumstances; indeed, a license to practice law is
required by statute in almost every jurisdiction to do specific tasks such as
representing another individual in court or dispensing legal advice. At the
same time, it is helpful for students to gain appreciation for the knowledge
and capability exhibited by professional and support staff in other fields.
Increased awareness of community resources and the development of ties
to reliable contact persons can benefit students who may have an ethical
duty as lawyers not only to advise clients about the law but also to refer to
"other considerations such as moral, economic, social, and political factors
that may be relevant to the client's situation" (American Bar Association
1996: 267-272).

Finally, limitations are placed on the practice of law by those who are
still in law school. Supervision by an on-site licensed attorney is essential.
Though students are permitted to perform myriad law-related tasks under
supervision, they generally must complete a designated number of credits
before they are permitted to do so, even under the auspices of an externship
or clinical program. Nonlegal service-learning placements avoid these particular restrictions and allow students to take part beginning in their first
year of law study.

However, one potential problem with this line of reasoning surfaced relatively early in the placement process. Although community partners were
eager for law student participation — anticipating that law students would
bring a skill level, along with a sense of maturity and professionalism,
greater than might be expected of the typical undergraduate — it was clear
that some agencies were decidedly interested in using the legal talents of my
students. Fortunately, Sima Thorpe, director of CCASL and herself a former
legal services paralegal, had developed excellent relationships with the community partners, and we were successful in explaining the strict limits on
law student involvement with their organizations.

Implementation

Solving a second dilemma — student receptivity — would depend on my
effective presentation of service-learning's benefits to my class. I had concerns about the lack of forewarning regarding the addition of a service-

learning component. Lawyers — and their law student counterparts — usually take the concept of advance notice very seriously because it is an essential part of the constitutional principle of due process. Again, I enlisted Sima Thorpe's aid by inviting her to my class. In her role as CCASL director, she was accustomed to providing background information in an eloquent and upbeat fashion. As I had hoped, our shared enthusiasm for the proposed undertaking was contagious, and the initial student response was positive.

In light of my course objective of increasing student awareness, I decided to require service-learning of all the students. However, I required that students commit only 20-25 hours total to actual on-site involvement with their community partners and offered a broad spectrum of placements. Two students out of the original 28 who were enrolled did drop the course due in part to the newly imposed obligation. In previous semesters, I had assigned three papers of varying lengths to the students for evaluation purposes. I announced that this time I would substitute service-learning for the midterm paper. I asked the students to complete journal entries that would be submitted periodically for my review. I planned to use a form of contract grading; that is, students would receive maximum credit if they responded fully to the questions I posed to them for each journal submission. Although some of my fellow teachers do use this approach, it is unusual because our law school — like many others — has a B-minus forced grading curve, at least for required courses and for any class with an enrollment greater than 50. The students were enthused that it was theoretically possible for everyone to get an A for this portion of the course.

My service-learning goals for Women and the Law were to (1) provide students with an alternative, hands-on approach to learning course concepts; (2) familiarize students with the day-to-day problems of women and girls, particularly those who are low-income or in transition; (3) assist non-profit service providers in the community through the use of student participants; (4) promote a longer-term commitment to public interest work by students; and (5) integrate the social justice mission of the university into the substantive coursework at the law school. These goals were memorialized in a formal contract with each student.

The 26 class members (21 women and five men) were placed with 15 different agencies that ran the gamut from more traditional legal work to activities completely unrelated to the law. The two legal placements involved assisting women litigants in domestic relations cases (under the auspices of the local bar association's Volunteer Lawyer Project) and advising unmarried new mothers of their legal rights (part of the Childbirth and Parenting Alone program sponsored by Catholic Charities and headed by a law school alumna).

Nonlegal placements included such organizations as the Spokane Sexual Assault Center (assistance to and support for rape survivors), the Alternatives to Domestic Violence Program sponsored by the YWCA (services to battered women and their children), the YWCA Multi-Cultural Center (information and other resources for non-English-speaking and immigrant women), the Children's Ark (residential program for teen moms), the Women and Children's Free Restaurant (preparing and serving meals to families recovering from domestic abuse), and the Women's Drop-In Center (information, referrals, and activities for women, including the homeless and those with disabilities). I did not select community partners with an adult male client base; however, three of the placements provided services to both girls and boys: Odyssey (support group for gay and lesbian teens), Crosswalk (temporary housing and other necessities for street kids), and Campfire Boys and Girls (service projects, educational and leisure activities for at-risk older elementary school children). Students at these placements were not forbidden to interact with males, but their primary focus was on working with girls. A few students developed their own placements with my approval at agencies such as the Indian Community Center and Big Brothers/Big Sisters.

In the placement process, one unexpected occurrence underscored the importance of the issue of sex discrimination — an issue basic to the Women and the Law course. Some of the community partners were unwilling to accept male students because of the sensitive nature of the work those agencies do, such as dealing with victims of sexual assault. As a result, it was more difficult to place the five male students, who discovered firsthand how it feels to have options limited solely due to their sex, and this provided the basis for fruitful class discussion.

Another placement obstacle concerned the length of time that it took to get students established in the organization of their choice. Most students had their placements squared away by the third week of the semester, but a few of the community partners required background checks for all new staff. Although I was assured that this would be handled "expeditiously," the state police responsible for conducting the background investigations defined that term more loosely than did I. As a result, the enthusiasm of the students whose applications were delayed did wane a bit. A couple of the placements required training as a prerequisite, training not scheduled to comport with the semester-long time frame under which we were operating. In a few other instances, we were penalized by having set up placements with designated agency representatives who subsequently left without notifying their successors of the arrangements in place. Naturally, solutions to all these problems are readily apparent in hindsight: Get started early, eliminate placements with onerous up-front requirements, and create a paper trail for future reference. But, at the time, it was a bit frustrating.

Assessment

I, along with most of my law school faculty colleagues, have no formal training in education. My octogenarian parents are still somewhat amazed that anyone allows me — without a "teaching certificate" — to teach anything. I must concede there are times when having greater awareness of terminology and techniques would be advantageous. Whenever I see the word "assessment," I am uncertain whether it means classroom assessment (feedback from students about their learning), student assessment (evaluation and grading of students), program assessment (gauging program quality), or teacher assessment (student evaluation of teaching performance) (Hess and Friedland 1999). I purposely use the term here in all its ambiguity because the student journal submissions touch on each of these meanings.

I gave questionnaires to the students and to their agency supervisors to get overall feedback at the end of the semester. But I was uncertain how to monitor student learning on an ongoing basis. Journaling seemed a natural way to receive periodic input, and although this could be characterized as classroom assessment because it emphasizes student learning, in effect I was using it to gauge the effectiveness of their out-of-classroom experience.

To formalize the project and differentiate journaling from keeping a personal diary (and stave off the inevitability of my getting bifocals), I requested that journal entries be typed. Students handed in copies of their journals for my review every three weeks. For the first journal entry, I asked the students to provide basic background information about their placements and then to address three basic questions: (1) What new information have you acquired as a result of your work thus far? (2) How do you *feel* about your experience? (3) Have you had any specific problems in your placement? (I asked this in order to make adjustments if needed.) For the second submission, I repeated the initial questions and added two more: (1) What is your most memorable experience to date? (2) In what ways has your placement resulted in your possibly exploring course issues from a different perspective? For the students' final entry, I wanted to know what changes they would make in the availability of services or the way services were delivered to the specific population they were working with. I also requested feedback on whether they believed service-learning was appropriate for the Women and the Law course.

The journal entries were not submitted anonymously, as is the norm for law school grading purposes. Students did use exam numbers on the other two assigned course papers. The first submissions varied greatly in format, content, and length. Because I did not dictate the use of a particular format, some submissions read like stream-of-consciousness musings, others resembled legal briefs. The individual personalities of the students emerged in a way uncommon in the law school setting. For once, they were given the opportunity to express themselves creatively, albeit with some structure provided by the questions posed. At the same time, content — as distinct from the manner of presentation — was important to me.

From some students I received a detailed log of activities that really did not speak to any of the questions I asked. For some, it was difficult to get in touch with their feelings about their experience; others emoted on each page. I hoped for a balance and indicated such in my comments. Although I had heard some horror stories about teachers receiving 400-page journals, I did not establish a minimum or maximum page limit. Most students wrote about 10 pages. I did receive a few papers in excess of 20 pages, and a couple of students wrote only four or five pages the first time. In retrospect, it seems reasonable to provide information up front on the page length expected. I made detailed comments at the end of each submission. I focused on ways the students could better respond to the questions presented, because that was the part of the exercise that I was actually grading. I was a bit more lavish in my praise than is usual for law school assignments, because I was convinced that almost all the students were trying hard to make their service-learning experience a positive one for their community partners, the clients, and themselves. Grading was somewhat of a challenge, but I tried to do as promised and concentrate on assessing their answers to my specific queries.

There were other minor quandaries to address. Two of the agencies were quite concerned about confidentiality issues. I assured them that the journals would be read only by me and that students would not reveal anything that would identify specific clients. For the handful of students who did not get started in a timely fashion, adjustments had to be made in the due dates for their journal submissions. The other issue I faced was student work that — even factoring in the informal presentation style — evidenced writing problems, such as poor grammar, sentence structure, and the like. (Yes, effective written communication is sometimes challenging even for graduate students!) I was apprehensive about correcting these mistakes, particularly where the content was good. If I noticed some writing difficulties, I wrote a brief comment to that effect at the end of the journal entry and offered assistance. I decided to allow the student to make the call on whether additional input from me was desired. Only one student sought my help with writing problems.

Most of the submissions I received were thoughtful and reflective. Some were quite amusing. Many were extremely heartfelt and touching. The students' own words are the best way to convey their sentiments:

Although we didn't have specific tasks to perform at the Women's Drop-In Center, it was still exhausting in an emotional respect. I'm so used to socializing and being surrounded by law students, law professors, and lawyers. Hanging out with women at the Center involved stepping out of my comfort zone and talking about things that aren't part of my everyday world such as drug use, abuse, children who are in jail or who have been taken away. Sometimes it took a lot of effort not to look shocked or weird-ed out [sic] by what I saw or heard. I am truly happy that I got to know these women because it reminds me that the world is made up of different people, not just the people who go to school with me.

(Third-year female student)

At first it seemed as though this would be a pretty easy . . . job, but in actu-ality I learned that providing service is much more difficult than trying to solve someone's legal problems. This experience has taught me that some problems may have no ready solution, and maybe the best thing that one can offer someone else is just a willingness to listen. Sometimes I do feel sorry for the women here because their lives are so hard. Many of these women do not feel empowered, but they gain strength in themselves by talking to one another. They empathize with one another and give practical advice in dealing with similar problems they've experienced. It's cathartic. This service project has educated me better in humanity than any other I've taken in law school. I know I may have clients with the same concerns and if I cannot relate to them, I will not be an effective advocate.

(Third-year female student)

I am struck by the girls here at Crosswalk. It must be so scary. I think back about dealing with problems when I was in high school and my biggest concern was whether I was having a bad hair day or which would be exactly the right college for me. These girls are so vulnerable, yet so expe-rienced at the same time. Many didn't spend the night after eating dinner. I wondered where they went, where did they sleep? Was it wet? Were they cold? Were they lonely?

I've learned so much in such a short time. Public service seems like such a vital part of education. I'm always complaining that law students don't have enough time to do everything, but some things are too important to put off until later.

(Third-year female student)

Service-Learning Redux

When I prepared to offer a service-learning component in my class the sec-ond time, I felt apprehensive in comparison with my somewhat cavalier approach during the first go-around. Was the initial success merely a fluke? A novelty whose appeal might wear off? I wasn't certain. I knew that this time I had several advantages.

First, student reaction was no longer a major concern, because students knew about the service-learning requirement at the time of enrollment. They also had the benefit of the "good buzz" about the experience from their predecessors.

Second, I was now aware that the placement process could take longer than expected. Fortunately, technological advances allowed necessary background checks to be handled in a manner that was expeditious by anyone's standard. The service-learning coordinator and I also began making the placement arrangements several months in advance, unlike the last-minute approach used previously. This allowed us to make the placements as congruous as possible with the objectives of the course.

Third, I could steer a greater number of students toward those placements where, based on past feedback, there were the best opportunities for service and for learning. I relied not only on the input I had received in my own course but also on the growing body of collective wisdom that resulted when other faculty in the women's studies program added or expanded service-learning components in their courses.

Fourth, I now had familiarity with the community partners and would be able to assist students better in choosing an appropriate placement based not only on their interests but also on their temperaments. For example, two students had been placed with a particular organization; one had a particularly meaningful experience, whereas the other sometimes experienced frustration with her immediate supervisor. By reading the journal entries, I knew it was a dramatic difference in working styles that created this occasional tension. With this knowledge, I was able to screen for compatibility as well as interest.

Finally, I perceived that I might be able to help students make the linkages more readily between the work of their organization and the course materials. With increased knowledge of the range of services offered and the client base of the various community partners, I could segue from the theoretical to the practical and invite students to get involved in class discussions related to their specific placements.

This second experience, although not perfect, was an unqualified success: a high level of student satisfaction as evidenced by journal entries and the teacher evaluations, spirited class discussions, much appreciation on the part of the community partners, and greater consistency. So, all's well that ends well, right? Yes . . . and no.

The Undergraduate Experience

Gonzaga University has a Junior Year Abroad Program in Florence, Italy. During fall semester 1997, I taught a Gender and Justice seminar to participating students under the auspices of the political science department. The course, which was cross-listed with women's studies, was well received by the students. It was a terrific semester for me also. (Naturally, any course would benefit from being taught in a 500-year-old palazzo in the center of one of the most beautiful cities in the world.) I was excited about the prospect of teaching another undergraduate cross-listed political science/women's studies course. (Women's studies is an interdepartmental program, not a separate department at the university.) The opportunity to do so arose in spring 1999.

Although service-learning would seem to be a sound teaching methodology to use in political science, the members of that department had not yet incorporated it into their courses. Buoyed by my success not only in teaching Gender and Justice but also in using service-learning at the law school level, I decided to be a pioneer, despite my adjunct status.

The Gender and Politics class was composed of 14 women and two men, ranging from freshmen to seniors. It was possible to use many of the same Women and the Law placements because the broad themes of the courses were similar: examining gender equality and public policy issues of importance to women. The new service-learning coordinator, Mari Morando, who had been a political science major during her college years at the same university, worked diligently to establish new placements as well.

I suspected that this community work would be an easy sell because the course was listed in advance as a service-learning course, and the students were familiar with the concept. I again was adjusting the number of written projects to allow for journal submissions. All the students except one found a suitable placement in short order, and the sole exception was a student whose health problems prevented her from finishing the semester.

Everything seemed to be proceeding smoothly until I received the first journal entries. There were no 20-page tomes for bedtime reading this time around. Although many students had a positive experience, as reflected by their journals, it was readily apparent that a few were not making the connection to the course themes at all. It was my sense that others thought contract grading meant that scribbling down any random thoughts on the assigned topic would suffice. A few people handed in no initial journal entry whatsoever.

I concede that I didn't handle the aftermath well. Rather than tighten up the stipulations for the journal entries, I actually loosened them somewhat. I did not return them to the students as quickly as I had done in Women and the Law, because I was waiting to receive the delinquent submissions. In retrospect, I surmise that I sent the message that perhaps I did not value the service-learning component sufficiently. Although I am often more flexible than many of my law school colleagues are about course requirements, that does not translate into my willingness to accept subpar work or to grade easily — something I try to impress on my students. Another professor in the law school has acquired, along with a slew of best-teacher awards, the moniker "the velvet fist" because his laid-back classroom manner belies his exacting standards for grading. I may be viewed similarly on my home turf, but the political science students were not privy to the law school rumor mill.

Another approach I adopted was to set aside one 75-minute class period about midway through the semester for the students to talk to one another specifically about their service-learning experiences. This information-sharing session seemed to pique student interest and was helpful to me in getting feedback. The second set of journal submissions due a week later were of higher quality.

What other differences might account for the nearly universal acclaim for service-learning among the law students and its more lukewarm reception by the political science students? My overconfidence was undoubtedly a factor. Perhaps the younger age and lower maturity level of the undergraduate students affected the nature of their service opportunities. When I compared the experiences of the Women and the Law students with those of the Gender and Politics students who worked with the same community partners, it was clear that oftentimes the law students were given greater responsibility.

One concrete example involves the organization that provides support to gay and lesbian teens. A 30-year-old law student was allowed to facilitate peer counseling groups, whereas a 19-year-old political science student was excluded from group work of any kind because there was not a sufficient differential between her age and that of the youthful participants. She spent most of her time working with group members in planning an educational event. Although she was working directly with people and obtained valuable insight through informal conversations, her experience was qualitatively different. I finally caught on to this and carefully reviewed the work of the undergraduate students as expressed in their second journal entries. In many instances, there was more focus on organizing, planning, and publicizing activities than on direct, regular, and sustained service to clients. At this juncture, this was difficult to remedy because a routine had already been established with the community partners. Nor did I consult with the service-learning coordinator, who undoubtedly would have been a valuable resource for assistance in making necessary adjustments.

When I reviewed the student evaluations for Gender and Politics after the semester ended, two of the 14 mentioned their displeasure with the service-learning component. Five students made a favorable reference to its inclusion in the course. The remaining seven students had a neutral response. I do not know whether some students were put off by its unfamiliarity in a political science setting. Although the chair of the political science department had been supportive of my adding a service-learning requirement to the course, my sense is that the department is viewed as one of the more "academically rigorous" in the university, and perhaps service-learning combined with my laissez-faire approach to evaluation did not coincide with this image. Furthermore, since many undergraduates do not have cars, transportation to the off-site locations was more difficult and time-consuming. If, then, the nature of the service work itself was less satisfying, the cumulative effect of negative factors may have outweighed the positive. One class member, however, was sufficiently enthused to provide the impetus for establishing a service house on campus. Along with her roommates, she is continuing the service with her agency partner in providing sex education, relationship counseling, empowerment, and support to teen girls.

During the summer, I sat down and brainstormed with the chair of the women's studies program and then with Sima Thorpe, the CCASL director. They both reminded me that it was the first time I had taught this particular course. Each of them had me almost convinced that I was being too hard on myself. Perhaps my lawyerly quest to find a definitive answer and solve the problem had allowed me to overlook the simple fact that sometimes things just do not work out as planned. I realized that I missed the comfort and solace that women can bring to one another's personal and professional lives. This so-called "casserole and consolation" function, as the feminist teacher and author Carolyn Heilbrun once phrased it in a course I took from her, cannot be the end-all and be-all of women's empowerment. But it was what I needed at that point. Not completely mollified, I did, however, stop obsessing about my contributions to service-learning's less-than-stellar debut in the political science department. At the same time, I determined that developing a beneficial service-learning program requires vigilance.

Making Connections

One highlight of the service-learning experience for me personally has been the opportunity it has provided to connect with like-minded faculty members across the university through the faculty service-learning committee established by the vice president for academics under the auspices of the Center for Community Action and Service-Learning. The purpose of the committee is to provide resources, mentoring, support, and recognition to faculty involved in service-learning. The committee meets monthly for two hours, with a longer planning meeting once a semester and intermittent subcommittee meetings.

There are two notable differences between these meetings and the seemingly endless schedule of other meetings on campus: About 75 percent of the participants are women and there is an attempt to make the time spent on committee work not only productive but enjoyable. The largely female committee composition is a departure from the norm in an institution where women faculty are a distinct minority. As in feminist teaching, there is an emphasis on collaborative projects and problem solving while maintaining structure. There is a greater awareness of different communication styles. Simply put, it is a more comfortable atmosphere in which for me to do good work. Following the committee chair's marketing strategy — if you feed them, they will come — we have benefited from the cooking skills of the CCASL staff. The committee has enjoyed Persian delicacies and Italian cuisine while engaging in long-range planning.

CCASL is striving for widespread, interdisciplinary involvement of the various departments. Even if women faculty are more willing initially to adopt service-learning, the aspiration is certainly that a greater number of colleagues, male and female, will be open to the possibilities when they discover its benefits. CCASL has 25 faculty participants in 14 departments and the law school. It has been an integral link to what is happening state-wide, regionally, and nationally in service-learning. The availability of information through the CCASL website and the service-learning listserv has enabled faculty to locate resources with greater ease. For those of us less skilled in ferreting out this type of information, CCASL's facilitation of the process has been invaluable.

Spreading the Word

What of my colleagues in the law school? I wish I could report that a significant number of law teachers were impressed by the successful integration of service-learning into my course and were convinced to follow suit. In actuality, I think that, after much cajoling, one other woman professor is poised to add a service-learning component to one of her upper-class elective courses.

A growing number of law schools are implementing some form of a pro bono or public interest requirement for students and faculty (Rhode 1999). Although the emphasis at many institutions is only on volunteer legal work, our law school has implemented a public interest mandate that is not strictly legally focused. Service-learning courses do satisfy the public interest obligation for students. As a result, our faculty now have an added incentive to offer these courses.

At present, all members of my law school's faculty who were hired on tenure track have received tenure. Even though a few faculty teach new courses from year to year, all are experienced classroom teachers with a command of the subject areas they teach. I informally surveyed members of this group of established legal educators about their reluctance to incorporate service-learning into their courses. The deterrents they mention are the standard ones: time constraints, course coverage, logistics, evaluation of students, academic rigor, and personal commitment. I would add the temperament of the faculty member to the mix as well. Perhaps an overabundance of Myers-Briggs "STJ" types among law teachers makes them less willing to cede control of any aspect of their courses and less appreciative of the value of affective learning (Randall 1996: 104).

Others have written at greater length and in greater depth on ways to address faculty concerns (Galura 1993; Kupiec 1993; Levine 1994). Sometimes a personal one-to-one testimonial can be even more convincing. Or so I continue to tell myself. I can certainly allay my colleagues' concerns by providing practical advice about the ways in which I have surmounted some of these barriers.

Conclusion

Despite my lack of immediate success with the faculty at my school, there is growing interest in service-learning among law teachers generally. This is evidenced by the topic's inclusion on the programs of national legal education conferences and in law review articles during the past year (Dubin 1998; Omatsu 1999). There has been greater emphasis placed on preparing law students to face the challenges of law practice through skills training of various sorts (American Bar Association 1992). Service-learning can lead to a deeper understanding of client needs and foster a commitment to change social conditions that may affect clients. It is ideally suited for preparing law students to be members of a profession that purports to value service in the public interest. Service-learning is an effective means to reconnect substantive coursework to human experience in a way meaningful for all students — and women law students in particular — who lament the lack of connectedness in the traditional law school curriculum. For me, it has been the answer to the conundrum that previously perplexed me in my teaching.

Note

1. That textbook is Becker, Bowman, and Torrey's *Feminist Jurisprudence* (West, 1994).

References

American Bar Association. (1992). *Report of the Task Force on Law Schools and the Profession: Narrowing the Gap.* The MacCrate Report. Chicago, IL: American Bar Association.

———. (1996). *Annotated Model Rules of Professional Conduct.* 3rd ed. Chicago, IL: American Bar Association, Center for Professional Responsibility.

Combs, Mary Irene. (Spring 1990). "Non-Sexist Teaching Techniques in Substantive Law Courses." *Southern Illinois University Law Journal* 14: 519-523.

Critchlow, George. (1990-91). "Professional Responsibility, Student Practice and the Clinical Teacher's Duty to Intervene." *Gonzaga Law Review* 26: 416.

Dubin, John C. (July-August 1998). "The Clinical Design for Social Justice Imperatives." *Southern Methodist University Law Review* 51: 1481-1482.

Galura, Joseph, ed. (1993). *Praxis II: Service-Learning Resources for University Students, Staff, and Faculty.* Ann Arbor, MI: OCSL Press, University of Michigan.

Guinier, Lani, Michelle Fine, Jane Balin, Ann Bartow, and Deborah Lee Satchel. (November 1994). "Becoming Gentlemen: Women's Experience at One Ivy League Law School." *University of Pennsylvania Law Review* 143: 3-5.

Hess, Gerald F., and Steven Friedland. (1999). *Techniques for Teaching Law.* Durham, NC: Carolina Academic Press.

Kendall, Jane, and Associates. (1990). *Combining Service and Learning.* Raleigh, NC: National Society for Internships and Experiential Education.

Kupiec, Tamar Y., ed. (1993). *Rethinking Tradition: Integrating Service With Academic Study on College Campuses.* Denver, CO: Education Commission of the States/Campus Compact.

Levine, Myron. (Fall 1994). "Seven Steps to Getting Faculty Involved in Service-Learning: How a Traditional Faculty Member Came to Teach a Course on 'Volunteerism, Community, and Citizenship.'" *Michigan Journal of Community Service Learning* 1: 110-114.

Mintz, Suzanne D., and Garry W. Hesser. (1996). "Principles of Good Practice in Service-Learning." In *Service-Learning in Higher Education: Concepts and Practices,* edited by Barbara Jacoby and Associates, pp. 35-37. San Francisco, CA: Jossey-Bass.

Omatsu, Glenn. (April 1999). "Teaching for Social Change: How to Afflict the Comfortable and Comfort the Afflicted." *Loyola of Los Angeles Law Review* 32: 791-797.

Randall, Vernillia. (1996). "The Myers-Briggs Type Indicator, First Year Law Students and Performance." *Cumberland Law Review* 26: 104.

Rhode, Deborah L. (July 1993). "Missing Questions: Feminist Perspectives on Legal Education." *Stanford Law Review* 45: 1563-1565.

Rhode, Deborah L. (April 1999). "Cultures of Commitment: Pro Bono for Lawyers and Law Students." *Fordham Law Review* 67: 2436-2439.

Shalleck, Ann. (1993-94). "Clinical Contexts: Theory and Practice in Law and Supervision." *New York University Review of Law and Social Change* 21: 148.

Torrey, Morrison, Jackie Casey, and Karin Olson. (Spring 1990). "Teaching Law in a Feminist Manner." *Harvard Women's Law Journal* 13: 89-109.

Weiss, Catherine, and Louise Melling. (May 1988). "The Legal Education of Twenty Women." *Stanford Law Review* 40: 1346-1347.

Bibliography: Service-Learning and Women's Studies

Theory: Books

Alcoff, L., and E. Potter. (1993). *Feminist Epistemologies*. New York, NY: Routledge.

Anzaldua, Gloria. (1998). *Making Face, Making Soul — Hacienda Caras: Creative and Critical Perspectives by Women of Color*. San Francisco, CA: Aunt Lute Books.

Belenky. M., B. Clinchy, N. Goldberger, and J. Tarule. (1986). *Women's Ways of Knowing*. New York, NY: Basic Books.

Dubois, Ellen Carol, and Vicki C. Ruiz. (1990). *Unequal Sisters*. New York, NY: Routledge.

Garry, Ann, and M. Pearsall. (1989). *Women, Knowledge, and Reality. Explorations in Feminist Philosophy*. Boston, MA: Unwin Hyman.

Gilligan, C. (1982). *In a Different Voice*. Cambridge, MA: Harvard University Press.

Harding, Sandra. (1991). *Whose Science? Whose Knowledge?* Ithaca, NY: Cornell University Press.

hooks, bell. (1994). *Teaching to Transgress: Education as the Practice of Freedom*. New York, NY: Routledge.

Mayberry, Maralee, and Rose Ellen Cronan, eds. (1999). *Meeting the Challenge: Innovative Feminist Pedagogies in Action*. New York, NY: Routledge.

McCarthy, Kathleen, ed. (1990). *Lady Bountiful Revisited: Women, Philanthropy and Power*. New Brunswick, NJ: Rutgers University Press.

Noddings, N. (1984). *Caring: A Feminine Approach to Ethics and Moral Education*. Berkeley, CA: University of California Press.

Stanley, Liz, ed. (1997). *Knowing Feminisms: On Academic Borders, Territories, and Tribes*. London: SAGE Publications.

Theory: Articles

Ellsworth, Elizabeth. (1994). "Why Doesn't This Feel Empowering?: Working Through the Repressive Myths of Critical Pedagogy." In *The Education Feminism Reader*, edited by Lynda Stone, pp. 300-327. New York, NY: Routledge.

Grant, J. (1987). "I Feel Therefore I Am: A Critique of Female Experience as the Basis for a Feminist Epistemology." *Women and Politics* 7(3): 99-127.

Jones, Kathleen. (1990). "Citizenship in a Woman-Friendly Polity." *Signs* 15(4): 781-812.

Weiler, Kathleen. (November 1991). "Freire and a Feminist Pedagogy of Difference." *Harvard Educational Review* 61(4): 449-474.

Young, Iris Marion. (Spring 1986). "The Ideal of Community and the Politics of Difference." *Social Theory and Practice* 12: 1-26.

Pedagogy: Books

Fisher, J., and E. Reuben. (1981). *The Women's Studies Service Learning Handbook: From the Classroom to the Community.* A publication from the National Women's Studies Association, University of Maryland. Silver Spring, MD: Crestwood Press.

Greene, Maxine. (1995). *Releasing the Imagination: Essays on Education, the Arts, and Social Change.* San Francisco, CA: Jossey-Bass.

Pedagogy: Articles

Daniels, Cynthia R. (1997). "Women and Citizenship: Transforming Theory and Practice." In *Experiencing Citizenship: Concepts and Models for Service-Learning in Political Science*, edited by Richard Battistoni and William Hudson, pp. 119-126. Washington, DC: American Association for Higher Education.

Williams, Tamara. (In press). "Negotiating Subject Positions in the Service-Learning Context: Towards a Feminist Critique of Experiential Learning." In *Feminist Classroom for the 21st Century: Pedagogies of Power and Difference*, edited by Susan Sanchez-Casel and Aurie MacDonald. Garland Press.

Essential Readings in Service-Learning

American Association for Higher Education. (1997-2000). *AAHE's Series on Service-Learning in the Disciplines,* edited by Edward Zlotkowski. 18 vols. Washington, DC: AAHE.

Delve, Cecilia I., Suzanne D. Mintz, and Greig M. Stewart, eds. (1990). *Community Service as Values Education.* New Directions for Teaching and Learning, no. 50. San Francisco, CA: Jossey-Bass.

Eyler, Janet, and Dwight E. Giles, Jr. (1999). *Where's the Learning in Service-Learning?* San Francisco, CA: Jossey-Bass.

————— , and Angela Schmiede. (1996). *A Practitioner's Guide to Reflection in Service-Learning: Student Voices and Reflections.* Nashville, TN: Vanderbilt University.

Howard, Jeffrey, ed. (1993). *Praxis I: A Faculty Casebook on Community Service.* Ann Arbor, MI: University of Michigan, OCSL Press.

—————. *Praxis II: Service Learning Resources for University Students, Staff and Faculty.* Ann Arbor, MI: University of Michigan, OCSL Press.

Jacoby, Barbara, and Associates. (1996). *Service-Learning in Higher Education: Concepts and Practices.* San Francisco, CA: Jossey-Bass.

Kendall, Jane, and Associates. (1990). *Combining Service and Learning: A Resource Book for Community and Public Service, Vols. I/II.* Raleigh, NC: National Society for Internships and Experiential Education.

Michigan Journal of Community Service Learning. (Fall 1996). A publication of the University of Michigan. <http://www.umich.edu/~ocsl/MJCSL/>

Rhoads, Robert A., and Jeffrey P. F. Howard, eds. (1998). *Academic Service Learning: A Pedagogy of Action and Reflection.* New Directions for Teaching and Learning, no. 73. San Francisco, CA: Jossey-Bass.

Stanton, T., D. Giles, Jr., and N. Cruz. (1999). *Service-Learning: A Movement's Pioneers Reflect on Its Origins, Practice, and Future.* San Francisco, CA: Jossey-Bass.

Zlotkowski, Edward, ed. (1998). *Successful Service-Learning Programs: New Models of Excellence in Higher Education.* Boston, MA: Anker Publishing Co.

A Response to Service

Butler, Judith, and Joan Scott, eds. (1992). *Feminists Theorize the Political.* New York, NY: Routledge.

Funiciello, Theresa. (1993). "Filling the Gap: A Charitable Deduction" and "City Silos and the Pop-Tart Connection." In *Tyranny of Kindness: Dismantling the Welfare System to End Poverty in America.* New York, NY: The Atlantic Monthly Press.

Gordon, Linda. (1990). *Women, the State and Welfare.* Madison, WI: University of Wisconsin Press.

Greene, Maxine, Janet Miller, and William Ayers, eds. (1998). *A Light in Dark Times: Maxine Greene and the Unfinished Conversation.* New York, NY: Teachers College Press.

Illich, Ivan. (April 1968). "To Hell With Good Intentions." Address to the Conference on Inter-American Student Project, Cuernevaca, Mexico.

McKnight, J. (January/February 1989). "Why Servanthood Is Bad." *The Other Side:* 38-42.

McKnight, J. (1977). "Professionalizing Service and Disabling Help." In *Disabling Professions,* edited by Ivan Illich et al., pp. 69-91. New York, NY: Marion Boyers Publishers.

Pasco, P. (1990). *Relations of Rescue.* Oxford: Oxford University Press.

Sidel, Ruth. (1992). *Women and Children Last.* New York, NY: Penguin Books.

Walker, Rebecca. (1995). *To Be Real.* New York, NY: Doubleday.

A Tradition of Activism: Books

Brookman, Ann, and Sandra Morgan. (1995). *Women and the Politics of Empowerment.* Philadelphia, PA: Temple University Press.

Bystyzienski, Jill, and Joti Sekhon. (1999). *Democratization and Women's Grassroots Movements*. Blooomington and Indianapolis, IN: University of Indiana.

DuPlessis, Rachel Blau, and Ann Snitow, eds. (1998). *The Feminist Memoir Project: Voices From Women's Liberation*. New York, NY: Crown.

Ferree, Myra Marx, and Patricia Martin Yancey. (1995). *Feminist Organizations: Harvest of the New Women's Movement*. Philadelphia, PA: Temple University Press.

Nancy A. Naples, ed. (1998). *Community Activism and Feminist Politics*. New York, NY: Routledge.

Historical Foundations: Books

Addams, J. (1893). *Philanthropy and Social Progress*. New York, NY: Thomas Y. Crowell and Co.

———. (1981, orig. 1910). *Twenty Years at Hull House*. New York, NY: Macmillan.

———. (1985). *On Education*. New York, NY: Teachers College Press.

Amidei, Nancy. (1991). *So You Want to Make a Difference: A Key to Advocacy*. Washington, DC: OMB Watch. <www.ombwatch.org>

Coles, Robert. (1987). *Dorothy Day: A Radical Devotion*. Reading, MA: Addison Wesley.

Day, Dorothy. (1952). *The Long Loneliness: An Autobiography*. San Francisco, CA: Harper and Collins.

Frankel, Nora Lee, and Nancy Dye Schrom, eds. (1991). *Class, Race and Reform in the Progressive Era*. Lexington, KY: University of Kentucky Press.

Goldman, Emma. (1934). *Living My Life*. Garden City, NY: Garden City Publishing.

Ginzberg, Lori. (1991). *Women and the Work of Benevolence: Morality, Politics and Class in 19th Century US*. New Haven, CT: Yale University Press.

Koerber, Linda. (1998). *No Constitutional Right to Be Ladies*. New York, NY: Hill and Wang Press.

Lasch-Qyinn, E. (1993). *Black Neighbors: Race and the Limits of Reform in the American Settlement House Movement, 1890-1945*. Chapel Hill, NC: University of North Carolina Press.

Lubove, Roy. (1973). *The Professional Altruist: The Emergence of Social Work as a Career, 1880-1930*. New York, NY: Athenaeum.

Miller, William. (1982). *Dorothy Day: A Biography*. San Francisco, CA: Harper and Row.

Pascoe, Peggy. (1990). *Relations of Rescue*. Oxford: Oxford University Press.

White, Deborah Gray. (1998). *Too Heavy a Load: Black Women in Defense of Themselves, 1894-1994*. New York, NY: Norton.

Weisenfeld, Judith. (1998). *African American Women and Christian Activism: New York's Black YWCA, 1905-45*. Boston, MA: Harvard University Press.

Historical Foundations: Articles

Addams, J. (1899). "The Subtle Problems of Charity." *Atlantic Monthly* 83(496): 163-178.

Baker, Paula. (February 1990). "The Domestication of Politics: Women and American Political Society, 1780-1920." *American Historical Review* 89(1): 620-647.

Morton, K., and J. Saltmarsh. (Fall 1997). "Addams, Day, and Dewey: The Emergence of Community Service in American Culture." *Michigan Journal of Community Service Learning* 4(1): 137-149.

Rauner, Judy. (Winter 1991-92). "Multicultural Perspectives in the History of American Volunteerism." *The Journal of Volunteer Administration* 10(2): 1-8.

Ryan, Mary P. (Spring 1979). "The Power of Women's Networks: A Case Study of Female Moral Reform in Antebellum America." *Feminist Studies* 5: 66-85.

Scott, A.F. (1990). "Most Invisible of All: Black Women's Vountary Associations." *The Journal of Southern History* 56: 3-22.

Sklar, Kathryn Kish. (1990). "Hull House in the 1890s: A Community of Women Reformers." In *Unequal Sisters*, edited by Ellen Carol Dubois and Vicki C. Ruiz, pp. 109-122. New York, NY: Routledge.

Appendix

Contributors to This Volume

Volume Editors

Barbara J. Balliet is associate director of women's studies at Rutgers University-New Brunswick. Her edited collection *Women Culture and Society* (1999) grew out of regular discussions among the faculty and graduate students teaching the introductory women's studies course there. A cultural historian, she is currently completing a book on gender and illustration in the 19th century. She received her PhD from New York University.

Kerrissa Heffernan is project associate in Integrating Service With Academic Study at Campus Compact, Brown University. Previously, Heffernan was the Arnow Weiler professor of liberal arts at Lasell College, and director of its Women's Studies Program. Additionally, she was the director of the Center for Public Service, and director of the Donahue Institute for Values and Public Life at Lasell. She is also the founder and director of Camp COLORS, a summer camp for preschool children with HIV.

Authors

D. Attyah is an artist/anthropologist living in San Francisco, and **S.A. Bachman** is an artist/educator teaching at the School of the Museum of Fine Arts in Boston. THINK AGAIN, an artist-activist collaborative founded by them, enjoys translating theory into straightforward ideas that people can actually use. Recently, THINK AGAIN's work has been included in *Ms* magazine as well as the exhibitions "Sex, Lies and Stereotypes," "No Human Is Illegal," and "The Culture of Class."

Karen Bojar is professor of English and women's studies at Community College of Philadelphia, where she has taught for the last 25 years. She co-developed the Introduction to Women's Studies course, which contains a service-learning component, and developed the service-learning course Community Involvement: Theory and Practice. She has had a long history in grass-roots feminist politics.

Blythe McVicker Clinchy is professor of psychology at Wellesley College, where she teaches courses in child and adult development and works on faculty development at the college's Learning and Teaching Center. She is coauthor of *Women's Ways of Knowing* (1986); coeditor of *Knowledge, Difference, and Power* (1996); and coeditor of *Readings in Gender and Psychology* (1998). Her writing and research focus on the evolution of conceptions of knowledge, truth, and value from early childhood through adulthood, and the implications of that evolution for the practice of education from nursery school through college.

Helen Damon-Moore is the director of service-learning and adjunct professor of education and women's studies at Cornell College. She teaches the courses Gender and Education, Community Service Seminar, and Introduction to Women's Studies. She is the author of *Magazines for the Millions: Gender and Commerce in the Ladies' Home Journal and the Saturday Evening Post* (1994). Her most recent publication is the entry "Advertising" in the *Reader's Companion to U.S. Women's History* (1998). She is currently working on a book-length study of the history of gender and service. Damon-Moore also coteaches a seminar on community service with Cornell College's president, Leslie Garner.

Kimberly Farah is associate professor and chair of the Chemistry Department at Lasell College. Her area of specialty is environmental chemistry and engineering.

Catherine Ludlum Foos is associate professor of philosophy at Indiana University East. She has served as senior fellow for Indiana Campus Compact's Faculty Fellows Program and is a member of a national consulting corps for service-learning cosponsored by AAHE and Campus Compact. She has published articles on service-learning in *Michigan Journal of Community Service Learning* and in the Philosophy and the Women's Studies volumes of AAHE's *Series on Service-Learning in the Disciplines*. She is also coeditor of a service-learning workshop curriculum guide published by Indiana Campus Compact.

Melissa Kesler Gilbert is on the faculty in the Women's Studies Program at Portland State University. She has published numerous articles and book chapters on women and work, family leave policies, feminist pedagogy, experiential role playing in the classroom, and women's community-based learning. Her current research is on the impact of service-learning on feminist community partners.

Jan L. Hitchcock is associate professor of social and behavioral sciences at Lewiston-Auburn College, University of Southern Maine. She teaches in a variety of areas, including life-span development and interdisciplinary topics such as cross-cultural psychology, spirituality, health, and violence. Her primary research interest is risk perception, and it is in this and related areas that she has involved students in service-learning projects. She completed her doctorate in personality and developmental psychology at Harvard University.

Debra J. Liebowitz is assistant professor of women's studies and political science at Drew University. She received her PhD from Rutgers University in 2000. Her research focuses on gender and transnational political organizing, with an emphasis on debates in international political economy and Latin American politics. She has published articles about gender, transnational political mobilization, and the North American Free Trade Agreement, as well as articles on gender and U.S. foreign policy. Liebowitz also has extensive experience developing experiential education programs that emphasize issues of gender, leadership, and public policy in this country as well as in Costa Rica, Mexico, and China.

Eve Allegra Raimon teaches in the Arts and Humanities Program at the University of Southern Maine's Lewiston-Auburn College. She has published essays on team-teaching about race from an interdisciplinary perspective and about the history of miscegenation in the United States. Her manuscript "Nationalism, Race and the Tragic Mulatto Figure in Nineteenth-Century Reform Fiction" is under revision.

Mary Trigg is program director of the Institute for Women's Leadership Scholars Program, and the assistant director of the Center for Women and Work at Rutgers University. She holds a PhD in American civilization from Brown University. Her areas of expertise include American women's history, women's education and leadership development, women and activism, and women and work. Her publications include articles in *Journal of Women's History, Initiatives, Transformations,* and *American National Biography,* among others.

Mary Pat Treuthart is a professor of law at Gonzaga University, where she teaches constitutional law and procedure, family law, and her course Women and the Law. She has an AB (1975) from Douglass College, a JD (1978) from Rutgers University School of Law-Camden, and an LLM (1989) from Columbia Law School.

Tobi Walker is a senior education associate at the Eagleton Institute of Politics at Rutgers University. She directs the New Jersey Civic Education Consortium, a statewide partnership project to expand and strengthen civic education in New Jersey. She also directs the NEW Leadership Development Network, a national program of the Center for American Women and Politics (CAWP) to train universities in CAWP's innovative political leadership program for young women. Walker holds an MA in political science/women and politics from Rutgers University.

Patricia A. Washington is assistant professor of women's studies at San Diego State University. A sociologist by training, she teaches and writes about the impact of social location (race, class, gender, sexual orientation, etc.) on individual and group access to institutional power and services.

Sally Zierler is professor of medical science in the Department of Community Health at Brown University, where she has served on the faculty of the School of Medicine since 1985. She has authored more than 60 articles and book chapters in the field of epidemiology, the majority of these addressing women's health. Zierler teaches courses in the methods of epidemiologic research, health of women, and theories of disease causation.

Series Editor

Edward Zlotkowski is professor of English and was founding director of the Service-Learning Project at Bentley College. He also is senior associate at the American Association for Higher Education.

About AAHE

AAHE's Vision AAHE envisions a higher education enterprise that helps all Americans achieve the deep, lifelong learning they need to grow as individuals, participate in the democratic process, and succeed in a global economy.

AAHE's Mission AAHE is the individual membership organization that promotes the changes higher education must make to ensure its effectiveness in a complex, interconnected world. The association equips individuals and institutions committed to such changes with the knowledge they need to bring them about.

About AAHE's Series on Service-Learning in the Disciplines

The Series goes beyond simple "how to" to provide a rigorous intellectual forum. *Theoretical essays* illuminate issues of general importance to educators interested in using a service-learning pedagogy. *Pedagogical essays* discuss the design, implementation, conceptual content, outcomes, advantages, and disadvantages of specific service-learning programs, courses, and projects. All essays are authored by teacher-scholars in the discipline.

Representative of a wide range of individual interests and approaches, the Series provides substantive discussions supported by research, course models in a rich conceptual context, annotated bibliographies, and program descriptions.

Visit AAHE's website (www.aahe.org) for the list of disciplines covered in the Series, pricing, and ordering information.